The Complete Idiot's Reference Card

D1404995

Program Manager: The 5

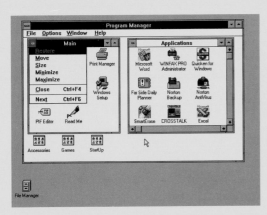

To	You
Select an open group	Click on it, or select it from the Window menu.
Open a minimized group	Double-click on it, or select it from the Window menu.
Highlight an item	Click on it, or use the arrow keys.
Start a program	Double-click on it, or highlight it and press Enter.
Move an item	Drag it or highlight it, and press F7.
Copy an item	Hold down Ctrl and drag it, or highlight it and press F8.
View an item's properties	Highlight it, and press Alt+Enter.

Windows' Wondrous Windows

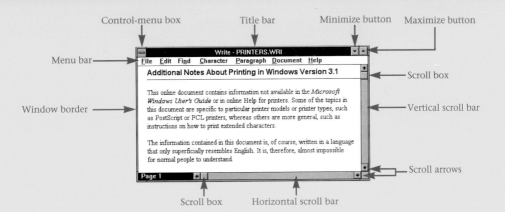

To	You
Size a window	Drag the borders or select Size from the Control menu.
Move a window	Drag the title bar or select Move from the Control menu.
Minimize a window	Click on the Minimize button or select Minimize from the Control menu.
Maximize a window	Click on the Maximize button or select Maximize from the Control menu.
Restore a minimized window	Double-click on the icon or select Restore from the Control menu.
Restore a maximized window	Click on the Restore button or select Restore from the Control menu.
Close a document window	Double-click on the Control-menu box or press Ctrl+F4.

Dialog Box Buttons: The Big Three

| OK | Select this button when you've finished with the dialog box and you want to put all your selections into effect. This is the "Make it so" button. |

| Cancel | Select this button when you panic and realize that you're looking at the wrong dialog box or if you've made a mess of your selections. This is the "Belay that last order" button. |

| Help | Select this button when you haven't the faintest idea what you're doing and you'd like the application to give you a hint. This is the "Please explain" button. |

Let's Do Launch

Here's a sampling of just a few of the 57 million ways you can launch your Windows applications:

In Program Manager, double-click on a program icon, or highlight the icon and press **Enter**.

In Program Manager or File Manager, select **R**un from the **F**ile menu, type in the name of the file that starts the program, and then select **OK**.

When starting Windows, type **win**, a space, and then the name of the file that starts the application.

Add the application to Program Manager's Startup group.

In File Manager, drag an application's data file and drop it on the file that starts the application.

Accessories to Complement Your Windows Wardrobe

Write

Full-fledged word processor; perfect for writing that great (insert nationality here) novel. See Chapter 20.

Paintbrush

Drawing and painting program; an ideal way to relive your youth. See Chapter 21.

Calendar

Simple day-timer; great for keeping track of power breakfasts, liquid lunches, cocktail parties—the usual business stuff. See Chapter 22.

Clock - 3/22

Displays the date and time, although this does mean you'll have one less excuse for being late. See Chapter 22.

Calculator

Performs quick calculations; lets you know if that check is going to bounce *before* you write it. See Chapter 22.

Cardfile

Stores addresses, phone numbers, and keeps simple databases of your belongings (all those Mantovani records, for example). See Chapter 22.

Mouse Movements

Point	Move the mouse pointer so that it rests on a specific screen location.
Click	Quickly press and release the left mouse button.
Double-click	Quickly press and release the left mouse button *twice* in succession.
Drag	Press and hold down the left mouse button, and then move the mouse.

Cool Tip #1

For those times when you zig instead of zag, many Windows applications include an Undo feature that reverses your most recent action. Just select Undo from the Edit menu, or press Ctrl+Z.

Cool Tip #2

Never shut off your computer while Windows is still running. Doing so can lead to lost data, trashed program groups, and unsightly warts.

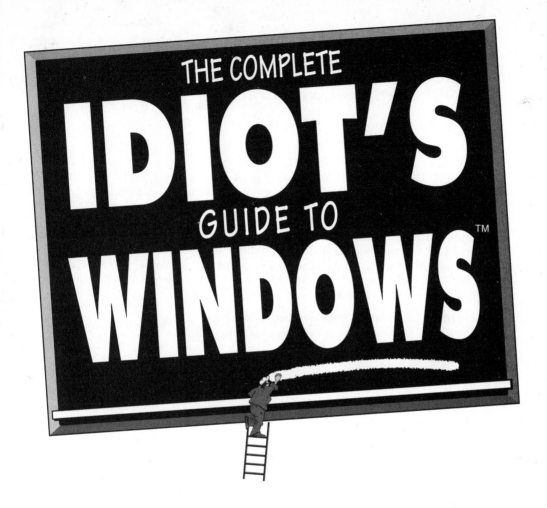

THE COMPLETE IDIOT'S GUIDE TO WINDOWS ™

by Paul McFedries

A Division of Macmillan Computer Publishing
A Prentice Hall Macmillan Company
201 W. 103rd St., Indianapolis, Indiana 46290 USA

To Sandy (my big sister), Chris (Beethoven wails!), Emily (Mrs. John Olerud?), Stephen (cowabunga, dude!), and my goddaughter Katy (the ringette and soccer star).

International Standard Book Number: 1-56761-546-5
Library of Congress Catalog Card Number: 94-79436

97   9

Interpretation of the printing code: the rightmost number of the first series of numbers is the year of the book's printing; the rightmost number of the second series of numbers is the number of the book's printing. For example, a printing code of 94-2 shows that the second printing of the book occurred in 1994.

Screen reproductions in this book were created by means of the Collage Plus program from Inner Media, Inc., Hollis, NH.

Printed in the United States of America

Publisher
Roland Elegy

Vice President-Publisher
Marie Butler-Knight

Managing Editor
Elizabeth Keaffaber

Acquisitions Manager
Barry Pruett

Product Development Manager
Faithe Wempen

Production Editor
Mark Enochs

Copy Editor
Barry Childs-Helton

Cover Designer
Scott Cook

Designer
Amy Peppler-Adams

Illustrator
Steve Vanderbosch

Indexers
Jeanne Clarke
Chris Cleveland

Production Team
*Brad Chinn, Kim Cofer, Lisa Daugherty, David Dean, Cynthia Drouin,
Jennifer Eberhardt, Beth Rago, Karen Walsh, Robert Wolf*

*Special thanks to Kelly Oliver for ensuring
the technical accuracy of this book.*

Contents at a Glance

Contents

Introduction

If you've ever tried to have a conversation with a so-called computer "expert," then you know those experts have this uncanny ability to make the rest of us feel like complete idiots within five seconds. They prattle on in their techno-jargon, throwing in the odd "of course" and "obviously" to make it clear that any fool with half a brain ought to know this stuff. Nuts to them, I say! Not only are we not idiots, but we're smart enough to know a thing or two ourselves.

- ☞ We're smart enough to know that it doesn't make sense to learn absolutely everything about Windows. We just need to know enough to get our work done, thank you.

- ☞ We're smart enough to know that life's too short to read five kazillion pages of arcane and mostly useless information. We have lives to lead, after all.

- ☞ We're smart enough to know that "cool" isn't defined by how many back issues of Popular Mechanics we keep in the bathroom. We simply don't need a lot of technical details (and we don't wear pocket protectors, either, so there!).

A Book for Smart Windows Idiots

If you're no fool, but the computer gurus of the world make you feel like one, then welcome to *The Complete Idiot's Guide to Windows*! This is a book for those of us who aren't (and don't even want to be) computer wizards. This is a book for those of us who have a job to do—a job that includes working with Windows—and we just want to get it done as quickly and painlessly as possible. This isn't one of those absurdly serious, put-a-crease-in-your-brow-and-we'll-begin kinds of books. On the contrary, we'll even try to have a little fun as we go along. (I do, however, feel compelled to apologize for some of the jokes in advance.)

You'll also be happy to know that this book doesn't assume you have any previous experience with Windows. This means that we'll begin each topic at the beginning and build your knowledge from there. But you won't find any long-winded discussions of boring, technical details. With *The Complete Idiot's Guide to Windows,* you'll get just the facts you need to know, not everything there is to know. All the information is presented in short, easy-to-digest chunks that you can easily skim through to find just the information you want.

Features of This Book

The Complete Idiot's Guide to Windows is organized into five sections:

Part I—Introducing Microsoft Windows

The three chapters that open the book are appetizers to get you started on the right foot. Chapter 1 lists the top 10 things you need to know about Windows. Chapter 2 tells you about Windows and answers a few common questions. Chapter 3 tells you how to install the program.

Part II—Universal Windows

Ninety percent of learning Windows involves learning a few simple techniques that can be applied to almost every Windows program. These universal skills are the subject of Part II. You'll learn how to start Windows, how to use the mouse and keyboard, and then we'll explore the various parts of the Windows screen.

Part III—Using Program Manager

Program Manager is your liaison to all the features of Windows. This section explains what Program Manager does and shows you how to start and work with other Windows programs.

Part IV—Using File Manager

File Manager is the Windows program that gives you an easy, graphical way to work with your computer's files, directories, and disks. The four chapters in this section explain the basic features of File Manager.

Part V—Working with Windows

The final section of the book covers miscellaneous topics that will help you get the most out of your Windows investment. You'll learn how to print and use fonts, how to customize Windows, and how to use some of the free programs that come with Windows.

The Complete Idiot's Guide to Windows also includes a glossary of computer and Windows terminology as well as a handy tear-out reference card that gives you easy access to Windows' commands.

To make the instructions easier to read, *The Complete Idiot's Guide to Windows* uses the following conventions:

- ☞ Text that you're supposed to type appears in **bold**.
- ☞ Text that appears on your screen and text you select also appears in **bold**.
- ☞ The selection letter for commands that you select will appear in bold, such as File.

Also, look for the following features that point out important information:

By the Way . . .
These boxes contain notes about Windows facts that are (hopefully!) interesting and useful.

Put It to Work
These are real-life, hands-on, practical Windows projects that you can try yourself.

There are always dangerous ways to do things on a computer, and this "OOPS!" icon will tell you how to avoid them.

This "Speak Like a Geek" icon defines geeky computer terms in plain English.

This "Techno Nerd Teaches" icon gives technical information that you can use to impress your friends (and then forget five minutes later).

There are always easier ways to do things on a computer, and this "E-Z" icon will tell you about them.

What's Wrong with This Picture

These examples show you some Windows pitfalls and how to get out of them.

Acknowledgments

I'd like to thank the members of the Academy. . . . Whoa, wrong speech! I'd like to thank Steve Poland, Seta Frantz, San Dee Phillips, Annalise Di Paolo and the other members of the Que family who contributed to this project (they're all listed at the front of the book).

Trademarks

All terms mentioned in this book that are known to be trademarks or service marks are listed below. In addition, terms suspected of being trademarks or service marks have been appropriately capitalized. Que cannot attest to the accuracy of this information. Use of a term in this book should not be regarded as affecting the validity of any trademark or service mark.

Windows is a trademark of Microsoft Corporation.

This page unintentionally left blank.

Part I
Introducing Microsoft Windows (Some Things to Check Out Before Diving In)

Okay, you've got a computer, you've got Microsoft Windows, you've got your favorite accessories (coffee, relaxing, background music, and so on). Hey, you're ready to go! However, just to build the suspense, this section presents some "look before you leap" stuff. (However, don't let me stop you if you're a dedicated leaper; feel free to head right into Part II.)

We'll begin with a chapter called "The Least You Need to Know." This gives you a quickie summary of the most important Windows tasks so you can get up and running fast.

If you've got some time and you want to know what this Windows stuff is all about, take a hike through Chapter 2, "Welcome to Windows." This chapter just talks about what Windows is and what it can do. It's kind of an appetizer for the rest of the book.

Finally, if you haven't yet installed Windows, Chapter 3, "The End of Innocence: Installing Windows," will show you how to do it quickly and painlessly.

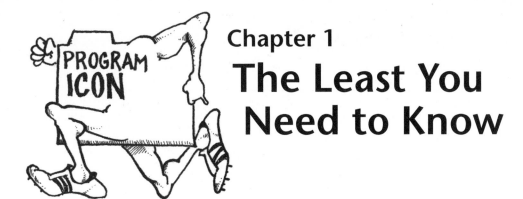

Chapter 1
The Least You Need to Know

I know, I know. You can't wait to get started. What is it? A looming deadline? Unfettered curiosity? A type-A personality? Well, not to worry. This chapter gets you up to speed quickly by presenting a "just-the-facts" description of the 10 most important Windows tasks. Of course, each of these items is discussed in more detail elsewhere in the book, so if you'd like to know more, I'll also point out the relevant chapters. If you're one of those people who likes to read ahead to the good bits, then this chapter's for you.

1. Starting Windows

To start Windows, you need to be at the DOS prompt. (The DOS prompt looks like C:\> or maybe just C>.) If your computer starts off in some kind of menu system, you need to exit the menu to get to DOS. Once you're in DOS, make sure you're logged on to the drive on which you installed Windows. To do this, just type the drive letter followed by a colon (:) and then press **Enter**. For example, to change to drive C, type **c:** and press **Enter**. Now peck out **win** on your keyboard, and press the **Enter** key. You'll know all is well if you see the Windows logo on your screen.

See Chapter 4, "Up, Up, and Away: Starting Windows," for more information.

2. Using Pull-Down Menus

Pull-down menus are hidden menus that list the various commands that are available for each Windows application.

To pull down a menu with a mouse, move the mouse pointer onto the menu bar area (the horizontal strip along the second line of an application's window), and then click on the name of the menu you want to pull down. From the keyboard, hold down the **Alt** key and press the menu name's underlined letter (the hot key). Here's a picture of Program Manager's File menu.

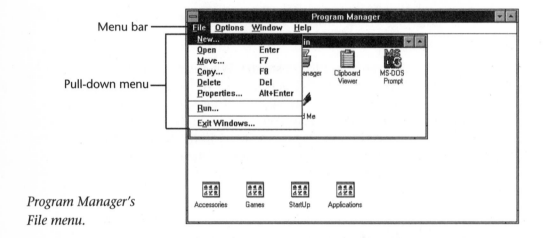

*Program Manager's
File menu.*

Once you have your menu displayed, you can then select any of the commands. With a mouse, you simply click on the command you want to execute. With your keyboard, you use the Up and Down arrow keys to highlight the command you want and then press **Enter**.

To learn more about pull-down menus, see Chapter 5, "Pull-Down Menus: Windows' Hidden Treasures."

3. Navigating Program Manager

Program Manager is always the first application you see when you start Windows. As its name implies, you use it to manage (for example, to set up, maintain, and start) the other programs on your computer.

Program Manager divides your system into groups of (hopefully) related applications. There are many ways to select a group, but these are the most common:

☞ Pull down the **Window** menu and select the group from the list at the bottom of the menu.

☞ If the group is already open, click on it with your mouse.

☞ If the group is minimized as an icon, double-click on it.

Once you have a group open, you can highlight an application's icon by simply clicking on it with the mouse or by using the arrow keys.

Chapter 9, "Program Manager: Your Faithful Windows Servant," gives you the complete lowdown on navigating Program Manager. If you're a new mouse user, read Chapter 4, "Up, Up, and Away: Starting Windows," to learn some mouse fundamentals.

4. Starting an Application

At its most basic, the whole purpose of Windows is to run neat applications. This is almost always accomplished using Program Manager. If you use a mouse, you can start an application by opening the appropriate program group and then double-clicking on the application's icon. From the keyboard, you need to open the program group. Use the arrow keys to highlight the application's icon, and then press **Enter**.

Check out Chapter 10, "The Real Fun Begins: Starting Applications," to learn more about starting and working with applications.

5. Opening a File

When you start an application, you'll usually see a new file displayed. If you'd prefer to work with an existing file, you need to open it. Here are the steps to follow:

☞ Pull down the application's **File** menu, and select the **Open** command. This displays the Open dialog box as shown here.

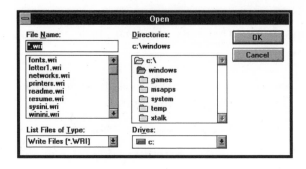

You use the Open dialog box to select the file you want to open.

☞ If necessary, use the Drives drop-down list box to select a different disk drive and the Directories list box to select a different directory.

☞ In the File Name list box, highlight the name of the file you want to open.

☞ Select the OK button.

For more information on the Open command, see Chapter 7, "Day-To-Day File Drudgery." To learn more about list boxes, buttons, and other dialog box stuff, see Chapter 6, "Talking to Windows Dialog Boxes."

6. Saving a File

One of the most gut-wrenching experiences in computerdom is to work on a document for hours and then lose everything because of a system crash or power failure. You can minimize the damage, however, by saving your work regularly. To do this, you just pull down the application's File menu and select the Save command. If you're saving a new file, the Save As dialog box will appear. Select the drive and directory where you want the file saved, and then use the File Name box to give the file a name. When you're ready, select OK.

See Chapter 7, "Day-To-Day File Drudgery," for more details about saving a file. To learn more about dialog boxes, see Chapter 6, "Talking to Windows Dialog Boxes."

7. Printing a File

Once you've finished working with a document, you'll want to print a copy. To do this, pull down the application's File menu and select the Print command. The Print dialog box that appears allows you to set the number of copies, the specific pages you want printed (if you have more than one), and various other settings (depending on the application). When you're ready to print, select the **OK** button (in some applications, you might have to select the Print button, instead).

For more printing particulars, take a look at Chapter 18, "Hard Copy: Windows Printing Basics." To learn more about dialog boxes, see Chapter 6, "Talking to Windows Dialog Boxes."

8. Undoing a Mistake

Many Windows applications include an Undo command that you can use to reverse your most recent action. This is great if you've just deleted your entire day's work or if you cut when you should have copied. (I know, I know, you don't make mistakes. But you probably know plenty of people who do, so you can pass this information on to them.) To use the Undo feature, pull down the application's Edit menu and select the **Undo** command.

I discuss the Undo command in more detail in Chapter 7, "Day-To-Day File Drudgery."

9. Switching Between Multiple Applications

Windows supports multitasking, which is just a fancy way of saying that you can run multiple applications at the same time. The number of applications you can run at once depends on how much memory you have in your computer, but even a bare-bones Windows system should be able to get two or three medium-size programs going.

Once you have your applications running, you need some way of switching between them. Fortunately, Windows has about 57 ways of doing this. Here's a summary of the easiest ones to use:

☞ If you can see any part of the application, click on it. If you've minimized the application and you can see the icon, double-click on it.

☞ If you have two applications open, press **Alt+Tab** to cycle back and forth between them. If you have more than two applications running, hold down **Alt** and press the **Tab** key repeatedly. Each time you press Tab, Windows displays the title and icon of one of the active applications as shown here. When you see the one you want, release the Alt key.

When you hold down Alt, each time you press Tab, Windows displays the title and icon of a running application.

☞ Double-click on any empty area of the desktop or press **Ctrl+Esc**. This displays a list—called the Task List—of all your running applications. Double-click on the application you want, or high-light it, and then click on the Switch To button.

Chapter 10, "The Real Fun Begins: Starting Applications," gives you more information on navigating running applications.

10. Quitting Windows

When you've finished with Windows, you can quit the program by pulling down Program Manager's File menu and selecting the Exit **Windows** command. Windows will display a dialog box asking you to confirm that you want to exit Windows. Select the **OK** button to continue.

See Chapter 4, "Up, Up, and Away: Starting Windows," for some additional stuff on quitting Windows.

Chapter 2
Welcome to Windows

In This Chapter

- ☞ What Windows is and what you can use it for
- ☞ How Windows makes your life easier
- ☞ Why you can still keep your old DOS programs

As strange as it may sound, I was actually at a baseball game when I first realized Windows was a Big Thing. Where I live, we have one of those state-of-the-art baseball stadiums with all the modern-day amenities: artificial turf, a McDonald's, and the main attraction: a huge 110-foot TV screen (the biggest in the world, I hear) that tells everyone when they're having fun.

Of course, with tens of thousands of people as a captive audience, you'd better believe this monster TV is going to show commercials. So there I was, sitting with 50,000 of the faithful when a commercial comes on for, you guessed it, Windows. The specifics of the ad have faded from memory, but I recall thinking that if Microsoft (the publisher of Windows) was willing to shell out the megabucks to peddle this new software at a major league baseball game, then something big was happening.

Actually, with Windows now selling over a million copies a month, "humongous" might be a better word. Windows is, truly, a phenomenon unlike any other in the world of personal computers. This chapter explores the Windows mystique and attempts to answer four basic questions:

- ☞ What's with all this Windows hoopla?
- ☞ Is Windows as easy to use as everyone says?
- ☞ I've got Windows; now what the heck do I do with it?
- ☞ Do I have to toss my DOS programs?

What's with All the Windows Hoopla?

Windows ads don't appear only on 100-foot TVs. You see them on normal-sized TVs, billboards, newspapers—you name it. Computer magazines (and even some real magazines) are stuffed full of articles like "57 Cool New Ways to Make Windows Bark Like a Dog!" Everywhere you go, people are talking about Windows (well, okay, almost everywhere). So why all the fuss?

Windows represents an entirely new way to get things done with a computer. The old way (that is, the DOS way) involved typing commands on your keyboard and waiting (or more likely, praying) for the computer to respond. There are two major drawbacks to this approach:

- ☞ Most of us are pathetic typists.
- ☞ Most of the things you have to type bear only the slightest resemblance to the English language; for example:

  xcopy c:*.* a: /d:04/15/93 /v

Yuck! Using DOS is like going to a fancy French restaurant where you have to write down your order. If you get anything wrong—like spelling crème as créme (or is the other way around?)—then you don't eat.

Windows changes all that because it works the way human beings do: visually. Your programs and any commands or options you need to choose are all represented visually on the screen (or they're a few mouse clicks or keystrokes away). Just think: no more convoluted commands and snaggled syntax to remember. In fact, Windows may be the first computer interface where you don't have to remember anything!

Is Windows Really As Easy to Use As Everyone Says?

Well, yes and no. I mean it's not like boiling water. On the other hand, it's not exactly brain surgery, either.

When you get right down to it, Windows, like just about anything else, is as easy or as hard as you make it. This is a fully loaded piece of software that comes with a veritable cornucopia of bells and whistles. It's possible to sink into its esoterica and never be heard from again.

How does Windows make it easier to use a computer? Imagery is the key. When you start up a Windows application, most of what you can do with the program is laid out visually in front of you. In our French restaurant example, Windows would be like ordering from a menu that has nice pictures of each of the dishes. You point to the selection you want, and voilà, your meal is served up piping hot. Windows even uses pictures to represent entire programs, as you can see here.

Each of the pictures in the Applications box represents an entire program.

In the box labeled "Applications," each of the pictures you see is a symbol for a specific application. You start the application by clicking on the picture with your mouse or selecting it with the keyboard. (If this isn't clear to you now, don't worry. It'll get clearer as we go along. In particular, Chapter 10, "The Real Fun Begins: Starting Applications," tells you everything you need to know about starting programs within Windows.)

> ### By the Way . . .
> There's no difference between a program and an application. However, application sounds more important, so that seems to be the word of choice these days. For variety's sake, I'll use both.

SPEAK LIKE A GEEK

The little pictures that Windows uses to represent programs are called *icons*.

Of course, cute little pictures are only part of the story. Another feature that makes Windows easy to use is the dialog box concept. You'll be learning about these in detail in Chapter 6, "Talking to Windows Dialog Boxes." As the name implies, a dialog box is simply a way for you and Windows to communicate. You'll see a dialog box any time Windows needs more information from you or if it needs you to confirm that what you asked it to do is what you actually want it to do. Here's an example of a confirmation dialog box.

A Windows dialog box asking you to confirm an action.

The third key to Windows ease-of-use is consistency. Certain operations, such as opening and saving files, are implemented the same way in almost all Windows applications. Also, most Windows applications look more or less the same. These consistencies across programs mean that you have that much less to relearn with each new program you use. Check out Part II, "Universal Windows," to find out about many of these consistencies.

Okay, I've Got Windows; Now What the Heck Do I Do with It?

TECHNO NERD TEACHES

Windows is an example of what the computer cognoscenti call a GUI—a graphical user interface. (You'll be pleased to know that GUI is pronounced "gooey.")

I'm not here to be an evangelist for Windows. I'm not going to tell you that Windows can do everything except wax the cat. Computers and the programs that run on them (including Windows) are like big pack animals.

However, donkeys live useful, productive lives and so, too, can Windows. For one thing, Windows will still allow you to do what people have been doing with personal computers for years: write letters, crunch numbers, draw pictures, and play cool games. Windows, though, brings a number of advantages to the table:

☛ Once you're comfortable with the Windows way of doing things (which won't take you very long), then you'll be able to do all those normal computer tasks easier and faster.

☛ Your finished product will be, generally speaking, more professional-looking.

☛ Windows lets you work on multiple things at once. For example, while a letter is printing out, you can use a different program (such as rewarding yourself with a couple of games of Solitaire).

Windows by itself is easily worth the price of admission (especially if it came bundled with your new computer), but there's actually a lot more fun stuff lurking in the Windows box. The Windows programmers have included, at no extra charge, a hatful of small programs (they're called accessories). With these programs you can

SPEAK LIKE A GEEK

The ability to run several programs at the same time is called *multitasking*. It simply means that Windows can walk and chew gum at the same time.

☛ Monitor your appointments.

☛ Store addresses and phone numbers (although this does mean you'll have one less excuse for not calling).

☛ Make quick calculations.

☛ Keep simple databases of your belongings.

See Part V, "Working with Windows," for information on these and other Windows tricks.

Do I Have to Toss My DOS Programs?

In a word—no. The creators of Windows looked at the tens of millions of people using DOS programs and figured they'd better keep these people happy. So they made sure that DOS applications would work reasonably well under Windows. They'll run a bit slower, and some of the more misbehaved programs might give Windows a little gas, but they'll run. I'll tell you more about combining DOS and Windows programs in Chapter 10, "The Real Fun Begins: Starting Applications."

The Least You Need to Know

This chapter gave you a brief introduction to Windows. Some key points to remember:

- ☞ Windows is selling over a million copies a month.

- ☞ Windows' visual approach makes using a computer easier.

- ☞ You can communicate with Windows by using dialog boxes. These are windows that appear on the screen to ask you for more information or to confirm a command you requested.

- ☞ To make Windows easier to use, all Windows applications implement certain key features in the same way.

- ☞ DOS and Windows are designed to work together, so you can keep (and use) all those old DOS programs.

Chapter 3

The End of Innocence: Installing Windows

In This Chapter

- ☛ Preparing to install Windows
- ☛ The installation procedure
- ☛ What to do if Windows won't install
- ☛ Touching stories of innocence lost and Christmases of long ago

My favorite thing about computers is probably the moment a new software package arrives. It sits there in its shrink wrap, filling me with great expectations. The wrapper gets torn off, the box gets mangled, the contents—the manuals, the disks, the registration card—are spilled and scattered. Then, inevitably, it must be installed to bring it to life on our computers.

If you've just purchased Windows, this chapter leads you gently out of the age of innocence and shows you how to install the program on your computer.

> ## By the Way . . .
>
> If your computer is new, Windows may already have been installed by the manufacturer. If you're not sure, turn on your computer, and see if it loads Windows, or try typing **WIN** at the prompt that appears, and then pressing **Enter**. If Windows is installed, skip this chapter and go to Chapter 4, "Up, Up, and Away: Starting Windows." The technoids at the factory know their hardware and will have set up Windows just right for your system.

Starting from DOS

You should see one of the following four things on your screen:

The DOS prompt, which looks something like this:

    C:\>

You may see a letter other than **C**, or you may see something like **C>** or **C:\DOS**. In any case, your computer is ready for the Windows installation, so you can skip to the next section. (The exception to this is if you see an **A** in the prompt. This means there was a disk in one of your floppy drives when you started your computer. Remove all disks from your computer, and start again.)

The MS-DOS Shell program. If you see **MS-DOS Shell** at the top of your screen, hold down the **Alt** key, and press the **F4** key. This will return you to DOS.

Some kind of menu system. Many computers are set up with a menu system that gives the user a list of programs to run. Look for an option called "Exit to DOS," "Quit," or something similar. You can also try pressing the **Esc** key.

Windows itself. If Windows loads every time you start your computer, you'll only need to go through the Windows installation if you're upgrading to a new version. If you're not sure which version you have, the

Windows logo that appears when Windows starts will tell you, or you can check with the person or company that set up your system, and ask them which version of Windows you have. If you are upgrading, tell Windows you want to exit by holding down the **Alt** key and pressing **F4**. Windows will ask you to confirm that you want to exit (yes, it's one of those dialog boxes I mentioned in the last chapter). To do this, just press **Enter**.

The No-Brainer Installation

When I was a kid, I used to get nervous whenever I got Christmas presents that said "Some assembly required" on the box. I knew what this meant. It meant I couldn't play with the toy right away.

Installing computer software still fills me with the same apprehension. Most installation programs are written by people who assume that everybody will know what they mean when they say, "Change the BUFFERS setting in your CONFIG.SYS file to 30."

I'm happy to report that the Windows installation program (called Setup) is different. It even includes an Express option that the most computer illiterate among us will love. This option makes Setup itself do most of the work. All you have to do is shuffle the installation disks in and out at the appropriate times (which Setup will tell you). Sound simple? It is.

After typing **a:** and pressing **Enter** (in step 2), DOS may report this ominous-sounding message

Not ready reading drive A Abort, Retry, Fail?

Yikes! This means one of two things:

There is no disk in drive A. In this case, press **f** (for "Fail"). Then type **b:**, and press **Enter**. This should give you the B prompt (**B:\>** or something similar).

OR

If drive A is a 5 1/4-inch floppy drive, the latch is not closed. Close it and press **r** (for "Retry").

Step 1: Get the Installation Disks Ready

Liberate the installation disks from their plastic wrapper and look for the one that says "Disk 1" on its label (it should be on top of the pile). Keep the others nearby.

Step 2: Insert Disk 1

Place Disk 1 in the appropriate drive (the one that matches the size of disk you have). To insert a floppy disk, hold it so that the label is facing up and next to you. Then insert the disk into the drive as far as it will go. The 3 1/2-inch disks will snap into place with a satisfying click. The 5 1/4-inch disks require you to close the small latch above the slot.

If the disk is in drive A, type **a:** (that is, the letter "a" followed by a colon) and then press **Enter**. If it's in drive B, type **b:** and press **Enter**. If you don't know drive A from a hole in the ground, don't worry:

☞ If you have only one floppy drive, it's definitely drive A.

☞ If you have both a 5 1/4- and 3 1/2-inch drive, the 5 1/4-inch drive is usually drive A.

☞ If you're still not sure, just try typing **a:** and pressing **Enter**. If you see the A prompt (something like **A:\>**), then you're okay.

Step 3: Start the Setup Program

This is the easy part. Simply type **setup** and press **Enter**. Setup chugs away for a few seconds and then displays the Welcome to Setup screen.

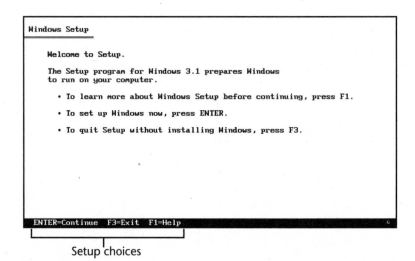

*The Welcome to
Setup screen.*

Setup choices

At this point, take a look at the bottom line of the screen. This line tells you which keys you can press and what they'll make Setup do next. In this case, you have three choices:

☞ Press **Enter** to continue the installation.

☞ Press **F3** to exit Setup.

☞ Press **F1** to get more information about what Setup is about to do.

Go ahead and press **Enter** to move to the next step.

Step 4: Selecting the Express Setup

So far, Setup hasn't shown us anything that's much different from other installation programs. But that all changes at the next screen.

Here, Setup gives you a choice between the Express Setup or the Custom Setup. Here's a summary of the differences:

Express Setup is designed with beginners and nontechnical users in mind. With this method, Setup automatically detects the hardware and software on your system and sets up Windows appropriately.

Custom Setup is for "techies" and experienced users who are very familiar with both Windows and their computer configuration and who don't mind wrestling with Setup's numerous options.

To choose the Express Setup, simply press **Enter**. Setup begins examining your system and copying files to your hard disk.

Step 5: Finishing the Installation

The rest of the installation procedure involves nothing more than answering some simple questions and feeding disks into your computer when prompted by Setup.

One of the questions asks you what kind of printer you have. As you work through the installation disks, you'll eventually see a box on your screen called Printer Installation. This box supplies you with a long list of printer names and asks you to select yours from the list. Just use the Up and Down arrow keys on your keyboard to scroll through the list. When you find the one you want, press **Enter**. If you don't have a printer, or if you really don't feel up to it, just press the **Esc** key.

By the Way . . .

If you're not sure what kind of printer you have, don't lose any sleep over it. You can always set up your printer later on. Chapter 18, "Hard Copy: Windows Printing Basics," tells you everything you need to know.

The Least You Need to Know

This chapter showed you how to get Windows out of the box and onto your computer. Here's a quick (but absolutely vital) summary:

☞ Put Setup Disk 1 in the drive. Then, at the DOS prompt, type **setup** and press **Enter** to start the installation process.

☞ Avoid premature graying by using the Express setup to install Windows quickly and easily.

☞ Follow the on-screen prompts to swap disks in and out of the drive.

Part II
Universal Windows (The Stuff You'll Be Using in Every Windows Application)

One of the cool things about Windows is what technoid types refer to as its "consistent interface." In English, this just means that you'll be able to use a lot of the techniques you learn in a Windows application today in a different Windows application tomorrow. These consistencies are what I mean by "universal Windows"—it's the subject of the five chapters in this section.

Chapter 4
Up, Up, and Away: Starting Windows

In This Chapter

- ☛ Starting Windows
- ☛ Mouse and keyboard basics
- ☛ The elements of the Windows screen
- ☛ Fascinating tales of motorcycles and brass tacks

Many years ago, against all reason and the protests of friends and family, I bought my first motorcycle. The fact that I couldn't afford it didn't bother me at all.

It was the first time I'd bought anything new, and I could hardly wait for the dealer to finish the preparations so I could pick it up. I can remember my feelings of exhilaration as I rode my new machine off the lot. It took some time to get used to the controls and the feel of the thing, but I was just happy to be riding.

What does all this have to do with Windows? Well, not very much, unfortunately, except that, now that Windows is installed and ready to go, it's time for your first test drive. As they did with my motorcycle, the controls will feel a little strange at first. But the more you ride the easier things will get, so let's get under way. . .

Starting Windows

Before you get too far into this section, you should check to see whether or not you even have to read it. First, a short quiz: When you start up your computer, do you eventually see a box on your screen that says Program Manager at the top? If so, then you're already in Windows! Skip ahead to the section titled "What's with This Mouse Thingy?"

Finding the DOS Prompt

You need to be at the DOS prompt to start Windows. (The DOS prompt looks like **C:\>** or **C>** or any variation of these.) If there is no prompt, then you're likely in some other program. Here are some possibilities:

The MS-DOS Shell program. If you see **MS-DOS Shell** at the top of your screen, hold down the **Alt** key and press **F4** to return to DOS.

Some kind of menu system. Your computer may be set up with a menu system that gives you a list of programs to run. Look for an option called Exit to DOS or Quit or something similar. You can also try pressing the **Esc** key.

The Two-Step Program for Starting Windows

Without further ado, here are the steps you need to follow to get Windows up and running:

1. If necessary, change to the drive on which you installed Windows by typing the drive letter, followed by a colon (:), followed by the Enter key. For example, to change to drive C, type **c:**, and press **Enter**.

2. Type **win** and press **Enter**.

OOPS!

Some people have reported having problems with Windows if they start typing before the program is finished loading. These may be just tall tales, but why take chances?

Don't Wait Up—This Could Take Awhile

Once you start Windows, you'll see the Windows logo on your screen. This gives you something to look at while Windows cranks itself up to speed. Be forewarned, however: depending on how much horsepower your computer has, Windows may take half a minute or more to load. You might want to keep a good book handy to pass the time (*War and Peace* is a good choice).

By the Way . . .

If, for some reason, you really don't want to see the Windows logo when you start the program, no problem. Just type **win :**, instead (that's win followed by a space, followed by a colon). Don't forget to press **Enter**, too.

When Windows Finally Loads

Here's what you'll see when Windows finally decides it's ready.

Minimize button   Program Manager window

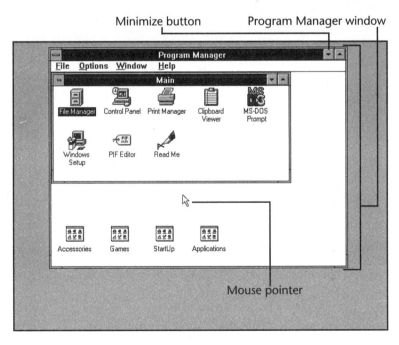

Mouse pointer

The Windows opening screen shows the Program Manager application.

The boxes that you see in the Windows screen are called *windows*. (Ah, now we're getting somewhere.) Get used to them because everything in Windows happens inside a window.

SPEAK LIKE A GEEK

The arrow that moves on your screen when you move a mouse is called the *mouse pointer*.

The larger box is an application called Program Manager. This is your liaison to all of Windows' functions and commands and to all of your programs. I'll use Program Manager as an example to teach you Windows fundamentals over the next few chapters. Part III, "Using Program Manager," gives you more specific information on Program Manager itself.

What's with This Mouse Thingy?

Learning how to use a mouse just might be your most important Windows survival skill. Why? Because most of Windows is designed with the mouse in mind, and you'll find that it makes many everyday tasks just plain faster and easier. If you can use a fork without poking yourself in the eye, then you'll have no trouble wielding a mouse.

The basic idea is simple: you move the mouse on its pad or on your desk, and a small arrow moves correspondingly on the screen. By positioning the arrow on strategic screen areas, you can select objects, run applications, and alter the shape and size of windows. Not bad for a rodent!

The Basic Mouse Technique

Using a mouse is straightforward, but it does take some getting used to. Here is the basic technique:

1. Turn the mouse so that its cable extends away from you.

2. Place your hand over the mouse in such a way that

   ☞ The part of the mouse nearest you nestles snugly in the palm of your hand.

   ☞ Your index and middle fingers rest lightly on the two mouse buttons (if your mouse has three buttons, rest your fingers on the two outside buttons).

☛ Your thumb and ring finger hold the mouse gently on either side.

3. Move the mouse around on its pad or on your desk. Notice how the mouse pointer on the screen moves in the same direction as the mouse itself.

Controlling the Darn Thing!

While moving the mouse pointer is simple enough, controlling the pesky, little thing is another matter. Most new mouse users complain that the pointer seems to move erratically, or that they move to one part of the screen and run out of room to maneuver. To help out, here are a few tips that will get you well on your way to becoming a mouse expert:

☛ Don't grab the mouse as if you were going to throw it across the room. A light touch is all that's needed.

☛ The distance the mouse pointer travels on the screen depends on how quickly you move the mouse. If you move the mouse very slowly for about an inch, the pointer moves about the same distance (a little more, actually). However, if you move the mouse very fast for about an inch, the pointer leaps across the screen.

☛ If you find yourself at the edge of the mouse pad but the pointer isn't where you want it to be, simply pick up the mouse and move it to the middle of the pad. This doesn't affect the position of the pointer, but it does allow you to continue on your way.

Mouse Actions

Here's a list of the kinds of actions you can perform with a mouse:

Point   This means that you move the mouse pointer so that it rests on a specific screen location.

Click   This means that you quickly press and release the left mouse button.

Double-click   As you might expect, double-clicking means that you quickly press and release the left mouse button twice in succession.

Drag   This simply means that you press and hold down the left mouse button and then move the mouse.

Put It to Work

It's a happy coincidence that the best Windows application for improving your new mouse skills also happens to be a very addictive game: Solitaire. To start Solitaire, first double-click on Program Manager's **Games** icon to open the Games window. Now double-click on the **Solitaire** icon. Here's a summary of the mouse actions you'll be using to play the game:

- ☞ Click on the deck to deal more cards.

- ☞ Drag the cards to move them between the row stacks.

- ☞ Double-click on a card to place it on the suit stack.

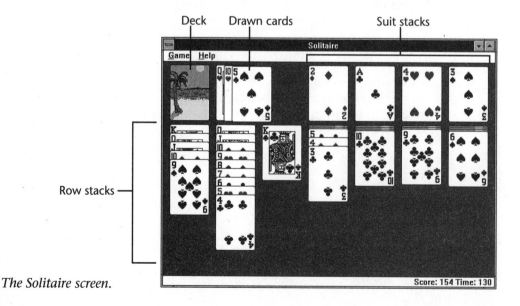

The Solitaire screen.

Windows Keyboarding for Nontypists

Although a mouse is handy for many Windows tasks, it's by no means essential. In fact, many Windows commands have built-in keyboard shortcuts that can be real time-savers. Does this mean that you have to become an expert typist to use Windows? Hardly. I've been using computer keyboards for years, and I wouldn't know what touch typing was if it bit me in the face.

The Keyboard Layout

Although there are a number of different keyboard styles available, they all share a few common features. In particular, all keyboards are divided into three sections: an alphanumeric keypad, a numeric keypad, and a function keypad, as you can see here.

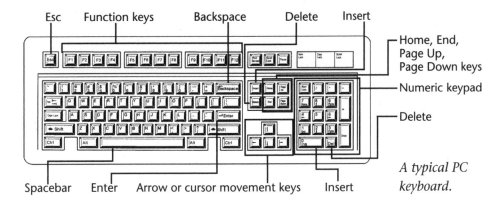

A typical PC keyboard.

Using the Alphanumeric Keypad

The alphanumeric keypad is the section of the keyboard that contains the letters, punctuation marks, and other special characters that you use most often (and some, like ~ and ^, that nobody uses). This section also contains several other keys that you use to execute Windows commands and functions, including the Ctrl, Alt, and Shift keys. Generally, you don't use these keys by themselves but as part of key combinations.

For example, try holding down the **Ctrl** key and pressing the **Esc** key. This causes the Windows Task List to pop up on your screen (you'll learn about the Task List in Chapter 10, "The Real Fun Begins: Starting Applications").

This method of holding down one key while pressing another is called a *key combination* and is used extensively in Windows. Since it's so much work to say "hold down the Ctrl key and press the Esc key," in this book, I'll simply say "press **Ctrl+Esc**." (By the way, to remove the Task List, just press **Esc** by itself.)

Using the Numeric Keypad

On each type of keyboard, the numeric keypad serves two functions. When the Num Lock key is on, you can use the numeric keypad to enter numbers. If Num Lock is off, the keypad cursor keys (the Left and Right arrow keys, the Up and Down arrow keys, Page Up, Page Down, Home, and End) are enabled and you can use these to navigate a window or list. Some keyboards (called extended keyboards) have a separate cursor keypad so you can keep Num Lock on all the time.

Using the Function Keys

The function keys are located either to the left of the alphanumeric keypad or across the top of the keyboard. There are usually 10 function keys (although some keyboards have 12), and they're labeled F1, F2, and so on. In Windows, you use these keys either by themselves or as part of key combinations. See the "Exiting Windows" section at the end of this chapter for an example.

The Parts Department: Elements of the Windows Screen

Okay, now that you're up to speed with the mouse and the keyboard, it's time to take a look around. This section gives you a brief rundown of the various parts of the Windows screen.

The Famous Desktop Metaphor

Ivory tower computer types like to invent metaphors for the way the rest of us use a computer. The idea is that more people will use a computer if using a computer is more like the way we do things in real life.

Windows uses the desktop metaphor. The idea is that the Windows screen is analogous to the top of a desk. Starting an application is like taking a folder full of papers out of storage and placing it on the desk. To do some work, of course, you need to pull papers out of the folder and place them on the Desktop. This is just like opening a file within the application (it could be a letter, a spreadsheet, a drawing, whatever). Most applications also come with *tools*, such as rulers, calculators, and pens, that are the electronic equivalents of the tools you use at your desk.

The Windows desktop metaphor is so prevalent that most people (geeks and otherwise) refer to the Windows screen as simply the *Desktop*.

Windows' Window Features

Here's a picture of Program Manager that points out the features that are common to most Windows applications.

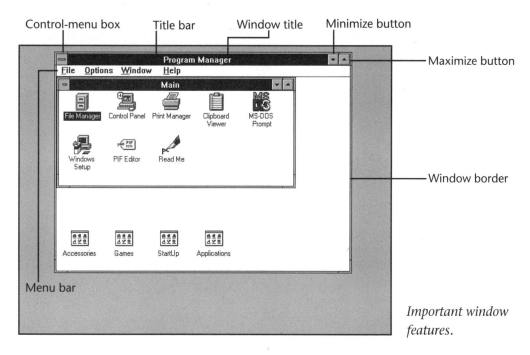

Important window features.

Window title   The name of the window (this isn't rocket science).

Title bar   The area along the top of the window that contains the window title.

Window border   The thin bar that surrounds a window.

Maximize button   The object with the upward-pointing arrow in the upper-right corner of a window. You click on this button to increase a window to its maximum size. See Chapter 8, "Why They Call It 'Windows,'" for information on maximizing windows.

Minimize button   The object with the downward-pointing arrow in the upper-right corner of a window. You click on this button to decrease a window to an icon. See Chapter 8, "Why They Call It 'Windows,'" for information on minimizing windows.

Control-menu box   The square in the upper-left corner of a window. Selecting this object displays the window's Control menu that enables you to easily work with the window from the keyboard. See Chapter 5, "Pull-Down Menus: Windows' Hidden Treasures," for information on using the Control menu.

Menu bar   Most application windows have a menu bar below the title bar. The menu bar contains one or more menu options that, when you select them, display pull-down menus. See Chapter 5, "Pull-Down Menus: Windows' Hidden Treasures," for information on using pull-down menus.

Exiting Windows

When you've finished working with Windows, you need to exit the program. If you use a mouse, you can follow these steps:

Never turn off your computer while Windows is still running. Doing so could result in lost data, damage to the Program Manager and other files, and accelerated hair loss.

1. Click on File in Program Manager's menu bar, and a menu of choices appears. This is your first look at a pull-down menu. We'll be exploring these magical beings in the next chapter.

2. At the bottom of the menu, click on Exit Windows. A message appears on the screen telling you what you already know: that you're about to end your Windows session.

3. Click on the button that says **OK**. Windows quits and returns you to DOS.

If you use a keyboard, here are the steps you need to follow:

1. Press **Alt+F** to display the menu of choices.

2. Press the Down arrow key until the Exit Windows option is highlighted.

3. Press **Enter**. Windows tells you that you're about to end your Windows session.

4. Press **Enter**. Windows quits and returns you to DOS.

If having to select the Exit Windows command from the File menu seems like a lot of work just to exit, there is a quicker way: simply press **Alt+F4** (this is one of those shortcut key combinations that I told you about earlier).

The Least You Need to Know

This chapter got you started with Windows. You learned how to get Windows up and running, how to use the mouse and keyboard, what the various parts of the Windows screen were, and how to exit the program. That's a lot! You might want to take five before moving on. In the meantime, here's a quick summary of what we covered:

☛ Type **win** and press **Enter** to start Windows. To avoid the brainwashing effects of the Windows logo, type **win :** and press **Enter**, instead.

☛ With practice, you'll find that a mouse is the easiest way to use most Windows functions. However, keyboard lovers can take heart: most Windows applications include a number of shortcut keys that you can use to do things quickly.

☛ To exit Windows, click on File in Program Manager's menu bar, click on Exit Windows in the menu that appears, and then click on **OK**. Keyboard users can simply press **Alt+F4** and then **Enter**.

☛ Motorcycles are loud and dangerous and are generally owned by fun-loving gadabouts who grow up to be free-lance writers.

This page unintentionally left blank.

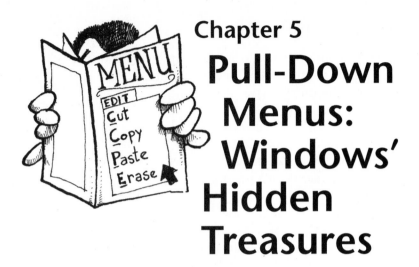

Chapter 5
Pull-Down Menus: Windows' Hidden Treasures

In This Chapter

- What are pull-down menus?
- Using pull-down menus with a mouse
- Using pull-down menus with the keyboard
- Strange but true tales of sofa cushions, desk drawers, and buried treasure

Life, as they say, is full of surprises, and one of my favorite surprises is lifting up the sofa cushions every few years and seeing what new collection awaits me. There is, of course, the usual assortment of flora and fauna: lint, crumbs, old Doritos, that kind of stuff. But you can also come across some buried treasure: coins, keys, old TV Guides—you name it.

The prospect of finding buried treasure is also what I like about the subject of this chapter: Windows' pull-down menus. These menus, which are normally hidden from view, contain all kinds of fun surprises, and they give you access to all the features of your Windows programs.

Desktop Metaphor Redux

In the last chapter, I introduced you to the desktop metaphor used by Windows. I'm returning to this metaphor now because it's perfect for describing pull-down menus. Here's what I mean:

To get your work done, it's not enough to simply shuffle papers all day. You usually need to do something to those papers, whether it's writing on them, stapling them together, making calculations, or whatever. To accomplish these tasks, you need the proper tools: a pen, a stapler, a calculator, and so on. With a few exceptions, you likely store most of these items in drawers instead of leaving them on top of your desk. When you need something, you just pull open the drawer (nudge, nudge) and select the item you want.

The choices you see in a pull-down menu are called *commands*. You use these commands to tell the application what you want it to do next.

In Windows, a pull-down menu is just like a desk drawer. When you need to access a *command* in an application, you simply open the appropriate menu and select that command.

Why You Pull "Down" Instead of "Up" or "Out"

Why are they called "pull-down" menus? Well, all Windows' applications include a menu bar, which is the horizontal strip on the second line of the application's window. (See Chapter 4 for a rundown of the various window parts.) Here's a look at Program Manager's menu bar.

Menu bar options   Menu bar

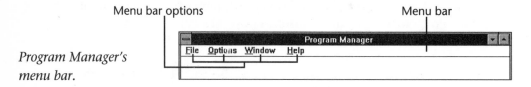

Program Manager's menu bar.

Selecting any one of the menu bar options (there are four in Program Manager: File, Options, Window, and Help) displays a menu of choices.

Here's what you see when you pull down Program Manager's File menu:

File pull-down menu

Program Manager's
File pull-down menu.

By the Way . . .

One of the easiest ways to become unproductive in a hurry is to waste time searching for the command you want in a Windows application's pull-down menu. When I'm learning a new application, I always check out the lay of the land by pulling down all the available menus and seeing what commands each has.

How to Use Pull-Down Menus with a Mouse

If you have a mouse, using pull-down menus is a breeze. All you do is move the mouse pointer into the menu bar area and then click on the name of the menu you want to pull down. For example, clicking on Window in Program Manager's menu bar pulls down the **Window** menu.

Once you have your menu displayed, you can then select any of the commands (there are some exceptions to this; see the section titled "More Fun Pull-Down Menu Stuff" for an explanation). To do this, you simply click on the command you want to execute. Depending on the command you select, one of three things will happen:

The command will execute. For example, with Program Manager's Window menu pulled down, click on the **Accessories** command. Lo and

You may find that you occasionally pull down a menu and then discover that you don't want to select any of its commands. You can remove the menu either by clicking on any empty part of the screen or by pulling down a different menu.

behold, the Accessories window appears. (To close the Accessories window, just double-click on the little square in the upper left corner of the window.)

Another menu will appear. In this case, click on the command you want to execute from the new menu.

A dialog box will appear to ask you for more information. See Chapter 6, "Talking to Windows Dialog Boxes," for details on using dialog boxes.

How to Use Pull-Down Menus with the Keyboard

Although a mouse makes pull-down menus easy to use, there's no law against using your keyboard. In fact, the keyboard method may even be quicker because you don't have to reach all the way over to the mouse. The secret to using pull-down menus from the keyboard is to look for the underlined letter in each menu bar command (they all have them). For example, in Program Manager, look at the "F" in File, the "O" in Option, and so on. These underlined letters are the super-duper hot keys. How do they work? Simple. You just hold down the **Alt** key, and then with Alt still held down, press the hot key on your keyboard. For example, hold down **Alt** and then press **W**. This pulls down Program Manager's Window menu.

By the Way . . .

It's traditional to abbreviate a phrase such as "hold down the Alt key and press W" to the much simpler phrase "press **Alt+W.**" Far be it from me to break with tradition (especially when it means less work for me), so I'll use this convention throughout the rest of the book.

Once you have a menu displayed, you need to select one of the commands. This is simple enough. Just use the Up and Down arrow keys to highlight the menu command you want, and then press **Enter**.

Depending on the command you select, one of three things will happen:

The command will execute. For example, in Program Manager's **Window** menu, highlight the **Accessories** command, and press **Enter**. Windows opens the Accessories window. (To close the Accessories window, press **Ctrl+F4**.)

Another menu will appear. In this case, use the arrow keys to select the command you want from the new menu, and then press **Enter**.

A dialog box will appear to ask you for more information. See Chapter 6, "Talking to Windows Dialog Boxes," for details on using dialog boxes.

What's Wrong with This Picture?

Here's a scenario that happens to me more than I'd care to admit. I'll be working away, and I'll decide to pull down a menu to run a command. So I hold down Alt and then, just as I'm about to press the appropriate hot key, I change my mind. So I release Alt and start typing again. However, all my computer does is beep rudely at me. Can you see what's wrong with this picture?

Answer: The problem is that any time you press Alt, Windows expects you to select a pull-down menu. So it activates the menu bar and waits for you to press a hot key. If you don't press a legitimate key, Windows admonishes you with a beep. The solution is to deactivate the menu bar by pressing either **Alt** or **Esc**.

More Fun Pull-Down Menu Stuff

You now know what pull-down menus are, how to pull them down, and how to select a command. I think rewarding yourself with a treat at this point would be a good idea.

What do you do if you pull down a menu and you discover that you don't want to select a command? Remove the menu by tapping the **Alt** key or by pressing **Esc** twice (yes, it has to be twice). If you find that you've pulled down the wrong menu, just use the Left or Right arrow keys to cycle through the other menus.

Okay. You may have noticed a few strange things about pull-down menus. For example, did you notice that every command in a pull-down menu has one underlined letter? Or that some commands are followed by three ominous-looking dots? Or that some commands also list a key or key combination? You can take advantage of some of these things to make your life easier. The rest of this section summarizes these features. I'll be using Program Manager's File menu as an example, so pull it down now if you want to follow along.

Underlined Characters: More Hot Keys

Every command in a pull-down menu has one underlined character. This is the command's hot key, and it means that, when the menu is displayed, you can select that command by simply pressing the underlined letter on your keyboard. For example, in Program Manager's File menu, you could select, say, the Exit Windows command simply by pressing x.

Shortcut Keys: The Fast Way to Work

Some menu commands also show a key or key combination on the right-hand side of the menu. These are called shortcut keys, and they allow you to bypass the menus altogether and activate a command quickly from your keyboard. For example, you can select the Move command in Program Manager simply by pressing F7. (For more information about Move and other Program Manager commands, see Part III, "Using Program Manager.")

Once you've worked with your favorite Windows applications for a while, you'll likely find that you often ignore the menus in favor of the program's shortcut keys. It's just a faster way to work. (For quick access to many of Windows' shortcut keys, take a look at the tear-out reference card that comes free-of-charge with this book.) Some smart applications (such as Word for Windows) even let you create your own shortcut keys.

Arrowheads (Menus, Menus, and More Menus)

In some applications, you'll see an arrowhead (►) to the right of a menu command (there are, unfortunately, no examples of this in Program Manager). This tells you that yet another menu will appear when you select this command.

When a menu command displays another menu, the new menu is called a *cascade menu.*

The Ellipsis (The Three-Dot Thing)

An ellipsis (...) after a command name indicates that a dialog box will appear when you select the command. A dialog box is a window that an application uses to ask you for more information. For example, if you select the Exit Windows command from Program Manager's File menu, a dialog box appears to ask you to confirm that you really want to exit the program. See Chapter 6, "Talking to Windows Dialog Boxes," for more details about dialog boxes.

What You Can't Do: The Dimmed Commands

You'll sometimes see menu commands that appear in a lighter color than the others. These are called *dimmed commands* and the dimming indicates that you can't select them (for now, anyway). Generally speaking, if you see a dimmed command, it means that you must do something else with the program before the command will become active.

Using the Control Menu

Besides the pull-down menus attached to the menu bar, each Windows window also has a Control menu. You use the Control menu to manipulate certain features of the window such as its size and position (see Chapter 8, "Why They Call It 'Windows,'" for details).

To display a window's Control menu with a mouse, simply click on the Control-menu box.

Control-menu box—

Control menu—

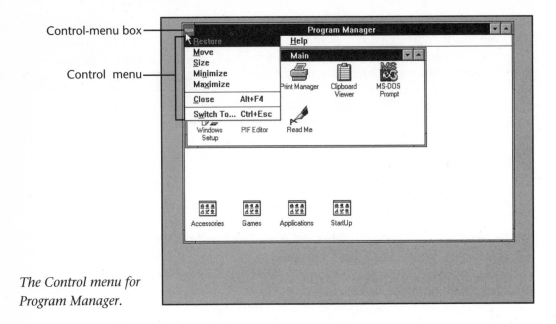

The Control menu for Program Manager.

It is, of course, impossible to remember when you use **Alt+Spacebar** and when you use **Alt+hyphen**. What I do is look at the bars inside the Control-menu boxes. In an application window, the bar is long like the Spacebar (so you press **Alt+Spacebar**), while in a document window the bar is short like a hyphen (so you press **Alt+hyphen**). Don't mention it.

Using the keyboard is a little more complicated:

☞ If you're working with the window of an application (such as the Program Manager window), press **Alt+Spacebar**.

☞ If you're working with a window within an application (such as Manager's Main program group), press **Alt+hyphen** (-).

The Least You Need to Know

This chapter explained Windows' pull-down menus and showed you how to use them with both a mouse and keyboard. Here's a summary of what you now know:

- Pull-down menus are a lot like desk drawers because they "store" tools (commands) that you use with your applications. All of this proves that there is apparently no end to the usefulness of the desktop metaphor.

- To pull down a menu with the mouse, simply click on the menu name in the menu bar. To pull down a menu with the keyboard, look for the menu's hot key, and then, while holding down **Alt**, press the key on your keyboard.

- Once a pull-down menu is displayed, you can select a command by clicking on it with your mouse. From the keyboard, you use the Up and Down arrow keys to highlight the command and then press **Enter**.

This page unintentionally left blank.

Chapter 6
Talking to Windows Dialog Boxes

In This Chapter

- ☞ What is a dialog box?
- ☞ Getting around in dialog boxes
- ☞ Learning about dialog box buttons, boxes, and lists

Communication is in. Everywhere you go, people are "establishing a dialogue," "networking," or dealing with "interpersonal dynamics." Experts from all fields are appearing on sleazy daytime talk shows to remind us to "listen to each other" or risk a dysfunctional fate.

Windows, being the hip, modern program that it is, is also getting into the act. As you work with Windows applications, endless little windows will appear on your screen to prompt you for more information. These are called dialog boxes, and they're Windows' way of saying "Talk to me!" This chapter looks at these chatty little beasts and offers some helpful tips for surviving their relentless onslaught.

Where Do They Come From?

Dialog boxes may sometimes seem to appear out of nowhere, but they generally show up after you select certain commands from an application's pull-down menu. Whether or not a dialog box appears depends on whether or not the application needs more information from you. For example, suppose you pull down a menu and select a command called Jump. Here's a dialog box you might see.

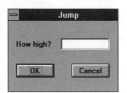

A dialog box you might see in response to a "Jump" command.

The application is telling you it needs more information. On the other hand, suppose you select a "Don't Jump" command, instead. This command needs no further embellishment, so it's not likely that a dialog box would appear.

By the Way . . .

You can always tell when a command will generate a dialog box by looking for three dots (...) after the command name. These three dots (an ellipsis) tell you that some kind of dialog box will appear if you select the command.

Put It to Work

By far, the best way to learn about dialog boxes is to open a few and try things out for yourself. To that end, I'll use the rest of this chapter to lead you through a concrete example: adding a new icon to a Program Manager group. To prepare, you only have to do one thing: make sure one of the Program Manager windows (Main, Accessories, and so on) is active. It doesn't matter a whole lot which one is active, but Accessories is probably a good choice. If Accessories appears as an icon in your Program Manager, double-click on it, or select Accessories from the **W**indow pull-down menu.

Dialog Box Basics

Before we can talk any more about dialog boxes, we need to get a specimen on the screen. To do this, pull down Program Manager's File menu, and select the New command. Program Manager displays the dialog box shown here.

Dialog box title

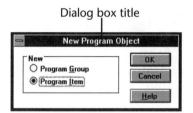

Program Manager displays the New Program Object dialog box when you select New from the File menu.

The first thing to notice about dialog boxes is that they have several features in common with other windows that you've seen, including borders and a title bar (the title of this dialog box is "New Program Object"). What's different is what's inside. The various objects you see are called controls because you use them to control the way the dialog box works.

Navigating Controls

Before you learn how these controls operate, you need to know how to navigate them. (This section applies only to keyboard users. Mouse users select a control merely by clicking on it.) There are two separate techniques:

Tab Key   Press the **Tab** key to move forward through the controls ("forward" means that you move either left-to-right or top-to-bottom, depending on how the dialog box is laid out). Press **Shift+Tab** to move backward.

Arrow keys   You'll often see several similar controls surrounded by a box. This means that the controls form a group. In the New Program Object dialog box, for example, the box labeled "New" groups together the Program Group and Program Item controls. You first use the Tab key to get into the group, and then you use the arrow keys to move within the group itself.

Any time you see a dialog box control with an underlined letter, it means that you can select the control by simply holding down the **Alt** key and pressing the underlined letter on your keyboard. For example, to select the Program Item control, you'd press **Alt+I**.

To get the hang of these techniques, you really need to get your feet wet and try them out. Feel free to use the New Program Object dialog box for your experiments. Simply moving around in the dialog box won't harm anything.

Working with Option Buttons

When I was in school, I always hated multiple-choice questions. I figured I could bluff my way through an essay question. But with multiple-choice, it's the law of the jungle: you're either right or wrong.

Windows' equivalent of the multiple-choice question is the option button. You're given two or more choices, and you're only allowed to pick one. (Argh, the pressure!)

The New Program Object dialog box contains two option buttons: Program Group and Program Item.

As you can see, an option button consists of a small circle with a label beside it that tells you what the option is. Remember that the purpose of a dialog box is to get more information from you. When you selected the New command from the File menu earlier, you told Program Manager that you wanted to create something new. This dialog box is Program Manager's way of asking, "What kind of new thing?" To help out, it also

If your mouse or keyboard skills aren't quite up to snuff yet, you may select the wrong option button. No problem. Just select the correct one, and Windows will automatically deactivate the incorrect one.

shows your available options: a Program Group or a Program Item. (Don't worry too much about what these terms mean. I'll explain it all in Part III, "Using Program Manager.") Your mission is to select one of these options, and then move on.

Selecting an Option Button

How do you select an option button? If you have a mouse, simply click on the option you want (you can either click on the button itself or on the name). Notice how a black dot appears inside the circle when you select an option.

To select an option from the keyboard, you need to press **Tab** until one of the option buttons in the group is *active* (it's surrounded by a dotted outline), and then use the arrow keys to move through the group to the option you want. In the New Program Object dialog box, select the Program Item option.

Working with Command Buttons

The other three controls in the New Program Object dialog box are labeled OK, Cancel, and Help. These are called command buttons and when you select one, you're telling Program Manager (in this case) to execute the command written on the face of the button.

Applications use command buttons for all kinds of things, but OK, Cancel, and Help are the most common. Here's what they do:

Select this button when you've finished with the dialog box, and you want to put all your selections into effect. This is the "Make it so" button.

Select this button when you panic and realize that you're looking at the wrong dialog box or if you've made a mess of your selections. This is the "Belay that last order" button.

Select this button when you haven't the faintest idea what you're doing and you'd like the application to give you a hint. This is the "Please explain" button.

Selecting Command Buttons

To select a command button with a mouse, just click on the button. To select a command button from the keyboard, press **Tab** until the command button you want is active (its name is surrounded by a dotted outline), and then press **Enter**.

Putting Your Knowledge to the Test

To continue with our example, follow these steps:

1. Make sure you've chosen the Program Item option button in the New Program Object dialog box.

2. Select the **OK** command button. Windows displays another dialog box, called Program Item Properties, as shown here.

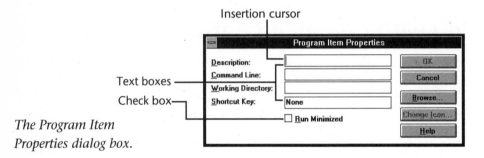

Insertion cursor

Text boxes

Check box

The Program Item Properties dialog box.

Working with Check Boxes

The real world is constantly presenting us with a series of either-or choices. You're either watching *Oprah* or you're not; you're either eating Heavenly Hash or you're not. Windows handles these yes-or-no, on-or-off decisions with a control called a check box. The check box presents you with an option that you can either activate (check) or not. In the Program Item Properties dialog box, for example, the Run Minimized control is a check box. This control is on when an "X" appears in the square, and it's off when the square is empty.

To select a check box with a mouse, click on the box or on its name. To deselect the box (remove the X), just click the box again.

To select a check box from the keyboard, press **Tab** until the check box you want is active (its name is surrounded by a dotted outline), and then press the **Spacebar**. To deselect the check box, press the **Spacebar** again.

Although we don't need the Run Mini-mized option for our example, you might want to try it out just the same. Just make sure it's off before continuing.

Working with Text Boxes

A text box is a screen area you use to type in text information, such as a description or a file name. When it's active, a blinking, vertical bar appears in the box.

To use a text box with a mouse, click anywhere inside the box, and then type in your text.

To use a text box from your keyboard, press **Tab** until you see the *insertion point cursor* in the box you want, and then begin typing.

Continuing with Our Example

To proceed with our example, make sure you

1. Select the **Description** text box in the Program Item Properties dialog box.

2. Type in **Windows Version Thingy**. (Actually, you can type anything you want because this is only a descrip-tion. You'll see what it does later on.)

3. Tab to the Command Line text box. Instead of filling this box with your own text, I'll show you how to get Windows to do it for you in the next section.

4. Select the **Browse** button. Windows displays yet another dialog box (I told you these things were relentless). This one is called the Browse dialog box.

Every group of command buttons always has a default button that has a darker outline than the others (you need to look closely to see this). To select this button, just press **Enter** from anywhere in the dialog box. When you first open the New Program Object dialog box, for example, the OK button is the default. Also, you can simply press **Esc** instead of selecting the **Cancel** button.

The blinking, vertical bar you see inside a text box is called the *insertion point cursor*.

If you make a typing mistake, press the **Back-space** key until the offend-ing letters are deleted.

List boxes

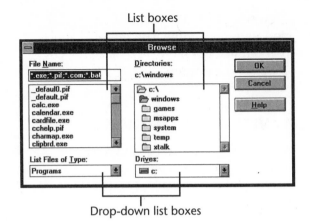

Drop-down list boxes

Another dialog box?
This one's called the
Browse dialog box.

Working with Drop-Down List Boxes

A drop-down list box is similar to a pull-down menu in that when you select one, Windows displays a list of options. (So why aren't they called "pull-down" list boxes? Beats me.) Drop-down list boxes usually contain lists of related items such as file names or disk drives.

To use a mouse to select an item from a drop-down list box:

1. Click on the downward-pointing arrow on the right side of the box. This opens the list to display its options.

2. Click on the item you want. If you don't see the item you want, use the scroll bar to view more of the list. (If you're not sure how a scroll bar works, see the next section.)

To use your keyboard to select an item from a drop-down list, follow these steps:

1. Press **Tab** until the drop-down box is highlighted.

2. Press the Down arrow key to open the list.

3. Use the Up and Down arrow keys to highlight the item you want.

4. Press **Enter**.

The Browse dialog box has two drop-down list boxes: List Files of Type and Drives. For our example, you don't need to select anything from these lists.

A Brief Scroll Bar Primer

You'll be learning more about scroll bars in the next chapter, but I'll give you a brief introduction here so you'll be able to use both drop-down list boxes and regular list boxes.

Some lists contain too many items to fit inside their box. In this case, a scroll bar appears on the right hand side of the box to make it easier to navigate the list. The box inside the scroll bar (called, appropriately enough, the scroll box) tells you where you are in the list. For example, if the scroll box is halfway between the top and the bottom of the scroll bar, then you're approximately halfway down the list.

Here's a tip that can save you oodles of time. Once the drop-down list is open, press the first letter of the item you want. Windows leaps down the list and highlights the first item in the list that begins with the letter you pressed. You can also use this tip for the regular list boxes that you'll learn about in the next section.

To navigate a list with the scroll bar, use the mouse techniques below:

To scroll through the list one item at a time, click on either of the arrows at the top and bottom of the scroll bar.

To jump quickly through the list, click inside the scroll bar between the scroll box and the top (to move up) or between the scroll box and the bottom (to move down).

To move to a specific part of the list, drag the scroll box up or down.

Working with List Boxes

A list box is a small window that displays a list of items such as file names or directories. A highlight bar shows the currently selected item in the list.

To use a mouse to select an item from a list box, you can

Double-click on the item if it's visible.

Use the scroll bars, if necessary, to display the item, and then double-click on it.

To select a list box item from your keyboard, follow these steps:

1. Press **Tab** until an item in the list is highlighted.

2. Use the Up and Down arrow keys (or PgUp and PgDn if the list is a long one) to highlight the item you want.

3. Press **Enter**.

Finishing Off the Example

Our example is almost complete. Here are the final steps:

1. Move to the File Name list box.

2. Select the file **WINVER.EXE**. Windows returns you to the Program Item Properties dialog box. Notice that the Command Line text box is filled in for you.

3. Select the **OK** button. Windows returns you to the Accessories program group. You should see a new icon in the group called Windows Version Thingy (or whatever you entered in the Description text box). To try it out, double-click on it, or press **Enter**. A dialog box will appear that tells you which version of Windows you're using. To get rid of the dialog box, click on **OK**, or press **Enter**.

The Least You Need to Know

This chapter showed you the ins and outs of using dialog boxes to communicate with Windows. We covered a lot of ground, and you learned all kinds of new things. If it's not all clear in your head right now, don't worry about it because, believe me, you'll be getting plenty of practice. Meanwhile, here's some important stuff to remember:

- ☞ Windows applications use dialog boxes to ask you for more information or to confirm that the command you've selected is what you really want to do.

- ☞ Keyboard jockeys use the Tab key to move through the dialog box controls. Inside a group of controls, use the arrow keys.

- ☞ Many controls have underlined letters. You can select these controls by holding down **Alt** and pressing the letter on your keyboard.

This page unintentionally left blank.

Chapter 7

Day-To-Day File Drudgery

In This Chapter

- ☞ Opening and saving a file
- ☞ Navigating a file
- ☞ Editing a file
- ☞ The usual assortment of rambling diatribes

It may sound strange to say, but Windows is the reigning sex symbol of personal computing. Think about it—all those lush screens, the siren call of those seductive icons, the cheesecake graphics. This is one good-looking program.

But even sex symbols sometimes have to take out the garbage and feed the cat. In Windows, this means opening and saving files, cutting and pasting text, printing out documents. This day-to-day stuff is Windows without its makeup on, and it's the subject of this chapter.

To get the most out of this chapter, you probably should follow along using an actual Windows application. I'll be using Write—the word processor that comes with Windows—for my examples, but it doesn't matter a whole lot which one you use. Just make sure that the application has both a File and an Edit pull-down menu. If you'd like to use Write as well, you'll find its icon in Program Manager's Accessories group. To start Write, double-click on the icon, or use the arrow keys to highlight it, and then press **Enter**. See also Chapter 20, "The Write Stuff: Word Processing with Write," for additional instruction on the features of Write.

Getting to Work: Opening a File

When you start most Windows applications, you'll usually see a new, blank file. Most of the time, though, you'll want to work with an existing file. This means that you have to open the file you want by pulling down the application's File menu (well, at least that makes sense) and selecting the Open command. You'll see the Open dialog box.

Current directory

Current drive

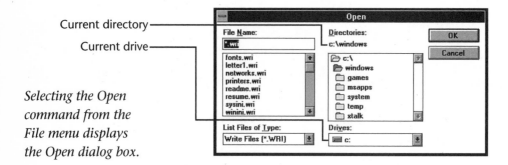

Selecting the Open command from the File menu displays the Open dialog box.

The purpose of the Open dialog box is to give you a reasonably coherent view of the files on your hard disk. The idea is that you browse through the files and then select the one you want to open. You'll be seeing this dialog box (or a variation of it) more often than you want, so let's take a closer look at just how you go about selecting a file.

Apartment Hunting Made Easy

To make this process of searching for a file a little more comprehensible, let's set up a simple analogy: the apartment search. When you're looking for an apartment, you first decide what city you want to live in. Once you know that, you can narrow your search to a specific area of the city. Finally, you narrow your search even further by deciding what type of apartment you want (bachelor, 1-bedroom, and so on). When all this is done, you end up with a short list of possible apartments and you select the one you want from this list. Okay, let's put this analogy to work.

Step 1: Selecting the Correct Drive (the City)

Files can be stored on your hard disk or on floppy disks, so the first step is to make sure that you're dealing with the right drive. In our apartment hunting analogy, this is like selecting a city in which to live. The Drives drop-down list box displays the current drive. You can use it to select a different drive, if necessary.

> If you're going to select a floppy drive from the Drives list, make sure there's a disk in the drive. Otherwise, your computer will make a rude noise, and Windows will display a dialog box telling you it **Can't read from drive a:** (or whatever drive you selected). If this happens, insert a disk, and then select the **Retry** button.

For all the gory details on drop-down list boxes, see Chapter 6, "Talking to Windows Dialog Boxes."

Step 2: Selecting the Correct Directory (the Neighborhood)

Just as cities are divided into neighborhoods, disks are divided into storage areas called *directories*. Use the Directories list box to select the correct directory for your file.

If you forget how to select items from a list box, see Chapter 6, "Talking to Windows Dialog Boxes."

Step 3: Displaying the Proper File Type (the Type of Apartment)

There are many different kinds of apartments, and there are many different kinds of files. And although a directory may contain dozens or even hundreds of files, there are only a few that you really need to look at. (For example, files created with Write generally end with .WRI.) Use the List Files of Type drop-down list box to narrow the number of files displayed.

Step 4: Selecting a File (the Apartment)

Now you're ready to make your selection. You've narrowed your search and the finalists are displayed in the File Name list box. Double-click on the file you want to open or highlight it, and then select **OK**.

By the Way . . .

If the sight of words such as directory and drive make you nervous, relax: this is the normal reaction of any sane person when confronted with DOS stuff. Just nod your head knowingly as you work through this chapter, or better yet, see Part IV, "Using File Manager," for some painless explanations.

Save Your Work, Save Your Life

Most people learn about saving files the hard way. For me, it was a power failure that wiped out an entire day's writing. Believe me, that kind of thing can make you old before your time. Why is saving necessary? Well, when you open a file, the program copies it from its safe haven on your hard disk to the volatile confines of your computer's memory. When you shut off your computer (or if a power failure forces it off), everything in memory is wiped out. If you haven't saved your file to your hard disk, you'll lose all the changes you made.

Saving a File

Fortunately, Windows makes saving your work as easy as shooting fish in a barrel. To save the file you're working on, pull down the application's File menu and select the **Save** command. That's it!

Well, actually, that's not quite it. If you're saving a new file, you'll see the Save As dialog box on the screen. (It looks almost identical to the Open dialog box from the last section.) Select the drive and directory in which you want to store the file, and then enter a file name in the File Name box.

The Strange but Useful Save As Command

Your application's File menu probably also includes a Save As command. This command is a lot like Save, except that you can save the file to a new name or a new location. This is useful for creating a new file that is very similar (but not identical) to an existing file. Instead of creating the new file from scratch, just open the existing file, make the changes, and then use the Save As command to save your changes to the new file. The old file remains as it was. When you select the Save As command, you'll see the same Save As dialog box that I told you about in the last section.

A Fresh Beginning: Starting a New Document

TECHNO NERD TEACHES

Of all the arcane restrictions that have been foisted on us by DOS, file names are probably the weirdest. They can be a maximum of eight characters, followed by a period, followed by another three characters. Windows applications make things a little easier because the period and the 3-character extension are usually added automatically. So when you're naming a file, just enter a descriptive name that's eight characters or less. Just to make our lives even more confusing, there are a few other restrictions you have to follow when naming a file. See Chapter 13, "File Finagling," for the gory details.

As I mentioned earlier, most applications display a new file when you first open them. However, you can open a fresh file anytime you want. All you do is pull down the application's File menu, and select the New command.

Printing a File

Printing is a pretty big subject in Windows, so I've devoted an entire chapter to it later on (Chapter 18, "Hard Copy: Windows Printing Basics"). To whet your appetite, though, I'll give you the basic steps here. To print a file, pull down the File menu, and select the Print command. This will display a Print dialog box.

*Write's Print
dialog box.*

At this point, you enter the number of copies you want printed, which pages you want to print, and so on. When you're ready, select **OK** (some Print dialog boxes have a Print button, instead).

Closing a File

Some weakling Windows programs (such as Write) only allow you to open one file at a time. In this case, you can close the file you're currently working on by either opening another file or by quitting the application altogether.

However, most full-featured Windows programs let you open as many files as you want. Things can get crowded pretty fast, though, so you'll probably want to close any files you don't need. To do this, select the file you want to close, pull down the File menu, and then select the Close command. If you made changes to the file, a dialog box will appear to ask you if you want to save those changes.

By the Way . . .

Working with multiple files in an application is an essential Windows survival skill. See Chapter 8, "Why They Call It 'Windows,'" to learn the basics.

Using Scroll Bars to Navigate a File

Depending on the application, an opened file will appear either in its own window or as part of the application's window. In either case, you'll often find that the entire file won't fit inside the window boundaries. When this happens, you need some way to move to the parts of the file that you can't see.

From the keyboard, you can use either the basic navigation keys—the arrow keys as well as Page Up and Page Down—or the special key combinations that vary from application to application.

By the Way . . .

I've found a few key combinations that seem to work in many applications. For example, the **Home** key will often take you to the beginning of the current line and the **End** key will often take you to the end of the line. Also, try **Ctrl+Home** to get to the beginning of the file and **Ctrl+End** to get to the end.

Mouse users, as usual, have all the fun. In this case, they get to use scroll bars.

Scroll bars are a lot like elevators. They look a bit like elevator shafts, and serve a dual purpose: they can tell you where you are, and they can take you somewhere else.

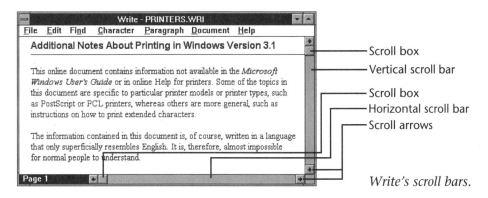

Write's scroll bars.

Where Am I? The Scroll Bar Knows

Thanks to my innately lousy sense of direction, I always seem to get lost in any file that has more than a couple of screens of information. Fortunately, I have scroll bars to bail me out. The idea is simple: the position of the scroll boxes tells me my relative position in the file. So, for example, if the vertical scroll box is about halfway down, then I know I'm somewhere near the middle of the file. They're just like the floor indicators on an elevator.

Can I Get There from Here? Navigating with Scroll Bars

The real scroll bar fun begins when you use them to move around in your files. There are three basic techniques:

☛ To scroll vertically through the list one line at a time, click on the vertical scroll bar's Up or Down scroll arrows. To scroll horizontally through the list one column at a time, click on the horizontal scroll bar's Left or Right scroll arrows.

☛ To leap through the file one screen at a time, click inside the scroll bar between the scroll box and the scroll arrows. For example, to move down one screenful, click inside the vertical scroll bar between the scroll box and the Down scroll arrow.

☛ To move to a specific part of the file, drag the vertical scroll box up or down, or drag the horizontal scroll box left or right.

Editing Files

You know how to open a file, how to save it, and how to get around in it. What's missing? Oh yeah, you've got to do some work eventually!

Of course, most of what you'll do in a file depends entirely on the application you're using, but let's look at a few basic skills that you can use in almost any application.

Highlighting Text

Most files have some sort of text in them that you can format (for example, add bolding or underlining) or cut and paste. Before you can do any of these operations, though, you need to *highlight* the text you want to work with.

To highlight text with a mouse, simply drag the mouse over the characters you want. From the keyboard, position the cursor to the left of the first character, hold down the **Shift** key, and then press the Right arrow key until the entire selection is highlighted. Use the Down arrow key if you need to highlight multiple lines.

Copying a Selection

One of the secrets of computer productivity is a simple maxim: Don't reinvent the wheel. In other words, if you've got something that works (it could be a picture, a section of text, whatever) and you need something similar, don't start from scratch. Instead, make a copy of the original, and then make whatever changes are necessary to the copy.

Happily, most Windows applications make it easy to copy. In fact, once you've highlighted what you want to copy, all you need to do is pull down the application's Edit menu and select the Copy command. You then position the cursor where you want to place the copy (it could even be in another file), and then select **Paste** from the Edit menu. A perfect copy of your selection appears instantly.

If you highlight some text and then press any letter on your keyboard, you'll be dismayed to see your entire selection disappear and be replaced by the letter you pressed. (This also happens if you press a number or even the Enter key.) This is, unfortunately, normal behavior that can cause problems for even experienced word-processor jockeys. To fix the problem, use the application's Undo command immediately (see "To Err is Human, To Undo Divine," below).

Many people also use the Cut command to delete things from their files. This is fine, but it's usually faster to simply press the **Delete** key.

Cutting a Selection

If you need to move something from one part of a file to another (or from one file to another), you can do so by making a copy, pasting it, and then going back to delete the original. But there's an easier way. Once you've selected what you want to move, pull down the Edit menu and select the Cut command. Your selection will disappear from the screen, but don't panic; Windows is saving it for you. Now position the cursor where you want to move the selection, and then choose Paste from the Edit menu. Your stuff miraculously reappears in the new location.

The Undo command only works on the last thing you did. If you do something else (such as type some text), you won't be able to reverse your mistake. For this reason, always select the **U**ndo command immediately after your blunder.

To Err Is Human, To Undo Divine

At some point in your computing career, usually when you least expect it, you'll have the "uh-oh" experience. This occurs anytime you do something that you shouldn't have, such as consign a vital piece of an irreplaceable file to deletion purgatory.

Fortunately, many Windows applications now come with an Undo feature to get you out of these jams. The Undo command restores everything to the way it was before you made your blunder.

To use the Undo feature, pull down the application's Edit menu, and select the Undo command. Depending on what you did, the command may actually say something like Undo Paste.

The Least You Need to Know

Now that was a chapter! You learned all kinds of practical stuff from opening and saving files to basic cut-and-paste techniques. Whew! Here's a summary of what you need to know:

☛ The **F**ile menu contains, not surprisingly, your basic file commands: **N**ew, **O**pen, **S**ave, and Save **A**s.

☛ Mouse users can take advantage of a window's scroll bars to navigate their files quickly.

☛ The **E**dit menu supplies you with three handy commands for working with highlighted material: **C**opy, Cu**t**, and **P**aste.

☛ If you make a mistake, immediately select **U**ndo from the application's **E**dit menu.

This page unintentionally left blank.

Chapter 8
Why They Call
It 'Windows'

In This Chapter

- ☞ Activating windows
- ☞ Moving and sizing windows
- ☞ Maximizing and minimizing windows
- ☞ A fascinating detour into the realm of etymology

In ancient times, long before glass was in common use, people would build their homes with holes in the walls to let in air and light. Because these holes allowed them to see out and allowed air in, they were called "wind eyes." Over time, of course, people began covering these holes with glass and the phrase "wind eyes" turned into the modern word "windows."

I tell you this story by way of introduction to the subject of this chapter: the windows in Windows. In a sense, the old meaning of the word "window" fits quite nicely here. In Windows, you can "see through" a window to look at what's on your computer. But these windows also "let in" your input in the form of keystrokes or mouse clicks. It might help to keep all this in mind as you work with Windows' windows. Just remember that each window on the screen is a view of something on your computer and that you can "reach through" the window and make changes to what you see.

So Many Windows, So Little Space

Isn't there an old saying that talks about a person's greatest strength also being their greatest weakness? It's possible I just made it up but, in any case, it certainly applies to Windows. Why? Well, Windows' greatest strength is the way it organizes your computer visually. Things appear all nicely laid out in their own window, and you can see everything that's going on.

Windows' second greatest strength is that it allows you to work on a bunch of things at the same time. This means that you can have Program Manager running in one window, your word processor in another, your spreadsheet in a third, and so on. As if that isn't enough, Windows also allows you to open up multiple windows in a single application! So in your word processor, for example, you could have a window open for your letter to Mom, one for your shopping list, one for your memo to the execs on the coast, and so on.

Too Many Windows

The problem with all these windows is that things can get confusing, really fast. If you don't believe me, take a look at this Word for Windows screen.

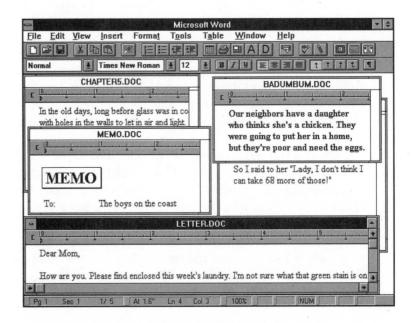

Opening multiple documents in a single application can quickly get out of hand.

What a mess! And there are only five documents open in this picture. If you have enough memory, you could conceivably open dozens of documents.

What's needed here are some simple techniques for managing windows. Fortunately, Windows offers a number of methods for regaining control of your screen. I'll use the rest of this chapter to get you up to speed on the easiest and fastest of these methods.

> ### By the Way . . .
> To keep things simple, this chapter only works with multiple windows in a single application. It's a whole other kettle of fish when you start talking about managing multiple applications. I'll postpone that until Chapter 10, "The Real Fun Begins: Starting Applications."

Anytime you find yourself with a bunch of windows on your screen, you can simplify your life immeasurably if you keep the following maxim in mind: You can only work in one window at a time. In other words, no matter how many windows may be open, the window you're currently working in (it's called the *active window*, by the way) gives you its complete and undivided attention. You can therefore safely ignore everything else going on around it.

Which Window Is Active?

With this in mind, the first stop on our window management tour will be to learn how to make a window active. How will you know when you've succeeded in making a window active? Just look at the window's title bar. If the window is active, its title bar will show the title in white letters on a dark background. If it's an inactive window, the title will appear in dark letters on a white background. (If you changed colors, look for a cursor or highlight inside the window, instead.) Here's an example.

The Main window is inactive, so the title bar shows dark letters on a white background.

How to tell the difference between an active and inactive window.

The Accessories window is active, so the title bar shows white letters on a dark background.

When you pull down the **Window** menu, you'll notice that each of the listed windows has an underlined number beside it. These are the hot keys that Windows has assigned to each window. So, to activate a window quickly, pull-down the **Window** menu, and then press the corresponding number on your keyboard.

Activating a Window

Any Windows application that lets you open multiple windows will normally have a Window option in its menu bar. Program Manager does, so let's use it as an example. Click on **Window**, or press **Alt+W** to pull down the **Window** menu. The various Program Manager windows (Main, Accessories, and so on) are listed at the bottom of the menu. To activate a window, simply select it from this menu. (Recall that you select pull-down menu commands by clicking on them or by using the arrow keys to highlight them and then pressing **Enter**.) What could be easier?

Well, there actually is an easier way to activate a window, but it only works in certain conditions. Specifically, if you have more than one window open on your screen and you can see any part of the window that you want to activate, then simply click anywhere inside the window with the mouse. Now that's easy.

Activating a window is important, but it's only the first step towards gaining full control over how your windows appear on the screen. The rest of this chapter shows you a number of the basic Windows techniques.

Windows on the Move

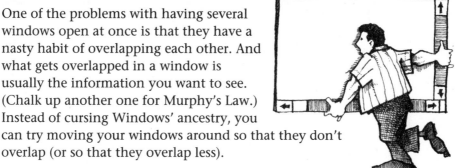

One of the problems with having several windows open at once is that they have a nasty habit of overlapping each other. And what gets overlapped in a window is usually the information you want to see. (Chalk up another one for Murphy's Law.) Instead of cursing Windows' ancestry, you can try moving your windows around so that they don't overlap (or so that they overlap less).

If you use a mouse, you can move a window like this:

1. Using the steps you learned earlier in this chapter, activate the window you want to move.

2. Point the mouse at the window's title bar, and drag the window to its new location. (Recall that you drag something by pointing at it, holding down the left mouse button, and then moving the mouse.) As you drag, the new position of the window appears as a gray outline.

3. When you have the outline in the position you want, release the mouse button. Windows redisplays the window in the new position.

If you use a keyboard, here are the steps to follow:

1. Activate the window you want to move.

2. Pull down the window's Control menu by pressing **Alt+Hyphen** (-).

3. Highlight the **Move** command and press **Enter**. You'll see a gray outline appear around the window border.

4. Use the arrow keys to move the window outline.

5. Once the outline is in the location you want, press **Enter**. Windows redisplays the window in the new location. If you decide you don't want to move the window after all, you can press the **Esc** key at any time.

Sizing Up Your Windows

Another way to reduce window clutter is to change the size of the open windows. For example, you can reduce the size of less important windows and increase the size of windows you do the most work in. The secret to sizing is the window border. The idea is that you drag part of the border (either the top, bottom, left, or right) with your mouse to create the new dimensions. Here are the explicit mouse steps:

It's possible to size two borders at the same time. All you have to do is position the mouse pointer on a window corner. When you drag the mouse, the two sides that create the corner will move.

1. Activate the window you want to size.

2. Point the mouse at a window border you want to adjust. You'll know the pointer is positioned correctly when it changes into a two-headed arrow.

3. Drag the border to the position you want. The new border appears as a gray bar.

4. Release the mouse button. Windows resizes the window.

5. Repeat steps 2–4 for any other borders you want to size.

If you prefer to use the keyboard, you need to follow these steps:

1. Activate the window you want to size.

2. Pull down the window's Control menu.

3. Highlight the **Size** option and press **Enter**. A gray outline appears around the window border.

4. To select a border to size, press the corresponding arrow key. For example to size the right border, press the right arrow key.

5. Use the arrow keys to size the window outline.

6. Once the outline is the size you want, press **Enter**. Windows redisplays the window in the new size. If you decide you don't want the window resized, just press **Esc**.

Letting Windows Do the Work: Cascading and Tiling

All this moving and sizing stuff is fine for people with time to kill. The rest of us just want to get the job done and move on. To that end, most Windows applications include Cascade and Tile commands that will automatically arrange your windows for you.

The Cascade command arranges your open windows in a cool, waterfall pattern, as shown here.

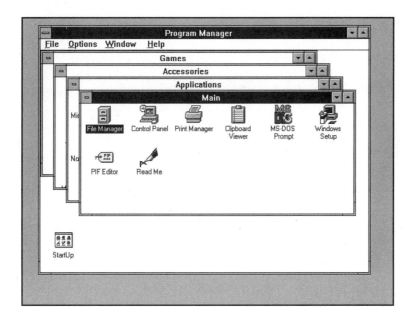

What the Cascade command does.

This is good for those times when you want things nice and neat, but you don't need to see what's in the other windows. To cascade your windows, select the Cascade command from the **W**indow menu.

The Tile command divides up your screen and gives equal real estate to each window, as shown here.

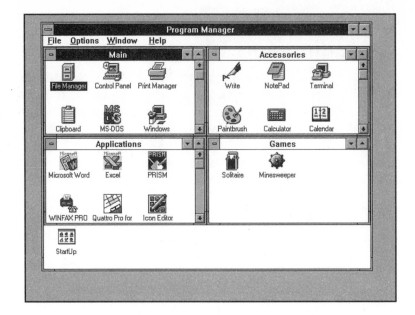

The Tile command gives each of your open windows an equal amount of screen space.

This pattern allows you to work in one window and still keep an eye on what's happening in the other windows. To tile your windows, select the Tile command from the Window menu.

The Minimalist Approach: Reducing a Window to an Icon

You'll often find that you have some windows that you know you won't need for a while. You could move them out of the way or make them smaller, but that takes time, and our goal is always to make things as easy as possible. Fortunately, there's an alternative: you can reduce the window down to a mere icon. This is called minimizing the window.

If you use a mouse, you can minimize a window in no time at all by simply clicking on the window's Minimize button, as pointed out in the following picture.

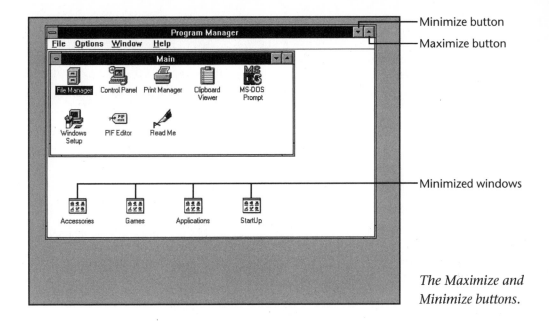

The Maximize and Minimize buttons.

It takes a bit more effort if you're using the keyboard. In this case, you need to pull down the window's Control menu and select the Minimize command.

Taking It to the Max: Maximizing a Window

To get the largest possible work area, you can maximize a window. This means that the window expands so that it fills the entire application window (except for the menu bar and title bar, of course).

If you use a mouse, all you have to do is click on the window's Maximize button. From the keyboard, pull down the window's Control menu and select the Maximize command.

Restoring a Window

When you maximize or minimize a window, Windows is smart enough to remember what the window used to look like. This allows you to easily *restore* the window to its previous size and position.

With a mouse, you have two options:

If you maximized the window, the Maximize button now appears with double arrows. This is called the Restore button (makes sense, doesn't it?). Simply click on this button to revert the window to its previous state.

If you minimized the window, you restore it by double-clicking on its icon.

From the keyboard, you need to do the following:

For a maximized window, pull down its Control menu, and select the Restore command.

For a minimized window, pull down the application's **Window** menu and select the window.

The Least You Need to Know

This chapter gave you the lowdown on the windows that give Windows its name. The emphasis was on gaining control over how your windows appear on your screen. Here's what you learned:

- ☞ The window you're working in is the active window.

- ☞ To display a document window's Control menu, press **Alt+Hyphen** (-).

- ☞ To move a window, drag its title bar, or select **Move** from its Control menu, and use the arrow keys. To size a window, drag its borders, or select **Size** from its Control menu, and make your adjustments with the arrow keys.

- ☞ To minimize a window, click on the Minimize button, or select the Minimize command from the window's Control menu. For maximizing, click on the Maximize button, or select the Control menu's Maximize command.

Part III
Using Program Manager (Or, How to Make Windows Make Something Happen)

Every time you start Windows, you get to see Program Manager's smiling face. This can be comforting in this world of changing allegiances, because you know that at least Program Manager will always be there for you.

The three chapters in this section will help you get better acquainted with your new friend. We'll start by taking a quick look around, and then Chapter 10 "The Real Fun Begins: Starting Applications," will show you how to use Program Manager to start other applications.

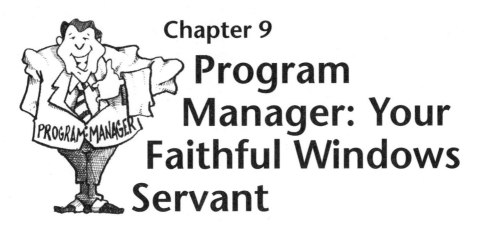

Chapter 9

Program Manager: Your Faithful Windows Servant

In This Chapter

- ☞ What does Program Manager do?
- ☞ All about groups, icons, and other Program Manager thingamajigs
- ☞ Setting up Program Manager your way
- ☞ The author relives part of his youth

Remember Alfred, stately Wayne manor's steadfast butler in the Batman TV series? Or how about Friday, Robinson Crusoe's devoted island side-kick? Or Cato, Inspector Clouseau's overzealous valet? These trusty servants are, I'm sure, the role models for Program Manager, your equally faithful companion that appears, rain or shine, whenever you start Windows.

Although you've already met your new servant, this chapter will help you get better acquainted. You'll learn just what it is that Program Manager does and how you can use it to handle some basic housecleaning chores.

What Does Program Manager Do?

Program Manager is probably the least complicated of all the applications that come with Windows. In fact, other than exiting Windows, Program Manager exists on this earth to do one thing, and one thing only: start your applications. That's it. There isn't anything that's worthwhile learning about Program Manager that your cat couldn't handle.

Program Manager makes things easy by showing you which programs are available on your system. To run a program, you simply select it with your mouse or keyboard. DOS, by contrast, gives you no clue about which programs are on your computer and makes you start programs by typing (shudder) a series of commands.

Program Manager's Parts: Groups and Items

Most restaurants (the ones without an emergency ward on the premises, at least) make things easier for you by organizing their menus into groups of related items: Appetizers, Entrées, Pretentious After-Dinner Drinks, that kind of thing. This is not unlike the way Program Manager organizes your applications.

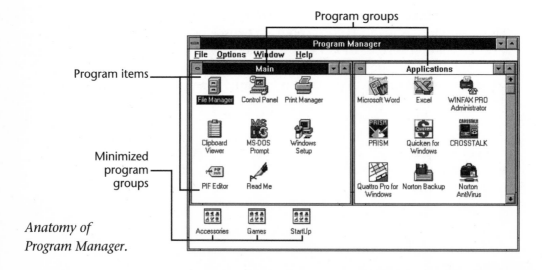

Anatomy of Program Manager.

The windows in Program Manager are called program groups. When you first install Windows, you automatically get four (or sometimes five) groups: Main, Accessories, Games, and Startup (you may also have an Applications group).These are usually fine for most people, but you're free to make changes to these groups or even add your own. (See Chapter 11, "Program Manager: Creating New Groups and Items," for the scoop on working with program groups.)

Inside each program group, you'll see a number of icons. These are called program items, and they represent applications on your computer. To run an application, all you do is select the icon with your mouse or keyboard. (See Chapter 10, "The Real Fun Begins: Starting Applications," for more information on starting programs.)

Navigating Program Manager

The first order of business is to learn how to move from group to group. Actually, because program groups are just windows, you're already an expert at this (if you've read Chapter 8, "Why They Call It 'Windows,'" that is). Just in case, though, here's a quick reminder of the easiest ways to select a group:

☛ Pull down the Window menu and select the group from the list at the bottom of the menu.

☛ If the group is already open, click on it with your mouse.

☛ If the group is minimized as an icon, click on it to select it (the group's Control menu will appear), or double-click on it to open it.

Once you have a group open, you'll need to be able to navigate among the icons. This is easiest (as usual) with the mouse where all you have to do is click on the icon you want. Keyboard users have to trudge through the icons using the Up, Down, Left, and Right arrow keys.

Arranging Things

If you've read Chapter 8, "Why They Call It 'Windows,'" then you know all about basic window techniques such as moving, sizing, maximizing, and minimizing. The good news is that you can use all of these procedures to whip your program groups into shape.

> ## By the Way . . .
> Moving groups minimized as icons can be easy or hard, depending on whether you use a mouse or keyboard. With a mouse, all you have to do is drag the icon. With the keyboard (take a deep breath), first hold down the **Ctrl** key, and press **F6** until the icon you want is highlighted. Now press **Alt+Hyphen** (-) to display the group's Control menu, and then select the **M**ove command. Next, use your keyboard's arrow keys to move the icon. When it's in the location you want, finish by pressing **Enter**. Whew!

Chapter 8 also showed you how to use the **C**ascade and **T**ile commands to organize your windows quickly. Well, Program Manager not only supports these commands, but it also provides you with handy shortcut keys. To cascade your program groups, just press **Shift+F5**. To tile them, press **Shift+F4**.

Arranging Program Items

Besides moving your groups around, you can also move the program items to different locations within each group. This is handy for moving important programs (such as Solitaire and Minesweeper) to the top of a group for easy access.

To move a program item with your mouse, simply drag the item to the location you prefer. (Can't remember how to drag? Just position the pointer over the item, hold down the left mouse button, and then move the mouse.) Sorry keyboard users, this is one of Windows' few mouse-only operations.

> ## By the Way . . .
>
> When you drag a program item, the mouse pointer will change into a ghostly representation of the icon. This is perfectly normal behavior designed to help you position the icon where you need it.

The Easy Way to Arrange Program Items

While moving program items is a handy skill, here's a picture of what can happen if you haven't quite got the hang of it, or if, like me, you're the type of person that likes to hang your clothes over the nearest chair.

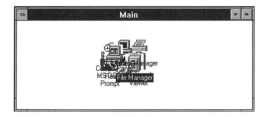

What happens when the Oscar Madisons of the world move their program items.

If you find yourself moving lots of icons around, you should consider letting Windows arrange them automatically. Pull down Program Manager's **Options** menu, and select the Auto Arrange command. Now, every time you move an icon, Windows will make sure it lines up nicely with the others.

> ## By the Way . . .
>
> You normally use the **Arrange Icons** command for program items, but you can also use it to straighten out any minimized program groups that are scattered willy-nilly. Just minimize every group, and then select **Arrange Icons** from the **Window** menu. (Chapter 8, "Why They Call It 'Windows,'" tells you how to minimize windows.)

Saving Your Settings

Because they use it so much, many people spend lots of time fine-tuning Program Manager's settings to get things just right. Unfortunately, many of these same people blow a gasket when they restart Windows the next day and find that Program Manager has simply gone back to the way it was before!

The problem is that Program Manager, like most applications, requires you to save your work. (Unlike most applications, however, Program Manager perversely doesn't ask you if you want to save your changes when you exit!) Program Manager doesn't have a Save command, per se, so you need to pull down the Options menu and select the Save Settings on Exit command. This tells Windows to save Program Manager's settings (such as the group and icon positions) every time you exit Windows.

By the Way . . .

The problem with the Save Settings on Exit command is that it waits until you exit Windows before it saves your configuration. If you're paranoid about losing your settings, try this: pull down the File menu, hold down the Shift key, and then select the Exit Windows command. You won't actually exit Windows, but your current settings will be saved.

The Least You Need to Know

This short chapter was designed to better acquaint you with Windows' humble servant, the Program Manager. Here's a short list of things you need to know:

☞ Program Manager's raison détre is to help you launch your applications.

☛ Program Manager's windows are called program groups. Each program group contains one or more program items that represent applications on your computer.

☛ You can manipulate program groups using the same techniques you'd use for any standard window.

☛ Use the Window menu's **Arrange Icons** command to line up your program items.

This page unintentionally left blank.

Chapter 10
The Real Fun Begins: Starting Applications

In This Chapter

- How to start your applications
- How to switch between your running applications
- How to quit applications
- Some good news (for a change) for keyboard users

Have you ever wondered where the phrase "get down to brass tacks" comes from? Apparently, old stores used to have brass tacks positioned a yard apart for measuring. When a customer was serious about buying some material, she "got down to the brass tacks" to measure the proper amount.

When we use the phrase now, of course, it means that we're ready to stop fooling around and get down to the essentials. That's what this chapter is all about. Here, you'll learn the various techniques you can use to start programs, how to switch between running applications, and, of course, how to quit applications you no longer need.

How Do I Start Thee?
Let Me Count the Ways

Microsoft, you'll be happy to know, is doing its part to ease the country's unemployment problem by hiring programmers to come up with new ways to do simple things. Starting applications is a good example. During a quick finger count, I came up with no less than ten (!) different ways to start an application in Windows.

Don't worry, I have no intention of giving you the sordid details on all 10 methods. In fact, even the four methods I will tell you about are probably overkill.

Starting Applications in Program Manager

By far the easiest and most often used method for starting applications is to simply select an icon from a Program Manager group.

If you use a mouse, first open the appropriate program group by clicking on it, if you can see it, or by double-clicking on its icon if it's minimized. Then all you do is find the icon you want (you may need to use the group's scroll bars—see Chapter 7, "Day-To-Day File Drudgery," for scroll bar basics) and double-click on it.

If you're a die-hard keyboard user, open the application's program group (if necessary) by pulling down the **Window** menu and selecting the group name from the menu. Now use your arrow keys to highlight the application's icon and then press **Enter**.

Using Program Manager's Run Command

What happens if none of your program groups contains an icon for the application you want to run? Use Program Manager's Run command to start the program. Begin by pulling down the File menu and selecting the **Run** command. The Run dialog box will appear.

Enter the program's directory and file name here.

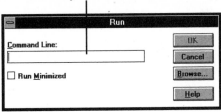

Use the Run dialog box to start any application on your computer.

If you know the name of the file that starts your application, type the complete file name in the Command Line text box. Be sure to include the file's drive and directory. For example, to start Word for Windows, you'd enter **c:\winword\winword.exe**. When you're done, select **OK** to run the application.

If you don't know the name of the file, select the Browse button. In the Browse dialog box that appears, use the Drives drop-down list box, and the Directories and File Name list boxes to select the file that starts your application. When you're ready, select the **OK** button to return to the Run dialog box. Now select **OK** to run the application.

Starting an Application When You Start Windows

If you know which application you want to run before you start Windows, it's a pain to have to wait for Program Manager to load and then to have to go through the steps to open the appropriate group and select the appropriate icon. Life's too short for all that. Instead, tell Windows to simply load your program when it loads itself. When you start Windows, type **win** as you normally do, and then type the full name of the file that starts your program. For example, here's what you'd type to start Excel (note that you need a space after win):

When you exit the application, you'll see Program Manager minimized at the bottom of your screen. This is normal. To restore Program Manager, double-click on the icon or, if the icon is highlighted, press **Enter**. (If the icon is not highlighted, hold down **Alt** and press **Esc** until it is.)

win c:\excel\excel.exe

If you're not sure which file name to use or which directory the program's in, your program manual should tell you.

An extra bonus to this method is that you don't have to look at the Windows logo during startup.

Using the Startup Group

The problem with the last two methods is that they're so, well, DOS-like. I mean, knowing whether to use the back slash (\) or the forward slash (/) is not a skill most people covet. Fortunately, there's an easier way to get Windows to load your applications automatically: the Startup group.

The Startup group is new to Windows version 3.1. If you're still using 3.0, you're out of luck.

The idea behind the Startup group is simple: the program items in the group run automatically every time you start Windows. This is great for loading things you use every day, such as a screen saver program or Windows File Manager.

To learn how to get stuff into your Startup group, take a look through Chapter 11, "Program Manager: Creating New Groups and Items."

By the Way . . .

Once your Startup group is working, there may be times when you start Windows and you don't want the applications to run. To tell Windows to bypass the Startup group, just hold down the **Shift** key while Windows is loading.

Working with Running Applications

Have you ever read the paper while watching TV? Or surreptitiously checked out a member of the opposite sex while talking to someone else? Well, this idea of doing two or more things at once is something that Windows eats for breakfast. Provided your system has enough memory to handle it, Windows is happy to let you open as many applications as you like.

Why would anyone want to do this? Well, there are plenty of things you do with your computer—such as printing verbose documents or recalculating humongous spreadsheets—that can seem to take forever. With multitasking, Windows handles these chores "behind the scenes," so you're free to move on to more important things (like finishing that game of Solitaire).

The ability to run several programs at the same time is called *multitasking*. It simply means that Windows, unlike some people, can walk and chew gum at the same time.

Switching Between Applications

While multitasking can be a real time-saver, you'll lose those savings if you can't switch quickly from one application to another. The rest of this section details the easiest methods for switching between running programs.

Easy Mouse Methods

I'm sure the keyboard mavens in the crowd are sick and tired of hearing about how much easier Windows is with a mouse. Well, don't worry; you'll get your revenge in the next section. For now though, here are a couple of absurdly easy mouse techniques for selecting an open application:

When you have multiple applications open, Windows doesn't actually run them simultaneously. Instead, it acts more like a traffic cop at an intersection, allowing one lane (program) to proceed, then switching to another. This all happens so fast, however, that it appears as though everything is happening at the same time.

- ☛ If you can see any part of the application window, click on it.
- ☛ If you've minimized the application and you can see the icon, double-click on it.

The "Cool Switch": Alternating Between Two Applications

Try an experiment. Make sure you have only Program Manager running. Next, use Program Manager to start up any application that strikes your fancy. Now press **Alt+Tab**. You're back in Program Manager! Press **Alt+Tab** again. Now you're back to the application you just started. You've just discovered the "Cool Switch"—the Alt+Tab key combination. When you've got two applications running (including Program Manager), the Cool Switch gives you a quick way to alternate between them.

The "Cool Switch" Revisited: Working with More Than Two Applications

What happens if you have more than two applications running? Not a problem. Just hold down the **Alt** key and start tapping the **Tab** key. Each time you press **Tab**, Windows displays the title and icon of one of the active applications, as shown here.

Hold down Alt and press Tab repeatedly to see the title and icon of each open application.

When you see the application you want, release the Alt key. Voilà, the entire application appears on your screen.

Cycling Through the Open Applications

The Cool Switch is a neat way to navigate your programs, but sometimes you need to see more than just the title and icon of an application before you switch to it. For example, you may need to see which files are open in an application, or you may simply forget what an application does.

The easiest way to do this is to hold down **Alt** and press **Esc**. Each time you tap the **Esc** key, one of your applications appears on the screen. If you've minimized the application, its icon will appear.

Switching Applications with the Task List

The Alt+Tab and Alt+Esc methods break down if you have a lot of applications running. (Remember: our goal here is to switch quickly between applications. Cycling through a dozen applications is not quick, and it's about as exciting as watching C-Span on a slow news day.)

The solution is to tell Windows to display a list—called the Task List—of all your running applications and then select the one you want from the list. Here's how to display the list:

With your mouse, double-click on any empty part of the desktop. If there is no empty space, pull down the Control menu from any application (by clicking on the box in the upper left corner of the application's window), and then select the Switch To command.

From the keyboard, press **Ctrl+Esc.**

As you can see here, the Task List just displays a handy list of your open applications. To switch to an application, highlight it (by clicking on it or by using the Up or Down arrow keys), and then select the Switch To button.

The Task List displays a list of all your running applications.

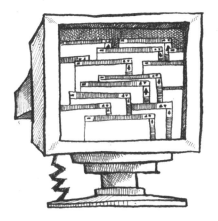

Arranging Application Windows with the Task List

Windows applications are like potato chips: bet you can't open just one. The problem, though, is that it doesn't take long before your screen is as crowded as a New York City subway at 5:00. For example, here's a screen that's a real mess, but there are only six applications running!

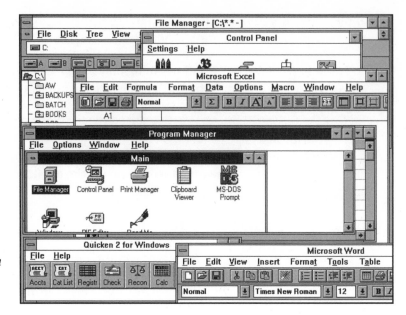

Having even just a few applications open can strangle the average screen.

If you find your screen getting messy, Windows offers a number of solutions.

Chapter 8, "Why They Call It 'Windows,'" outlines a whole raft of techniques for arranging windows within an application (moving, sizing, maximizing, minimizing, and more). The good news is that you can use most of these methods to arrange your application windows, as well.

If you want to cascade or tile your applications, however, the steps are a little different. You first need to display the Task List as I showed you earlier in this chapter. To cascade your applications, select the Task List's Cascade button. If you prefer to tile your applications, select the Tile button, instead.

By the Way . . .

Windows will only cascade or tile applications that aren't minimized. To include a minimized application in a cascade or tile operation, be sure to open the window first.

Quitting Applications

When you've finished with an application, you should shut it down. This will save you some memory and reduce the clutter on the screen. Once again, Windows has a variety of methods to choose from:

☞ Pull down the application's File menu and select the Exit command.

☞ Select Close from the application's Control menu.

☞ Double-click on the application's Control-menu box.

☞ Press **Alt+F4**.

☞ Display the Task List, highlight the application, and then select the End Task button.

The Least You Need to Know

This chapter showed you how to open, navigate, arrange, and quit your applications. Here's a summary:

☞ Windows has more ways to start an application than I can count. The easiest method, though, is to double-click on the Program Manager icon or, from the keyboard, highlight an icon and press **Enter**.

☞ Windows is content to run any number of programs at once, provided you have enough memory. Running multiple applications is called multitasking.

☞ The easiest ways to switch between running applications are the Cool Switch (**Alt+Tab**) and the Task List (double-click on the desktop or press **Ctrl+Esc**).

☞ You use the same methods to arrange your application windows that you use for all other windows. For cascading and tiling, use the appropriate Task List buttons.

☞ The easiest ways to quit an application are to select Exit from the File menu or to press **Alt+F4**.

This page unintentionally left blank.

Chapter 11

Program Manager: Creating New Groups and Items

In This Chapter

- Creating new program groups
- Creating new program items
- Moving and copying program items
- Deleting groups and items
- Various other cool ways to show Program Manager a good time

So far you've seen Program Manager on its best button-down behavior. However, all work and no play makes Jack (and anyone else) a dull boy, so it's time to loosen up a bit and get creative. This chapter shows you how to play around with Program Manager by creating your own groups and items, moving and copying items, and deleting items you no longer need.

Playing with Program Groups

When you first install Windows, Program Manager is set up with five standard groups: Main, Accessories, Games, Startup, and (usually) Applications. You may be surprised to know that it really doesn't matter to Program Manager whether you use these groups or not. This means you're free to rename groups, create your own groups, and even delete groups.

Renaming a Group

The name you see in a group's title bar or below a group icon is not set in stone. In fact, you can change a group name to anything that strikes your fancy. So, for example, if having a "Games" group doesn't present the right image at the office, you could rename it to, say, "Relaxation Enhancement Tools." To

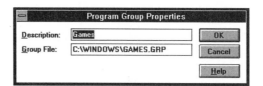

rename a group, first minimize it, and then select it by clicking on it or by holding down **Ctrl** and pressing **F6** until the icon you want is highlighted. Now, pull down the File menu, and select the **P**roperties command. This displays the Program Group Properties, as shown here.

Use the Program Group Properties dialog box to rename your program groups.

Program Group Properties	
Description:	Games
Group File:	C:\WINDOWS\GAMES.GRP

OK Cancel Help

Once you've selected the group you want to rename, you can display the Program Group Properties dialog box quickly by simply pressing **Alt+Enter**.

In the Description text box, enter the new name for the group and then select **OK**. Program Manager renames the group.

Creating a New Group

Creating a new program group is a snap. You begin by pulling down the File menu and selecting the New command to display the New Program Object dialog box. Select the Program Group option button and then select **OK**. This displays another dialog box called Program Group Properties. Use the Description text box to enter a name for the new group, and then select **OK**.

Put It to Work

Do you share your computer with other people either at work or at home? If so, then each of you probably uses a different mix of applications. One person might use mostly a spreadsheet and a presentation graphics program, while another uses a word processor and a desktop publishing application. And, of course, there are programs that *everybody* uses, such as File Manager and Solitaire. One way to simplify things would be to create personalized program groups for each person. You could name each group after the person who'll be using it, and then, using the techniques you'll be learning later on, you could copy the appropriate items to each group.

Deleting a Group

If you have any groups you never use, you should delete them to keep Program Manager clutter to a minimum.

To begin, minimize the group (so Program Manager will know you're deleting a group and not just an item in the group), if necessary, and then highlight the icon. Now pull down the File menu, and select the Delete command. Program Manager, ever cautious, will ask if you're sure you want to delete the group. If you *are* sure, select the Yes button (otherwise, choose No to cancel the whole thing).

To delete a minimized group quickly, highlight it, and then press **Delete**.

Once you've deleted a group there's no way to get it back except by rebuilding it from scratch. So be *very* sure you won't be needing a group before deleting it.

Put It to Work

When I was learning Windows, I could never remember where to find program items, such as Write or NotePad. Were they in Accessories? Main? Maybe I stuffed them into Applications? If you're in the same boat, one solution is to copy every application you use into a single "super group."

continues

continued

Now delete the other groups and then maximize the remaining group. The result, as you can see here, is that all your applications are nicely laid out in front of you, so they're easy to find and easy to select.

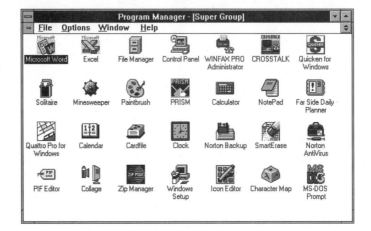

Reduce Program Manager to a single group for easy access to your applications.

Playing with Program Items

Once you have your groups set up the way you want, you can fine-tune things by playing around with the program items, too. The next few sections will show you how to work with an item's properties, how to create new items, and how to move, copy, and delete existing items.

To display the Program Item Properties dialog box quickly, highlight the item, and press **Alt+Enter**.

Changing the Name of an Item

The name you see below an icon is usually the name of the application itself. However, if you're feeling creative, you can assign whatever name you like. To give it a try, first highlight the program item you want to work with, and then select the **P**roperties command from Program Manager's File menu. In the Program Item Properties dialog box that appears, use the Description text box to enter a different name for the item. When you're done, select **OK**.

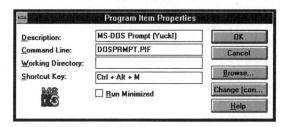

The Program Item Properties dialog box.

Assigning a Shortcut Key to an Item

One of the cool things you can do in the Program Item Properties dialog box is to assign a shortcut key combination to a program item. This means that you can start or switch to the application just by pressing these shortcut keys.

To display the Program Item Properties dialog box, highlight the item, pull down the File menu, and then select the Properties command. In the Shortcut Key box, press a letter or number. Program Manager will create a key combination using the Ctrl and Alt keys. For example, if you type **m**, the shortcut key becomes **Ctrl+Alt+M**. If you change your mind, press **Delete** or **Backspace** to remove the key combination. When you're ready, select the **OK** button.

Changing an Item's Icon

Whenever you create a new item for a DOS application (see the section "Creating a New Item" later in this chapter), Windows supplies you with the same boring icon each time. You don't have to accept this! Fight back by assigning your own icon (you can do this for Windows applications, too). Here are the steps:

1. Highlight the item you want to work with.

2. Select the Properties command from Program Manager's File menu to display the Program Item Properties dialog box.

3. Select the Change Icon button. If you're changing the icon of a DOS application, Program Manager will tell you that there are **no icons available**. If this happens, ignore this and select **OK** to continue. The Change Icon dialog box will appear.

4. The Current Icon box shows you the few dozen icons that are available in a file called PROGMAN.EXE. If you see one you like, highlight it.

    If you'd like to look at more icons, select the **Browse** button and select any of the icon files that appear in the File **Name** list. I'd recommend the file MORICONS.DLL. Select **OK** to return to the Change Icon dialog box.

5. When you've got the icon you want, select **OK** to return to the Program Item Properties dialog box.

6. Select **OK**.

Moving an Item to Another Group

Once you've highlighted the item you want to move, press **F7** to display the Move Program Item dialog box quickly.

Program items are not tied to the groups they inhabit. You're free to move them from group to group as often as you like.

With a mouse, all you do is drag the item to its new group (it doesn't matter if the group is open or minimized).

From the keyboard, begin by opening the appropriate program group and highlighting the item you want to move. Then pull down Program Manager's File menu, and select the **Move** command. Program Manager displays the Move Program Item dialog box.

Keyboardists use the Move Program Item dialog box to move a program item from one group to another.

Use the To Group drop-down list box to select the item's new home, and then select **OK**. Program Manager moves the item.

Copying an Item to Another Group

Ever have one of those busy days when you wish you could be in two places at once? Well, *you* may not be able to pull it off, but Program Manager can. In fact, you can make a copy of a program item in as many groups as you want. This is handy for applications you use a lot, or if you're setting up customized program groups for all the people who use your computer.

To copy an item with a mouse, hold down the **Ctrl** key and drag the item into the other group or onto the group's icon. From the keyboard, highlight the item you want to copy, pull down the File menu, and select the Copy command. In the Copy Program Item dialog box that appears, select the group receiving the copy from the To Group drop-down list box, and then select **OK** to perform the copy.

Once you've highlighted the item you want to copy, press **F8** to display the Copy Program Item dialog box quickly.

By the Way . . .

In Chapter 10, "The Real Fun Begins: Starting Applications," I told you about Program Manager's Startup group. Any program items you place in this group are run automatically every time you start Windows. (This is an easy way to start programs you use every day, such as File Manager and Clock.) If you want to take advantage of this new feature, you can use the copying techniques you learned here to copy items into your Startup group.

Creating a New Item

Most Windows applications have the common courtesy to add their own program item to one of Program Manager's groups (sometimes they're even cheeky enough to add their own group). If an application doesn't install its own icon, or if you have DOS applications you'd like to set up, here are the steps to follow:

1. Open the group that will store the item.

2. Pull down Program Manager's File menu, and select the New command. This displays the New Program Object dialog box.

3. Select the Program Item option button, and then select **OK**. Program Manager displays the Program Item Properties dialog box.

4. Use the Description text box to enter the name you want to appear under the icon.

5. Use the Command Line text box to enter the name of the file that starts your program. Be sure to include the drive and directory. If you're not sure about the file name, select the **Browse** button and choose the appropriate file from the Browse dialog box. (If you need more help, the program's manual should tell the name of the file that starts the program.) Select **OK** when you're done.

6. Select **OK** to add the new item.

Deleting an Item

To delete a program item you no longer use, highlight it, and select the Delete command from the File menu. Program Manager will ask you if you're sure you want to delete the item. Select the Yes button to continue with the deletion, or select No to cancel.

To delete an item quickly, highlight it, and then press the **Delete** key.

The Least You Need to Know

This chapter showed a number of methods for playing with your Program Manager groups and items. Here's what you need to take with you:

- ☞ To rename a group, select the **Properties** command from Program Manager's **File** menu, and enter the new name in the **Description** box.

- ☞ To create a new group, select the **File** menu's **New** command, and fill in the dialog box.

- ☞ To delete a group, highlight it, and then select **Delete** from the **File** menu.

- ☞ To rename a program item, select the **File** menu's **Properties** command, and enter the new name in the **Description** box.

- ☞ To create a new item, select the **New** command from the **File** menu, and fill in the dialog boxes.

- ☞ To move or copy an item, highlight it, select the **File** menu's **Move** or **Copy** command, and then choose the destination from the dialog box.

- ☞ To delete an item, highlight it, and then select **Delete** from the **File** menu.

This page unintentionally left blank.

Part IV
Using File Manager (and Good Riddance to the DOS Prompt)

For the most part, Windows does a pretty good job at shielding us from the harsh realities of the DOS world. We have Program Manager to start our applications, we have pull-down menus to access commands, and we have dialog boxes to talk to Windows. All very civilized, if you ask me.

However, the two worlds collide in File Manager. This is the program where you have to concern yourself with arcana, such as files, directories, and disks. Groan! But, as the chapters in this section will show you, it's really not as bad as all that. In fact, File Manager makes it easy by taking advantage of Windows' visual approach. DOS makes you jump through hoops just to find out what's on your hard disk, and then you have to figure out all kinds of bizarre and cryptic commands just to get anything done. File Manager, though, shows you a picture of what's on your hard disk, and as in all other Windows applications, you do things by simply selecting the appropriate pull-down menu commands. Easy as pie (really!).

Chapter 12
File Manager Basics

In This Chapter

- ☛ Files, directories, and disks explained (in English!)
- ☛ A tour of the File Manager screen
- ☛ Navigating File Manager
- ☛ Selecting files, directories, and disks
- ☛ The author compares a computer and a house (which just shows that he needs to get out more)

Most people who are new to Windows—and especially those who are new to computers in general—would rather have a root canal than work with File Manager. I mean this is one *intimidating* program; all those strange, cryptic names, the confusing layout, the DOS terminology (words like directories and disks). Shudder. To make things worse, File Manager doesn't have any cute icons like Program Manager does.

The good news, though, is that File Manager really isn't as bad as it seems. In fact, once you get comfortable with the layout and learn a few basic techniques, you'll probably feel right at home. In any case, File Manager is light years ahead of the DOS command prompt. Now *that's* intimidating.

This chapter gets you started with File Manager. We'll begin with some plain English explanations of files, directories, and disks, and then I'll show you around the File Manager screen.

SPEAK LIKE A GEEK

To make sure we're heading down the same path in this chapter, I should make sure that you know what a *hard disk* is. Put simply, a hard disk is your computer's main storage area. Every program you install—and every file you create and save—gets stored somewhere on the hard disk.

Your Computer Is Your Castle

When people ask me to explain files and directories to them (well, no, it doesn't happen all *that* often), I always tell them to think of their computer as a house. Not just any old house, mind you, but one with all kinds of servants waiting to do their bidding. (People usually start warming up to the analogy at this point.) The inside of the house, you can think of this as the computer's hard disk— has maids, valets, cooks, and so on; these are the applications installed on the hard disk (such as DOS and Windows). Outside the house there are gardeners, landscapers, and chauffeurs; these are the devices attached to the computer (such as the keyboard, printer, or modem).

SPEAK LIKE A GEEK

The files that run your programs are called— surprise, surprise—*program files*. The files used by you or your programs are called *data files*.

How Files Fit into All This

In the simplest possible terms, your computer's files are equivalent to the various elements in the house. As I've said, the people (the servants) are the files that run your programs. The inanimate objects in the house—the furniture, appliances, utensils, and so on—are the files used by you or your programs.

Directories: Continuing the House Analogy

Imagine a house with no rooms; four walls and a roof, that's it. Now imagine all your possessions scattered randomly throughout this house. Clearly, trying to *find* anything in such a place would be, if not impossible, at least frustrating.

The problem, of course, is that there is no organization. A normal house has many different rooms, and usually everything in one room is related in one way or another. So, if you were looking for either cooking utensils or food, you'd probably look in the kitchen instead of the bedroom (I said *probably*).

Your computer's hard disk also contains a number of rooms, and these rooms are called *directories*. In a properly organized hard disk, each directory normally contains a number of related files. For example, your Windows directory contains all the files that Windows uses as well as the files for the programs that come with Windows (Write, Paintbrush, and so on). You may also have a separate directory for each program installed on your computer.

Let's extend the analogy a little further. Some rooms in a house have a smaller room attached to them (such as a walk-in closet in a bedroom or a dining room in a living room). Even storage spaces such as pantries and cupboards are "room-like" because they store objects. All of these are examples of what we could call "subrooms." Directories can also have "subrooms," and these are called—you guessed it—*subdirectories*. For example, your word processing directory could have separate subdirectories for business memos and personal correspondence.

Hard Disk Structure (or, Your House Is Now a Tree)

When you or your programs create new directories, DOS organizes them in a special way. Everything begins with what is called the *root directory*. The idea is that all the other directories "branch out" from the root to form a tree (sort of). However, instead of using a tree to explain hard disk structure, I'm going to stick with our old friend, the computer house. In this case, the root directory is analogous to a hallway running from the front door to the back of the house. This hallway contains a few objects (files), but you mostly see doorways to other rooms (directories).

Transporting Stuff with Floppy Disks

The things inside the house had to get there somehow. They could have been brought in on foot in a bag or box; they could have been packed into a car; or they might have been loaded on a truck. And, of course, you could use any of these means to take stuff out of the house to a different location.

Computer geeks (proving that at least some of them have a sense of humor) refer to the floppy disk method of file transfer as *sneaker net*.

This is just what floppy disks do. All the files on your computer got there because someone loaded them from one or more disks. If you need to take some files elsewhere, the most common way to do it is to simply load them onto a disk and transport the disk to the new location.

Getting Ready for File Manager

Congratulations, we've now covered everything you ever need to know about files, directories, and disks! Now you're ready to tackle File Manager. Just keep the house analogy in mind and you'll have no problems.

Go ahead and start File Manager by selecting the **File Manager** icon from Program Manager's Main group. Here's the window you'll see (although the contents of your window will almost certainly be different from mine).

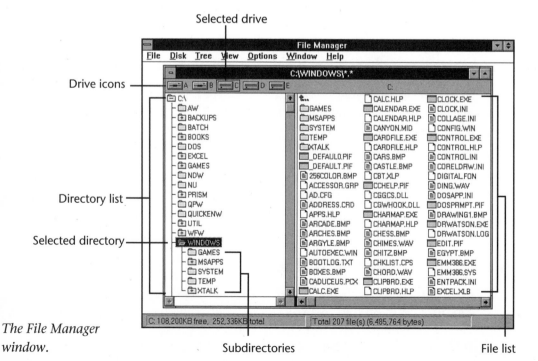

The File Manager window.

The File Manager Window

The idea behind File Manager is to show you what's inside your computer. This makes it easy to select files, directories, and disks and then to work with them. So when you start File Manager, the program opens a window that displays a snapshot of one area of your hard disk. It's like looking at a floor plan of one of the rooms in your computer house. Three areas of the window tell you what you're looking at: the *drive icons*, the *directory list*, and the *file list*.

The Drive Icons   File Manager displays these icons just below the window's title bar. They show you all the disk drives that are available on your system (both hard drives and floppy drives) and which drive you're logged onto. File Manager surrounds the icon of the current drive with a box.

The Directory List   This list displays the available directories on the current drive. The directory at the top of the list (it's C:\ if you're in drive C) is the root directory, and the others branch off from it. File Manager highlights the current directory.

The File List   This list displays the names of the files stored in the current directory as well as any subdirectories that exist.

Navigating File Manager

Half the battle with File Manager involves simply learning how to get around and select things. Once you're comfortable with that, the rest is a breeze.

Selecting a Disk Drive

To select a different disk drive with a mouse, simply click on the appropriate drive icon. If you're using your keyboard, press **Tab** until the current drive icon is highlighted, use the left and right arrow keys to highlight the drive you want, and then press **Enter**. File Manager opens a new window and displays the directories on the new drive.

An easier way to select a different disk drive is simply to hold down **Ctrl**, and press the letter of the drive. For example, to open drive A, you'd press **Ctrl+A**.

If you want to open a floppy disk drive, make sure you have a disk in the drive before doing so. Otherwise, File Manager will get upset and display an error message.

Selecting a Directory

To select a different directory with your mouse, simply click on the directory name. From the keyboard, press **Tab** until the current directory is highlighted, and then use the up and down arrow keys to select the directory you want. File Manager updates the file list to display the files stored in the new directory.

If the directory has subdirectories, you can display them with a mouse by double-clicking on the directory. With your keyboard, highlight the directory, and press the plus sign (+). To hide subdirectories, double-click on the original directory, or highlight it, and press the minus sign (–).

Selecting a File

To select a file from the file list, you can click on the file name with a mouse, or with the keyboard, press **Tab** until you're in the file list, and then use the arrow keys to highlight the file.

By the Way . . .

In Chapter 10, "The Real Fun Begins: Starting Applications," I showed you a few methods for getting your programs up and running. Now that you know how to get around in File Manager, I can show you how to start programs from there. All you have to do is find the file that starts the application and either double-click on it with your mouse, or highlight it, and press **Enter**. For example, select your WINDOWS directory and look for a file named SOL.EXE. Start this file, and you'll soon see Solitaire on your screen.

Program file icons versus data file icons.

Exiting File Manager

When you've finished with File Manager, use any of the following techniques to exit the program and return to Program Manager:

☛ Select the Exit command from the File menu.

☛ Press **Alt+F4**.

☛ Double-click on the **Control-menu** box.

File Manager displays a small icon to the left of each file. The type of icon tells you whether the file is a program file (a file that will start an application) or a data file (a file used by a program). As you can see in the figure, the program file icon looks like a small window while the data file icon looks like a piece of paper with a dog-eared corner.

The Least You Need to Know

This chapter introduced you to File Manager and tried to show you that it's not such a bad application after all. Here's a summary of what we did:

☛ File Manager is a lot easier if you understand at least a little about what files, directories, and disks are. The best way to visualize these things is to think of a house. Files are the people and objects in the house, directories are the rooms, and you use floppy disks to transport stuff to and from the house.

☛ Program files are your applications while data files are files used by your applications.

☛ File Manager gives you a snapshot of the selected disk drive. The directory list shows you the available directories and the file list shows you all the files in the selected directory.

continues

continued

☛   Mouse users select disks, directories, and files simply
by clicking on them. Keyboard users press **Tab** to
get to the appropriate area, and then use the arrow
keys to make their selection.

☛   You can start applications from File Manager by
double-clicking on the program file or by highlighting it and pressing **Enter**.

Chapter 13
File Finagling

In This Chapter

- ☞ Copying and moving files
- ☞ Renaming and deleting files
- ☞ Searching for files
- ☞ Drag-and-drop demystified
- ☞ Various other cool file techniques that are sure to impress your family and friends (at least those who are easily impressed)

In the last chapter, I tried to sell you on the idea that your computer was like a house, and that your computer's files were just the objects and people that populated the house. In this chapter, you learn some basic house chores, such as redecorating (moving files around), spring cleaning (deleting files), and loading up the car (copying files to a floppy disk).

Copying Files

You'll find that copying files, whether you're copying them from one part of your hard disk to another or between your hard disk and a floppy disk, will be one of your most common chores. This section shows you two ways to copy files: the old-fashioned way (using the Copy command) and the new-fangled way (using something called "drag-and-drop").

Copying Files with the Copy Command

The usual way to copy a file is to select it, pull down File Manager's File menu, and then select the Copy command. This displays the Copy dialog box, as shown here.

Selecting Copy from File Manager's File menu displays the Copy dialog box.

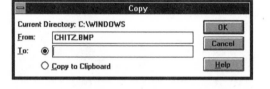

Once you've highlighted a file, you can display the Copy dialog box quickly by simply pressing **F8**.

In the To text box, tell File Manager where you want the file copied. To avoid confusion, you should enter both the drive and directory. For example, to copy a file to a directory called BACKUP on your C drive, you'd enter **c:\backup** in the To box. Similarly, to copy a file to drive A's root directory, you'd enter **a:**. When you're ready to copy, select the OK button.

Before copying a file to a floppy disk, make sure you have a disk in the appropriate drive. If you don't, your computer will make a rude noise, and File Manager will chastise you.

Drag 'Til You Drop (Or, Forget Everything I Just Told You, 'Cause This Is Way Easier)

If you have a mouse, there's a way cooler method—called *drag-and-drop*—for copying a file. What you do is hold down the **Ctrl** key on your keyboard and point your mouse at the file you want to copy. Now (with Ctrl still pressed) hold down the left mouse button and move the mouse to the new location (that is, a different directory or drive). As you move the mouse, you'll see a document icon attached to the mouse pointer (this is the dragging part). When you release the mouse button, the file is copied to the new location (this is the dropping part). This is about as fun as it gets with File Manager, so enjoy the moment while it lasts.

> ## By the Way . . .
>
> If you're copying a file to a different directory on your hard drive, drag-and-drop won't work if you can't see the other directory in the directory list. Bummer. The easiest way around this is to select New Window from File Manager's Window menu, then display the destination directory in the new window. Now select Tile from the Window menu, and you're back in business.

Moving Files

When you copy a file, the original stays intact and an exact replica is created in the new destination. If you don't want to keep the original, then you need to *move* the file, instead. This section looks at the two methods you can use to move files.

Press **F7** to display the Move dialog box quickly.

Using the (Yawn) Move Command

As you might expect, moving a file is quite similar to copying one. You first highlight the file you want to move, then you pull down the File menu, and select the Move command. In the Move dialog box that appears, enter the new destination in the To box and then select **OK**.

Using (Yeah!) Drag-and-Drop

Moving files is easiest when you drag-and-drop them to their new locations. You use the same technique that I outlined for copying files, except that you hold down **Alt** instead of Ctrl.

By the Way . . .

What happens if you're in the middle of a drag-and-drop and you're suddenly not sure whether you should be using Ctrl or Alt? Ah, good question. One way to figure it out is to simply associate Copy and Ctrl because both start with the letter C. If you want something more substantial, how about this: just before you release the mouse button to drop the file, take a look at the original file's icon. If it's still there, you're copying the file; if it's gone, you're moving it, as shown here.

File is being dragged to drive A.

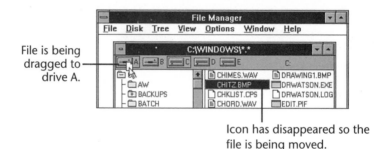

When you move a file, its icon disappears.

Icon has disappeared so the file is being moved.

More Drag-and-Drop Fun

Drag-and-drop is one of those features that can actually make it enjoyable to use a computer. But there's more to drag-and-drop than simply copying and moving files. A lot more. This section gives you two examples.

Opening a File Automatically When You Start an Application

Most applications display a new file when you start them up. If you want to work with an existing file, you have to go through the whole Open dialog box rigmarole. Forget that. Now (if you're using Windows 3.1) you can use drag-and-drop to not only start an application but have it *automatically* open the file you want!

Sound too good to be true? Well, let's try an example. Select the Windows directory in File Manager and adjust the file list so that you can see both PBRUSH.EXE (the file that starts the Paintbrush application) and any file that ends with BMP (try PAPER.BMP or REDBRICK.BMP). Drag the BMP file (you don't have to hold down Ctrl or Alt), and drop it on PBRUSH.EXE. File Manager will ask you if you're sure you want to start Paintbrush. Select **Yes** and Paintbrush loads with the BMP file opened. Gnarly!

> **By the Way . . .**
> This technique also works for applications that are already open. Just drag the file from File Manager, and drop it inside the application's window (or on its icon if it's minimized).

Creating New Items in Program Manager

Creating a new program item in Program Manager seems to require about 57 dialog boxes (the entire process is outlined in Chapter 11, "Program Manager: Creating New Groups and Items"). With drag-and-drop, you can do it in two simple steps (again, you need Windows 3.1 for this). First, adjust the Program Manager and File Manager windows so that you can see both the program group (it can be either minimized or open) and the file you want to use. Now all you do is drag the file and drop it on the group.

If you use a program file (that is, a file that loads a program, such as PBRUSH.EXE), then the new program item in Program Manager will simply start the application. However, if you use a data file (such as one of Paintbrush's BMP files), then the new item will start the application *and* load the file.

A File by Any Other Name: Renaming Files

If you don't like the name of a file, you can change it. So, for example, if the file CHITZ.BMP in your Windows directory bugs you because you don't know what the heck a "chitz" is, you can rename it to, say,

OOPS!

To avoid disastrous consequences, don't rename any files that your applications use (especially anything ending with EXE, COM, PIF, or DLL). To be safe, a good general rule is to rename only those files that you've created yourself.

GOOFBALL.BMP. Renaming is easy. Just highlight the file, and select the **Re**name command from the File menu. In the Rename dialog box that appears, enter the new name in the To box and then select **OK**.

By the Way . . .

File names usually contain a period flanked by a *primary name* (the part on the left) and an *extension* (the part on the right). When renaming a file, make sure you observe the sacred File Name Commandments handed down by the great DOS Nerd Gods:

    I.   Thou shalt not use more than eight characters for the file's primary name.

    II.   Thou shalt not use more than three characters for the file's extension.

    III.   Thou shalt separate the primary name and the extension with a period.

    IV.   Thou shalt not use a space or any of the other forbidden characters:

        + = \ | [ ] ; : , . < > ? /

    V.   Thou shalt not take the name of an existing file in the same directory in vain.

What's Wrong with This Picture?

Here's a list of file names, some of which violate the sacred File Name Commandments. Take a look through the list, and write down which commandment the name blasphemes (if any) and the reason.

   1. COWABUNGA.TXT

Commandment violated:

Reason:

2. WHATTHE.HECK

   Commandment violated:

   Reason:

3. NO_FRUIT.SIR

   Commandment violated:

   Reason:

4. IS THIS.OK?

   Commandment violated:

   Reason:

5. THISISIT

   Commandment violated:

   Reason:

6. DUH,SAID.HE

   Commandment violated:

   Reason:

Answers:

1. Incorrect: This name violates Commandment I because the primary name is nine characters long.

2. Incorrect: Commandment II is violated because this name uses a four-character extension.

3. Correct: The underscore character (_) is a legal character, and it's useful for making file names more legible.

4. Incorrect: This name actually has two mistakes. Both the space in the primary name and the question mark in the extension violate Commandment IV.

5. Correct: The extension is optional. (Notice that when there's no extension you don't need the period.)

6. Incorrect: The comma in the primary name violates Commandment IV. The two-character extension is okay.

Cleaning House: Deleting Files

It's axiomatic in real estate that property values will always rise because nobody's making any more land. This is true in hard disk real estate, as well. As applications (especially Windows applications) get bigger and bigger, your hard disk (remember how it seemed so *huge* when you first got it?) gets more and more cramped. This section shows you how to free up more disk space by deleting files you no longer need.

Saving You from Yourself

Deleting the wrong file can have disastrous effects on both your health and your career. For an extra margin of safety, tell File Manager that you want to be nagged whenever you try to delete a file. You do this by pulling down the Options menu and selecting the Confirmation command. This displays the Confirmation dialog box, as shown here.

For maximum safety, make sure that every one of the Confirmation dialog box's options are checked.

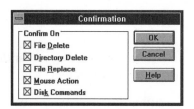

Make sure there's an X in the File **D**elete check box. This tells File Manager to confirm each deletion with you. Now is a good time to make sure all the other Confirmation options are checked, as well.

Deleting a File

Okay, it's time to take out the garbage. Here are the steps you need to follow to delete a file:

1. Highlight the file you want to delete.

2. Select **Delete** from the File menu. File Manager displays the Delete dialog box that shows the name of the file in the Delete text area.

3. If it's the wrong name, change it to the correct one. When you're ready, select **OK**. The Confirm File Delete dialog box appears.

4. Select **Yes** to delete the file.

Put It to Work

If you have a notebook computer with a 40- or 60-megabyte hard disk, it can be disconcerting to watch Windows take up 10 or 11 megabytes of this precious real estate. However, it's possible to downsize Windows by deleting some unnecessary files. For example, if you don't use wallpaper, you can delete all the files in the Windows directory that end with BMP. (To make this easier, you might want to read ahead to the section titled "Selecting Multiple Files.") Also, delete any accessories that you don't use. For example, if you don't use Recorder, delete the files RECORDER.EXE and RECORDER.HLP (the Help system file) in the Windows directory.

Undeleting with DOS 5 and 6

Some wag once said that there are two types of computer users: those who have accidentally deleted files and those who will. Microsoft finally tuned in to this reality by including a utility in DOS 5 and 6 that will "undelete" an accidentally erased file. The good news is that you can use this utility from within File Manager.

By the Way . . .

For best results, always try to use the Undelete utility *immediately* after erasing the file. The sooner you do it, the better your chances are of recovering the file.

What you need to do is pull down the File menu and select the **Run** command. Now, in the Run dialog box that appears, use the Command

Line text box to enter **undelete** followed by the name of the file and then select **OK**. For example, to undelete a file named CRUCIAL.TXT, you'd enter **undelete crucial.txt**. File Manager will disappear from the screen, and you'll see something like the following (your screen may look slightly different).

```
UNDELETE - A delete protection facility
Copyright (C) 1987-1993 Central Point Software, Inc.
All rights reserved.

Directory: C:\WINDOWS
File Specifications: CRUCIAL.TXT

    Delete Sentry control file not found.

    Deletion-tracking file not found.

    MS-DOS directory contains     1 deleted files.
    Of those,    1 files may be recovered.

Using the MS-DOS directory method.

    ?RUCIAL  TXT    41724  3-18-92  3:18a  ...A  Undelete (Y/N)?
```

Undelete scopes your system and looks for the file you want to undelete.

To confirm that you want to undelete the file, type **y**. Now, bizarrely, DOS asks you to enter the first letter of the file name (and they wonder why people hate DOS!). Just press the letter, and DOS will recover your file.

Making Life Easier: Selecting Multiple Files

So far, I've only shown you how to work with one file at a time, but if you've got, say, a dozen files to copy, then even drag-and-drop can get old in a hurry. The solution is to select *all* the files you want to work with and then do the copy (or move, delete, whatever).

Mouse Techniques

With your mouse, there are two methods you can use to select multiple files:

☞ To select random files in a directory, hold down the **Ctrl** key, and click on each file.

☞ To select several files in a row, click on the first file, hold down the **Shift** key, and then click on the last file.

Keyboard Techniques

For dedicated keyboardists, here's how to select multiple files:

☞ To select random files, use the arrow keys to highlight the first file, and then press **Shift+F8**. For the other files you want to select, highlight them, and then press the **Spacebar**. When you're done, press **Shift+F8** again.

☞ To select several files in a row, highlight the first file, hold down **Shift**, and then use the arrow keys to highlight the other files.

The Needle in a Haystack Thing: Searching for a File

Today's humongous hard disks can easily hold hundreds of files. If you use your computer a lot, then you know it's no sweat to add to this hard disk overpopulation with dozens of your own data files. So it's inevitable that you'll misplace the odd file from time to time. However, instead of wasting time scouring your directories, let File Manager's Search command do the work for you. All you do is select Search from the File menu to display the Search dialog box. Use the Search For text box to enter the name of the file you want to find, and use the Start From box to specify the directory you want to search. When you select **OK**, File Manager begins the search and displays the results in a separate window.

TECHNO NERD TEACHES

Wanna know why you have to tell DOS the first letter of the file you're trying to undelete? Well, it seems that when you erase a file, DOS, being the lazy operating system that it is, doesn't actually erase anything! Instead, it tells itself that the space used by this file is now available for other files to use. How does it do that? By changing the *first letter* of the file (ah!) to some weird character. By restoring the first letter, you restore your file. (This also tells you why you have to use Undelete right away; if you wait too long, some other file may come along and usurp your file's space.)

By the Way . . .

If you haven't the faintest idea which directory your file might be in, use your hard disk's root directory in the Search dialog box's Start From box. For example, if your hard drive is drive C, you'd enter C:\. Also, make sure the Search All Subdirectories check box is activated (that is, it has an X in it). These two things tell File Manager to search your entire hard disk for the file.

The Least You Need to Know

This chapter showed you how to work with the files that give File Manager its name. Here's a summary of the important stuff:

☛ To copy a file, select Copy from the File menu, and enter the destination in the Copy dialog box.

☛ To move a file, select Move from the File menu, and enter the destination in the Move dialog box.

☛ Drag-and-drop makes it easy to copy and move files. Just drag the file from the file list and drop it (that is, let go of the mouse button) on the appropriate directory or drive icon.

☛ To rename a file, select Rename from the File menu and enter the new name in the Rename dialog box.

☛ To delete a file, select Delete from the File menu.

☛ Use the File menu's Search command to search for a lost file.

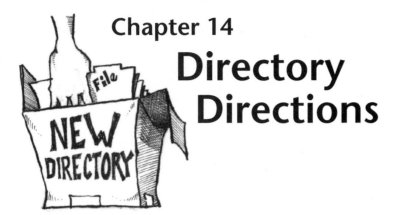

Chapter 14
Directory Directions

In This Chapter

- ☞ Working with directories
- ☞ Creating new directories
- ☞ Copying, moving, and deleting directories
- ☞ More drag-and-drop shenanigans

In our computer house analogy from Chapter 12, we likened your hard disk's directories to the various rooms in the house. Now in the real world, things like creating new rooms, copying and moving existing rooms, and deleting rooms altogether are pretty hard, if not downright impossible. In the computer world, though, these things are a piece of cake. I'll tell you all about them in this chapter.

Directory Structure: A Brief Recap

With your indulgence, I'd like to briefly revisit Chapter 12's directory structure concepts using the File Manager directory list shown here as a visual aid.

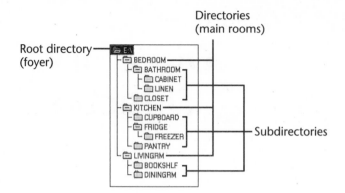

Root directory
(foyer)

Directories
(main rooms)

Subdirectories

*File Manager's
directory list.*

Everything begins at the top of the directory list with the *root directory*. (In the directory list shown I've used drive E, so the root directory is called **E:**. In, say, drive C, it would be **C:**.) In a house, this is equivalent to the main foyer or vestibule.

From this foyer, there is a hallway that runs the length of the house. This is represented in the directory list by the line that extends down from the root directory. As you "walk" down this hall, you see doors to the main rooms of the house. These other rooms are your hard disk's directories. In our example, there are three main rooms: a bedroom, a kitchen, and a living room. If you think of a room (and a directory) as just a place where you store stuff (files), then most rooms will have smaller rooms inside them. For example, the bedroom has two rooms of its own: a bathroom and a closet. In your computer, these are called *subdirectories*. As you can see, the process can extend indefinitely (the bathroom has a cabinet and a linen closet, for example).

By the Way . . .

You may see directories referred to as C:\WINDOWS\SYSTEM or E:\BEDROOM\BATHROOM\CABINET. All those back slashes can be confusing, but they're just used to separate the names of directories and their subdirectories.

Controlling the Directory List

For the directory list to be truly useful, you need to be able to control the display of the directories and subdirectories. The following table outlines the keys you can use to hide and display directories. To use these keys, just highlight the directory you want, and then press the appropriate key.

Press	To
+	Display the next level of subdirectories for the current directory.
*	Display all the subdirectories for the current directory.
Ctrl+*	Display all the directories and subdirectories for the current drive.
-	Hide the subdirectories for the current directory.

TECHNO NERD TEACHES

This house analogy is too comprehensible for the world's technical types. Instead, they prefer to think of the directory structure as a tree. This is, in fact, the origin of the name *root directory*. We're supposed to visualize a trunk growing out of the root directory from which spring branches (*directories*) which can have their own branches (*sub-directories*), and so on. (This is all fine, but it means that, when we look at File Manager's directory list, we have to visualize a tree growing upside down! Right.)

By the Way . . .

If you can't tell whether a directory has any subdirectories, pull down the Tree menu, and select the Indicate Expandable Branches command. This tells File Manager to display a plus sign (+) in the icon of any directory that has subdirectories.

Working with Directory Windows

What's a Windows application without all kinds of windows to make things confusing? File Manager is no exception. It lets you open different windows to get different views of the contents of your computer.

File Manager's windows are called *directory windows* because they show the contents of a specific directory in the current drive.

Opening a New Window

If you want to compare two directories, or if you want to see a different directory in order to drag-and-drop a file, then you need to open a second directory window. No problem. Just select the New Window command from File Manager's Window menu, and then use the new window to select the directory you want.

By the Way . . .

If you have a window configuration that you'd like to use all the time, you need to do two things. First, once you have your windows just the way you want them, pull down the File menu, *hold down the Shift key*, and select the Exit command. This only saves your configuration; it doesn't actually exit the program. Now pull down the **O**ptions menu, and if there is a check mark beside the Save Settings on **E**xit command (indicating that it's active), select it to deactivate it.

Keyboard mavens, press **Shift+F5** to cascade your windows, or **Shift+F4** to tile them.

Once you've opened more than one window, you can manipulate these windows just like those in most other Windows applications. You can size and move 'em, maximize and minimize 'em, and there are even Cascade and Tile commands in the Window menu.

What's Wrong with This Picture?

The following picture seems to be showing two listings of the files in drive B. Can you guess what's wrong?

A. The ratio of the CONFIG.SYS buffers to stacks dropped below 3.14159.

B. File Manager has gone to the Bahamas.

C. It was all done with mirrors.

D. You're hallucinating.

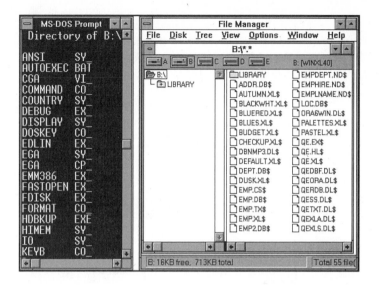

Both windows show a listing of files in drive B!

Answer: B. Here's what happened. To get the window on the right, I inserted a floppy disk in drive B and then displayed its contents in File Manager. To get the window on the left, I inserted a *different* disk in drive B, opened a Windows DOS session (by selecting the MS-DOS Prompt icon from Program Manager), and displayed the contents of the new disk (by typing **dir b:** and pressing **Enter**). Things aren't right!

The problem here is that File Manager isn't smart enough to know when you've changed floppy disks. *You* have to give it a kick in the pants and tell it to update its display. You do this by selecting the Refresh command from the **W**indow menu.

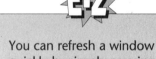

You can refresh a window quickly by simply pressing **F5**.

Adding On: Creating Directories

Adding rooms to a house is usually expensive, time-consuming, and messy. On the other hand, adding directories to your hard disk is free, fast, and easy. What could be better?

The first decision you need to make before adding a directory is *where* you want it. Do you want it to branch off from the root directory? If so, then you need to first highlight the root directory. Do you want it to be a subdirectory of an existing directory? In this case, you need to highlight the existing directory.

Once you've selected the location, pull down the File menu, and choose the Create Directory command. You'll see the Create Directory dialog box, as shown here. Use the Name text box to enter the name of the new directory, and then select **OK**.

Use the Create Directory dialog box to enter the name of your new directory.

By the Way . . .

I'm sorry to report that directory names have to follow the same arcane rules that I outlined for file names in Chapter 13, "File Finagling."

To display the Copy dialog box quickly, highlight the directory, and press **F8**. For the Move dialog box, press **F7**.

Copying and Moving Directories

The techniques for copying and moving directories are, mercifully, almost exactly the same as those for copying and moving files. And, as with files, you also have the choice of using the File menu commands or the drag-and-drop method.

Copying and Moving with the File Menu Commands

To copy a directory, just highlight it, and then select the Copy command from the File menu. In the Copy dialog box, use the To text box to enter a destination for the directory. The directory you're copying will become a *subdirectory* of whatever directory you enter in the To box.

Moving a directory is the same, except you select the Move command from the File menu. (Remember, too, that when you *move* something, the original is deleted after being copied.)

Avoid moving or renaming directories created by your applications. Most programs are finicky enough to expect to find their files in specific directories. Even changing a single letter of one of these directories, can put an application in a huff where it will refuse to run. As with files, only rename what you yourself have created.

Copying and Moving Directories Using Drag-and-Drop

Copying or moving directories is way more fun using the drag-and-drop method (you need Windows 3.1 for this, however). To copy a directory, hold down the **Ctrl** key, drag the directory, and drop it on the destination directory. File Manager will ask if you're sure you want to copy the directory. Select Yes to finish the operation. Remember that the copy of the directory becomes a subdirectory of the destination you chose.

To move a directory, you use the same steps except you hold down the **Alt** key, instead.

Renaming Directories

If you don't like the name of a directory, go ahead and rename it. All you have to do is highlight the directory, and then select the Rename command from the File menu. Enter the new name in the To box and then select **OK**.

The Wrecking Ball: Deleting Directories

The idea of "deleting" a room from a house conjures up fun images of wrecking balls tearing down walls. Your Windows wrecking ball is File Manager's Delete command. Here are the steps you need to follow to delete a directory:

1. Highlight the directory you want to delete.

2. Select Delete from the File menu. File Manager displays the Delete dialog box that shows the name of the directory in the Delete text area.

3. If it's the wrong name, change it to the correct one. When you're ready, select **OK**. The Confirm Directory Delete dialog box appears and asks if you're sure you want to delete the directory.

4. Select Yes. The Confirm File Delete dialog box appears to ask if you're sure you want to delete the first file in the directory.

5. To delete all the files in the directory, select the Yes to All button. To confirm the files one at a time, select the **Yes** button for each file.

A quicker way to display the Delete dialog box is to simply press the **Delete** key.

Just as an improperly wielded wrecking ball can do more harm than good, so, too, is the Delete command especially dangerous when working with directories. If File Manager isn't asking you to confirm either your directory or file deletions, select the **C**onfirmation command from the **O**ptions menu and make sure that each check box in the Confirmation dialog box is activated.

The Least You Need to Know

This chapter showed you how to work with directories in File Manager. Here's a summary:

☞ Directories are analogous to rooms in a house. The root directory is like the vestibule and the other rooms run off its main hallway.

☞ File Manager windows are called *directory windows*. You can manipulate them using the same techniques as you would any ordinary window.

☞ Use the **F**ile menu's **C**reate Directory command to create new directories.

☞ Use the **F**ile menu's **C**opy and **M**ove commands to copy and move directories. If you have a mouse, you can also use the drag-and-drop method.

☞ Use the **F**ile menu's **R**ename and **D**elete commands to rename and delete directories.

This page unintentionally left blank.

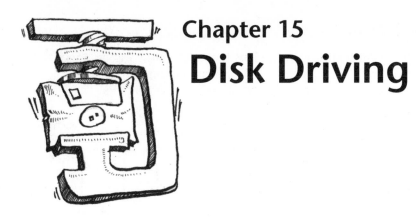

Chapter 15
Disk Driving

In This Chapter

- Painless facts about disks

- How to copy a disk

- How to format a disk

- The easy way to create a "bootable" disk

- Numerous, bizarre asides about things like oysters, peg boards, and the dark side of the Force

This chapter closes out our tour of File Manager (insert sigh of relief here). Our subject will be floppy disks: those fun little platters that your kids have been using for Frisbees. We'll begin with some background about disks (it's easy stuff, but your friends will be very impressed that you know it), then I'll show you how to copy and format your disk and how to make a *bootable* disk.

Types of Floppy Disks

In our endlessly useful computer house analogy, I likened floppy disks to storage containers you use to transport objects to and from the house. These containers can be small (like a box or suitcase) or large (like a car or truck), and different containers hold different amounts of stuff. Floppy disks, too, come in various sizes and capacities.

Floppy Disk Sizes

Although the technowizards in the labs have been showing off a few weird-sized disks recently, your basic floppy disks come in the two different sizes you see here: 5 1/4- and 3 1/2-inch.

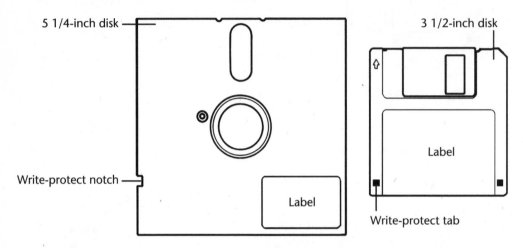

5 1/4-inch disk

3 1/2-inch disk

Write-protect notch

Label

Label

Write-protect tab

The 5 1/4-inch disks are usually black, and they come safely ensconced inside a flexible plastic case. (The flexibility of the 5 1/4-inch disks is where the "floppy" in floppy disk comes from.) The 3 1/2-inch disks come in all kinds of designer colors. Their cases are quite sturdy and they even have moving parts! They also fit nicely into a shirt pocket (if this doesn't feel like too much of a nerdy thing to do).

Which type of disk you use depends on the type of floppy disk drive you have installed in your computer. If you're not sure, you can tell easily enough just by looking at the drive. If the opening is a little more than 5 1/4 inches wide, then it's a 5 1/4-inch floppy drive. If it's about 3 1/2 inches wide, then it's a 3 1/2-inch floppy drive. This is not, as you can see, rocket science.

The Capacity of a Floppy Disk

A slightly more subtle issue is the *capacity* of a floppy disk. A disk's capacity is simply the number of bytes of information the disk is designed to hold.

Both 5 1/4- and 3 1/2-inch disks are available in two capacities: *double-density* and *high-density*. (Actually, the term "double-density" is relatively meaningless nowadays. It comes from the old days of computers—way back in the 80s!—when there were such things as "single-density" disks. Many people now refer to double-density disks simply as "low-density.") Table 4.1 summarizes the four most common floppy disk types.

SPEAK LIKE A GEEK

A *byte* is computerese for a single character of information. So, for example, the phrase "This phrase is 28 bytes long" is, yes, 28 bytes long (you count the spaces, too). To make things real confusing, a *kilobyte* is equal to 1,024 bytes and a *megabyte* is equal to 1,024 kilobytes. If you want to be cool, always say "K" instead of "kilobyte" and "meg" instead of "megabyte."

Table 4.1   The Most Common Floppy Disk Types

Disk type	Storage capacity
5 1/4-inch, double-density	360 kilobytes
5 1/4-inch, high-density	1.2 megabytes
3 1/2-inch, double-density	720 kilobytes
3 1/2-inch, high-density	1.44 megabytes

TECHNO NERD TEACHES

What's with this fetish for the number 1,024? You may be sorry you asked. You see, "kilo," as you may know, means "thousand," and it turns out that 2 to the power of 10 (2x2x2x2x2x2x2x2x2x2) is 1,024, which is close enough. Why *2* to the power of 10? Well, internally, computers can only deal with 2 states: on or off. A circuit either has an electric current (it's on), or it doesn't (it's off). (Amazingly, the world's computer geniuses have been able to create everything from Pac Man to Windows out of these two simple states.)

> ### By the Way . . .
>
> Normally, the only way to tell whether a disk is high-density or double-density is to look at the disk's markings. For a high-density disk, look for the words "High-Density" (of course) or the letters "HD." For a double-density disk, look for "Double-Density" or "DD."

Which type should you use? Generally speaking, you should use high-density disks only if you have a high-density disk drive. If you're not sure what kind of disk drive you have, your computer's packing slip or receipt (if you still have either one) should tell you. As a rule, the older the machine, the less likely it is that its floppy drives are high-density.

Inserting a Floppy Disk

Before your computer can do anything with a floppy disk, you have to insert it in its disk drive. Here's how it's done:

☞ To insert a 5 1/4-inch disk, first grasp the edge opposite the oval hole and make sure the label is facing up. (If the disk has no label, make sure the side with no seams is the one pointing up.) Now gently insert the disk into the drive slot as far as it will go. On most drives, you should feel a slight click once the disk is in place. Close the latch above the slot, and you're ready for action.

☞ For a 3 1/2-inch disk, grab it on the edge away from the sliding, silver rectangle with the label facing up. (If there's no label, "up" is the side opposite the round, silver doohickey.) Insert the disk into the drive slot until you here a satisfying clunk.

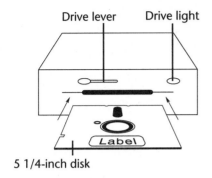

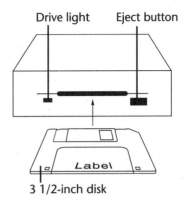

5 1/4-inch disk

3 1/2-inch disk

Removing a Floppy Disk

Most books are happy to tell you how to put a disk in a disk drive, but no one ever seems to get around to telling you how to get the suckers out! As a public service, here are the oh-so-simple directions:

The 5 1/4-inch disks are, literally, a snap to take out. First, remove any obstacles (such as your eye) from the front of the drive door. Then just open the latch, and voilà, your disk pops right out. (If for some reason, the disk doesn't pop out, just pull it straight out of the drive.)

The 3 1/2-inch disk drives have a button on the bottom right-hand side. Just push this button to remove a disk.

Disk Dos and Don'ts

Do:

☛ Place your 5 1/4-inch disks inside their protective pouches when not in use.

☛ Keep backup copies of important disks.

☛ Buy cheaper, no-name disks for everyday use.

☛ Buy top-quality disks for important needs, such as backing up your hard disk.

☛ Try to get out more.

Don't:

☞ Touch the magnetic surface of a disk.

☞ Expose a disk to direct sunlight or excessive temperatures.

☞ Place a disk near a strong magnetic or electronic source.

☞ Fold, spindle, or mutilate a disk.

☞ Use a pen or pencil to write on a label attached to a 5 1/4-inch disk (felt pens are okay).

☞ Try to remove a disk from a disk drive if the drive's light is still on.

☞ Eat oysters unless there's an "r" in the month. (Or is that *if* there's an "r" in the month? Hmmm.)

Copying Disks

Copying a floppy disk is one of those chores that only seems to come up now and then. For example, most software manuals tell you to make backup copies of the program's installation disks in case anything goes wrong. Here are the steps involved:

> ## By the Way . . .
> You can only copy a disk to another disk of the same type (that is, of the same size and capacity).

When copying floppy disks, the original disk is called the *source* disk, and the new disk is called the *destination* disk.

1. Insert the disk you want to copy in the appropriate drive. If you have two identical disk drives, insert the new disk in the other drive.

2. Pull down the Disk menu, and select the Copy Disk command. If you have more than one floppy drive, you'll see the Copy Disk dialog box shown here.

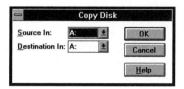

Use the Copy Disk dialog box to tell File Manager where to find the disks.

3. In the Source In drop-down list box, select the letter of the drive that contains the original disk. In the Destination In drop-down list box, select the letter of the drive that contains (or will contain) the new disk.

4. Select **OK**. File Manager scares the daylights out of you by telling you that "ALL" data in the destination disk will be erased. Remain calm, and select the **Yes** button. File Manager asks you to insert the "source" disk.

5. You've already done this, so select **OK**. File Manager begins reading the information from the disk (this may take a minute or two). When it's read all it can, you'll be prompted to insert the "destination" disk.

6. Insert the new disk (if necessary), and select **OK** to get File Manager to start copying the information to the new disk. Depending on the system you have, File Manager may ask you to swap the source and destination disks again. Just follow the prompts on the screen.

Formatting a Disk

You can't, of course, just stick any old piece of plastic in a disk drive and expect it to read and write information. Even official I-bought-it-at-the-local-computer-store floppy disks need to be set up first so that the information can be properly stored on the disk.

It's like the difference between a peg board and an ordinary piece of wood. Buying new disks (unless the box says they're "preformatted") is like buying a bunch of flat, featureless pieces of wood. You can try all day to stick pegs in 'em, but they'll just fall off. What you need to do is "format" the wood so you end up with peg board. *Then* you're in business.

The process of setting up a disk so that it can read and write information is called *formatting*.

Why aren't *all* disks preformatted? Well, most disks can be used with both DOS and non-DOS computers, and the different machines require different formats (think of peg boards with different sized holes). So the disk manufacturers simplify their lives by shipping their disks unformatted.

Fortunately, though, File Manager makes disk formatting about as painless as it can get. Begin by inserting the disk you want to format in the appropriate drive, and then select the Format Disk command from the Disk menu. You'll see the Format Disk dialog box.

The Disk menu's Format Disk command displays the Format Disk dialog box.

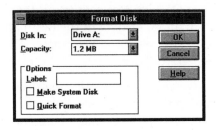

Here's a summary of the available options in this dialog box:

☞ Use the **Disk In** drop-down list box to select the letter of the drive that contains your disk.

☞ Use the **Capacity** drop-down list box to select the proper capacity of the disk.

☞ If you want to give the disk a name, fill in the **Label** text box. Follow the naming conventions outlined in Chapter 13, "File Finagling."

☞ The **Make System Disk** option allows you to create a "bootable" disk. See the section titled "Creating a Bootable Disk," below.

☞ The **Quick Format** option is a real time-saver when you're formatting used disks. Selecting this option will cut your format time down to a few seconds (it normally takes a minute or so).

When you've set up your options, select **OK**. File Manager warns you that formatting the disk will erase all the data on the disk. (It says this even if you're formatting a brand new disk. As I've said before, these machines aren't very smart.) Select **Yes** to start the format. File Manager displays a dialog box to show you the progress of the format. When it's done, the program will ask you if you want to format another. If you're done, select **No**. If you *do* want to keep formatting, select **Yes** to return to the Format Disk dialog box, insert the new disk, and repeat the process.

Put It to Work

Formatting can help protect you against computer *viruses*, those nasty, little programs designed by repressed, pimple-faced, pseudo-human nerds who have succumbed to the dark side of the Force. Most viruses are transmitted from machine to machine via floppy disks, so you should always be careful about which used disks you trust in your computer. If you've inherited some old disks, make sure there are no viruses lurking in the weeds by formatting each one before you use them.

Creating a "Bootable" Disk

The next time you start your computer, keep your eye on disk drive A. A few seconds after you throw the switch, the drive light should come on briefly. This means the drive is being set up for use, and once that's done, the light goes out again. A few seconds later, though, the light will reappear. In this case, your system is looking to see if there's a floppy disk in the drive. If there is, the computer will attempt to load DOS from the floppy disk. If the disk contains the proper files—specifically, the DOS *system files*—then DOS will load and you'll see an **A>** prompt instead of the usual **C>** prompt. This is called "booting from a floppy," and a disk with the DOS system files is called a "bootable disk."

What good is such a disk? Well, it's possible that, thanks to a virus or a system crash, you may lose access to your hard drive. If this happens, you just place your bootable disk in drive A and reboot your computer. With DOS control restored, you can then proceed to investigate the problem.

Formatting a Disk to Make It Bootable

The easiest way to create a bootable disk is to format it that way. Recall that the Format Disk dialog box included a **Make System Disk** option ("system disk" is the term the pointy-head types use instead of "bootable disk"). Just activate that option and format away.

By the Way . . .

DOS will only boot from a floppy disk in drive A, so make sure whatever disk you're using will be readable in drive A.

Making an Already Formatted Disk Bootable

If you've already formatted a disk, you don't have to bother reformatting it to make it bootable. Instead, insert the disk in drive A, and select the **Make System Disk** option from File Manager's **D**isk menu. In the Make System Disk dialog box that appears, select drive A and then select **OK**. File Manager copies the necessary files to the disk.

Testing the System Disk

For boring, technical reasons, File Manager won't always copy the system files to a formatted disk. If you get a message to that effect, try formatting the disk, instead.

Once you've created your bootable disk, you should try it out as soon as you can to make sure it works. All you do is place the disk in drive A, exit Windows, and then reboot your computer. If all goes well, your computer should ask you to enter the date and time (you can just press **Enter** in both cases), and then you'll see the A> prompt. Remove the disk, reboot your computer, and store the bootable disk in a safe place.

The Least You Need to Know

This chapter told you everything you'd ever want to know about floppy disks and how to use them. Here's a summary:

☞ Floppy disks come in various sizes and capacities. By far the most common are 5 1/4- and 3 1/2-inch disks.

☞ Today's disks mostly come in two capacities: double-density and high-density.

☞ To copy a disk, use File Manager's **C**opy Disk command from the **D**isk menu.

☞ To format a disk, use the **D**isk menu's **F**ormat Disk command.

☞ A bootable disk can help you recover from hard disk problems. You can create one either during a format (you need to select the **M**ake System Disk option in the Format Disk dialog box) or by selecting the **M**ake System Disk command from the **D**isk menu.

This page unintentionally left blank.

Part V
Working with Windows (When It's Time to Stop Playing Solitaire and Get Some Work Done)

Windows can be fun to play with, but one of these days, you've gotta get some work done. To that end, this section presents a number of chapters that cover practical (but not overly serious) topics. You'll learn such handy things as how to share data between your applications (Chapter 16), how to print (Chapter 18), and how to use Windows' fancy fonts (Chapter 19). You'll also learn how to take advantage of the free stuff that you get with Windows (Write, Paintbrush, Cardfile, and so on), and I'll even show you how to customize Windows (Chapter 17) and how to wrestle some common Windows problems to the ground (Chapter 23). Don't work too hard!

Chapter 16
It's Nice to Share: Moving Information Between Applications

In This Chapter

- ☞ Selecting information that you want to share
- ☞ Copying information from DOS and Windows applications
- ☞ Pasting information into DOS and Windows applications
- ☞ Setting up links between the data in your Windows applications
- ☞ Lots of fun stuff about commercials from long ago, weird business techniques, and your computer's IQ

The mind is a strange thing. Take my mind, for example (please). I'm constantly forgetting important things like friends' birthdays, paying the rent, doing the dishes. On the other hand, I vividly remember a commercial that was on TV, oh, about 20 years ago. It showed a father eating a chocolate bar and asking his daughter what she learned in school today. She replied, gazing longingly at the chocolate bar, "Shaaaring."

This chapter shows you what to do if one of your applications has the computer equivalent of a chocolate bar (a *bar* chart, perhaps?), and you want to share it with another program.

Sharing Info: The Basics

A friend of mine in the business world once told me a hilarious story about trying to work out a deal between two people who, for various reasons, refused to talk to each other. On one occasion, each person was hunkered down in a hotel suite (on different floors, of course), and both refused to meet on neutral ground. My friend had to shuttle back and forth between rooms to get anything done.

This behavior reminds me of DOS applications—trying to get them to share information is at best painful and is usually impossible. Windows changes all that by acting, as my friend did, as a go-between for all your applications (Windows *and* DOS). In fact, the whole procedure can be reduced to three easy steps:

1. Highlight the information you want to share.

2. Copy (or cut) the information.

3. Paste the information into the other application.

Highlighting Stuff in Windows Applications

When moving data between programs, the first step is to highlight the information you want to share. This is easiest with a mouse where all you do is position the pointer at the beginning of the selection, and then drag the mouse over the information you want. If you're selecting text, it will appear highlighted (that is, white letters on a dark background). If you're selecting a picture, you'll likely see a dotted line to indicate your selection.

> ### By the Way . . .
> Some applications may require an extra step. In Paintbrush, for example, you have to select either the Scissors or Pick tool before dragging the mouse. See Chapter 21, "Nurturing Your Inner Child with Paintbrush," for more information.

From the keyboard, position the cursor at the beginning of the selection, hold down the **Shift** key, and then use the arrow keys to highlight what you want. If you need to select a lot of information, you can also use the Page Up and Page Down keys to highlight large chunks at a time.

The following scenario will happen to you more than once: you highlight a large section of text and then accidentally press some other key on your keyboard. Yikes, you're entire selection disappears! Don't panic and, above all, don't press anything else. The application should have an **Undo** command on its **Edit** menu. Select this command to restore your text.

Cutting and Copying Information

Now that you have your information highlighted, you need to tell Windows what to do with it (yes, yes, I know what you'd *really* like to tell Windows to do with it). You have two choices: cutting and copying.

Cutting Stuff from Windows Applications

If you don't want to keep the highlighted information in the original application, then you can cut it right out of there. It's simple: just pull down the application's **Edit** menu, and select the Cut command. The selection will disappear from the screen, but don't be alarmed; Windows is on the job and has saved everything to a secret location.

Psst. Wanna know the name of this secret location? It's called the *Clipboard*. Any time you cut or copy information, Windows stores it in the Clipboard just in case you want it back. If you're curious how this thing works, cut or copy something, and then start up the Clipboard application from Program Manager's Main group. You'll see your information sitting there, waiting for your next move.

By the Way . . .

For sharing purposes, you can only cut stuff from Windows applications; it doesn't work for DOS applications.

TECHNO NERD TEACHES

386 is the aficionado's cool short form for the *80386*, a type of microprocessor. The microprocessor is the head honcho chip inside your computer that controls the whole shebang. Most people describe it as the "brain" of the computer, and I suppose that's as good a way to look at it as any. So what does 80386 mean? Well, it actually refers to certain hardware features of the microprocessor, but for our purposes, think of it as your computer's IQ. In that sense, a 386 machine is "smarter" than a 286, and a 486 is the genius of the group.

Copying Stuff in Windows Applications

When sharing information, you normally send only a copy of the data to the other application. This way, you keep the information in the original application in case you need it for something else.

Copying highlighted information in a Windows application is easy: just select the Copy command from the program's Edit menu.

Copying Stuff in a DOS Application

DOS applications are another kettle of fish. The steps you follow depend on whether you're copying text or graphics.

Copying Text in a DOS Application

The best way to copy text from a DOS application is to place the program in a window and highlight the text you want. However, you can only place DOS programs in windows if you have at least a 386 computer. Anything less just won't cut the mustard.

Here are the steps you need to plow through:

1. Open the DOS application, and place it in a window (if it's not already) by pressing **Alt+Enter**.

2. Pull down the window's **Control** menu by clicking on the square in the upper left corner or by pressing **Alt+Spacebar**.

3. Select the Control menu's Edit command. This displays a new menu of commands.

4. From this new menu, select the Mark command. A blinking cursor appears just below the Control-menu box.

5. Highlight the information you want to copy. You're screen will look something like the one shown here.

If your computer doesn't do much of anything when you press **Alt+Enter**, and you *know* you have at least a 386, then you're in the wrong Windows mode (you need to be in something called *enhanced mode*). Exit Windows, and try forcing it into the proper mode by starting it with the command **win /3**.

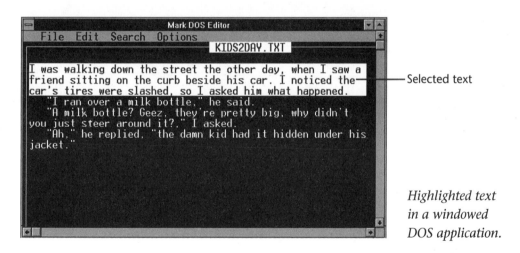

Selected text

Highlighted text in a windowed DOS application.

6. Press **Enter** to tell Windows to copy the selection.

Copying DOS Text with a 286

If you're still trudging along with an old 286 and you're starting to think that 386 and 486 users have all the fun, well you're probably right. However, this doesn't mean you're stuck. You can still copy text from a DOS application by simply pressing your keyboard's **Print Screen** key.

The advantage of this method is that it's simple. The disadvantage, though, is that you end up with a copy of the entire screen, warts and all, as you can see here.

Copying DOS text with the Print Screen key usually gives you more than you bargained for.

Once you paste a screen like this, you'll have to edit out the bits you don't need.

Copying Graphics in a DOS Application

If the DOS program has a picture that you want to copy, you first need to display the application in a window. (This means that 286 users are, once again, out of luck.) Set up your window so you can see the image, and then press **Alt+Print Screen**.

> **By the Way . . .**
>
> This method makes a copy of the *entire* window—you get the title bar, the scroll bars, everything. Unless you want these things, you should first paste the image into Paintbrush (I'll show you how to do this in the next section) and remove the extraneous matter from there. See Chapter 21, "Nurturing Your Inner Child with Paintbrush," for the lowdown on working with Paintbrush.

Pasting Information

Okay, you're finally ready to place your cut or copied information into another application. The method you use depends on whether you're pasting to a Windows or a DOS application.

Pasting Information to a Windows Application

This is a no-brainer: place the program's cursor at the point where you want the information to appear, and then select the **Paste** command from the Edit menu. That's it!

Pasting Information to a DOS Application with a 386 or 486

Pasting text into a DOS application takes a bit more effort. If you have a 386 or 486, position the cursor where you want the text to appear, place the application in a window (by pressing **Alt+Enter**), and then follow these steps:

1. Pull down the window's **Control** menu by clicking on the square in the upper left corner or by pressing **Alt+Spacebar**.

2. Select the Control menu's Edit command. A new menu of commands appears.

3. Select the **Paste** command from the new menu. The Clipboard copies your text before your very eyes!

Pasting Information to a DOS Application with a 286

286 users, you'll be happy to know that you, too, can paste text into your DOS applications. Here's how:

1. In the DOS application, press **Alt+Esc** to reduce the program to an icon. (If you can't see the icon, be sure to move or minimize any windows that are in the way.)

2. Display the icon's **Control** menu by clicking on it or by pressing **Alt+Esc** until the icon is highlighted and then pressing **Alt+Spacebar**.

3. Select the **Paste** command. Windows redisplays the program and pastes the text.

Linking Your Windows Applications

As you've seen, Windows makes it real easy to share information between applications (especially Windows applications). One of the problems with this simple cut (or copy) and paste approach, though, is that you need to repeat the whole procedure if the original information changes.

Consider the following scenario: you've got some spare time (hey, it could happen), so you decide to write a long-overdue letter to your mom. In fact, to show off your new skills, you decide to do it in Write and include some Paintbrush drawings that the kids have done. So you write your letter, copy and paste the drawings, and then print everything out a few days later. When your kids see the letter, though, they're upset because they changed the drawings last night and you haven't used their updated artwork (as a parent, of course, you're *supposed* to know these things). You don't see what the big deal is, so they show you:

Paintbrush picture pasted into Write

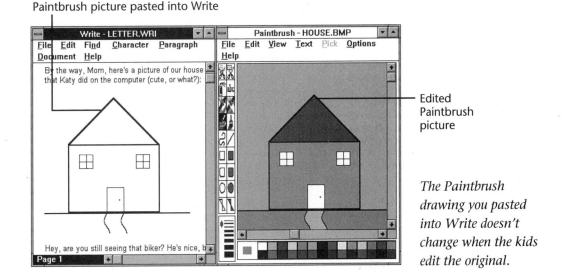

Edited
Paintbrush
picture

*The Paintbrush
drawing you pasted
into Write doesn't
change when the kids
edit the original.*

The problem here, of course, is that unless you know that any information you've pasted has changed, you're stuck with the old version.

The good news is that some *very* cool technology exists that allows you to tell Windows to keep an eye on things for you. By *linking* the pasted information, Windows will automatically update the pasted copy any time someone changes the original.

> ## By the Way . . .
>
> If you've heard people talking about Object Linking and Embedding (it's usually abbreviated as OLE, which is correctly pronounced as "oh-LAY"), this is the "linking" part.

How to Link Your Applications

Fortunately, linking your applications isn't a whole lot more complicated than a simple paste. Copy your information as you normally do (this only applies to Windows applications, however), and then switch to the other program (or open it if it's not already running). Pull down its Edit menu, and take a look at the commands. If you see a Paste Link command, select it. This will paste your information *and* tell Windows to maintain a link between the two applications. You don't need to do anything else; Windows handles all the hard stuff in the background.

If there's no Paste Link command, select Paste Special, instead. You'll see a Paste Special dialog box similar to the one shown here.

Use the Paste Special dialog box to set up a link between your applications.

Select the Paste Link button to paste the information and set up the link.

By the Way . . .

OLE is a fairly new technology, so not all Windows applications are up to speed with it yet. If your application doesn't have a Paste Link command in its Edit menu (or a Paste Link button in its Paste Special dialog box), then it can't handle linking.

Put It to Work

Linking is perfect for projects involving more than one person. A good example would be a family newsletter. You could do most of it in Write, include recipes from Cardfile, pictures from Paintbrush, and so on. By linking all these objects to the Write newsletter, you never have to worry about someone making a change and not telling you.

Editing a Linked Object

If you need to make changes to a linked object, you could, of course, just open the original application, load the file, and edit it, confident in the knowledge that the pasted copy will be updated automatically.

Alternatively, you could edit the *pasted* version of the object. This is easiest with a mouse where all you do is double-click on the object. Windows will load the object's original application automatically. For example, suppose you've pasted and linked a Paintbrush picture in a Write document. Double-clicking on the picture starts Paintbrush and loads the picture.

If you prefer to use your keyboard, highlight the linked object, pull down the Edit menu, and look for one of two things:

☞ A command, such as Edit Paintbrush Picture Object. Selecting this command opens the original application and loads the object.

☞ The Links command (this command is in the File menu in some applications). Selecting this command displays the Links dialog box. Select the Open Source (or just Open, in some cases) button to load the original application.

When you've finished editing the object, exit the application, and save your changes when prompted.

The Least You Need to Know

This chapter covered all kinds of fun stuff about exchanging information between Windows and DOS applications. Don't look now, but you're well on your way to becoming a real Windows maven! Just don't let it go to your head. Here's a summary of what a maven should know about this chapter.

☞ The first step when sharing information is to highlight the data you want to use.

☞ The second step is to copy (or cut) the information to the Clipboard. In Windows applications,

continues

continued

use the Edit menu's Copy (or Cut) commands. In windowed DOS applications, select Edit from the Control menu, and then select the Mark command.

☞ Once your information is on the Clipboard, open the other application, and select the Paste command from the Edit menu.

☞ If you think your data will be changing after it's pasted, set up a link between the two applications. In the Edit menu, select the Paste Link command, or choose Paste Special and then select the Paste Link button in the dialog box.

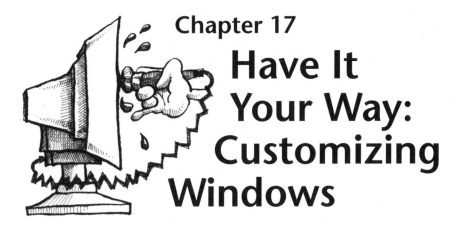

Chapter 17

Have It Your Way: Customizing Windows

In This Chapter

- ☞ Playing with Windows' colors
- ☞ Customizing the desktop
- ☞ Customizing your mouse
- ☞ Customizing your keyboard
- ☞ Miscellaneous musings on fritterware, the February blahs, and (once again) the desktop metaphor

Fritterware is the name given to any option-ladened software program that makes you fritter away your time playing around with its bells and whistles. Windows, with its seemingly infinite number of customization options, is the undisputed fritterware champ, and this chapter will prove it.

The Control Panel: A Quick Guide

All your Windows customizing chores are handled by a special application called the Control Panel. Before diving into the fun customization stuff, you should read this section first to get yourself familiar with the basic Control Panel operating procedures.

Starting Control Panel

You'll find the Control Panel icon in Program Manager's Main group. Double-click on this icon (or, from the keyboard, select **Main**, highlight the **Control Panel** icon, and press **Enter**) to start the application. You'll see a screen that looks something like this one.

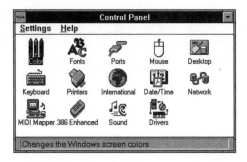

The Control Panel window.

Navigating the Control Panel Window

As you can see, Control Panel, with all those icons, looks like a scaled-down version of Program Manager. (The number of icons displayed in *your* Control Panel depends on your system and the equipment you have installed.) Each of these icons represents some aspect of the Windows environment.

Selecting an icon is easiest with a mouse where all you do is double-click. With the keyboard, you can use the arrow keys to highlight an icon, and then press **Enter**. Or you can pull down the **Settings** menu, and select the appropriate command.

Exiting Control Panel

When you're done with Control Panel, you can quit by selecting the Exit command from the **Settings** menu or by double-clicking on the Control-menu box with the mouse.

Doing Windows' Colors

The scene outside my window on this cold February morning is not a pretty one. I see leafless, lifeless trees; I see a few snowflakes descending lazily—the remnants, I suppose, of last night's storm; and I see a sky covered with colorless, foreboding clouds that promise more of the evil, white stuff. Yuck!

Believe me, the *last* thing I want to see on my computer screen is Windows' usual drab gray and blue colors. If you, too, feel like giving Windows a make-over, then the screen colors are a good place to start.

Selecting a Color Scheme

The easiest way to change Windows' colors is to select one of the predefined color schemes. These schemes control the colors of just about everything you see in Windows, including the desktop background, the pull-down menus, and all the window components (the title bars, borders, scroll bars, and so on).

To choose a scheme, begin by selecting Control Panel's **Color** icon. You'll see the Color dialog box, as shown here.

The name of the color scheme ⟶

These windows show you what the scheme looks like.

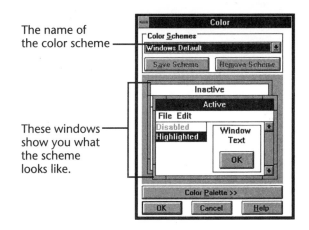

Use the Color dialog box to select a different color scheme.

The Color **S**chemes drop-down list box displays the name of the current scheme, and the two overlapping windows in the middle of the box show you what the scheme looks like. Use this list to try out some other schemes, and when you find one that strikes your fancy (Black Leather Jacket, perhaps?), select **OK** to return to Control Panel.

Creating Your Own Color Scheme

Some of the Control Panel's color schemes are, well, just plain silly (Hot Dog Stand? Rugby?). If none of them are *you*, then why not get creative and come up with your own scheme? Here's the basic procedure:

1. Select Control Panel's Color icon, and in the Color dialog box, select the Color **P**alette button to display more options.

2. Use the Screen Element drop-down list box to select which component of the Windows screen you want to change.

> ### By the Way . . .
> Mouse users can select screen elements quickly by simply clicking on the appropriate element in the fake windows on the left side of the dialog box.

3. Select a color for the component from the **B**asic Colors collection. Mouse users just click on a color; keyboard users have to press **Alt+B**, use the arrow keys to highlight a color, and then press the **Spacebar**. The fake windows on the left side of the dialog box show you what the new color will look like in action.

4. Repeat steps 2 and 3 for the other screen elements you want to change.

5. When you're done, select the S**a**ve Scheme button. The Save Scheme dialog box appears.

6. Enter a name for the scheme in the text box provided, and then select **OK** to return to the Color dialog box.

7. Select **OK** to get back to the Control Panel with your new color scheme in effect.

Customizing the Desktop

If you were listening way back in Chapter 4, "Up, Up, and Away: Starting Windows," then you'll remember me telling you about Windows' desktop metaphor. (You know, the one where Windows organizes everything on your screen the way you might organize things on your desk. Right, *that* desktop metaphor.) So it should come as no surprise that the background on which Windows struts its stuff is called the *desktop*.

You saw in the last section that you can change the color of the desktop (unless, of course, you *like* drab gray). That's pretty neat, but it's not all you can do. You can also change the *pattern* that appears on the desktop and, if you're really feeling your oats, you can even create your own pattern.

Selecting a Predefined Pattern

Like the color schemes you saw earlier, the Control Panel also comes with a selection of desktop patterns (and some of these have silly names, too). To pick out one of these patterns, select the **Desktop** icon to display the Desktop dialog box.

There's a lot of stuff in this dialog box, but for now, you only have to worry about the controls in the Pattern area at the top. In particular, the Name drop-down list box contains the names of the predefined patterns. Pick one that sounds interesting, and then select **OK** to see what it looks like. (You may need to minimize any running applications to get the full effect.)

Creating Your Own Pattern

Some of the predefined patterns are pretty cool (I like Thatches, myself). For true creative fun, you can come up with your own pattern. Here's how:

> ## By the Way . . .
> Sorry keyboard users, you need a mouse to create your own pattern.

1. From the Control Panel, double-click on the **Desktop** icon, and in the Desktop dialog box' Pattern area, select the Edit **Pattern** button. You'll see the Desktop-Edit Pattern dialog box, shown here.

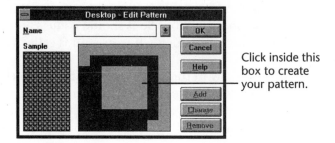

Use the Desktop-Edit Pattern dialog box to create your own desktop pattern.

Click inside this box to create your pattern.

2. Create a pattern by clicking inside the larger box in the middle of the Desktop-Edit Pattern dialog box. As you click, the Sample box shows you what the pattern will look like.

   To erase parts of the pattern, click again on a darkened square.

3. When you're done, use the Name text box to enter a name for the pattern.

4. Select the Add button to add it to the list, and then select **OK** to return to the Desktop dialog box.

By the Way . . .

Instead of creating your own pattern from scratch, select a pattern from the **Name** drop-down list box, and edit it.

Wallpapering the Desktop? Why Not!

In the real world, wallpapering is a chore that, for most people, ranks right up there with grouting the bathtub. Fortunately, this isn't the real world, and so wallpapering Windows is actually quite entertaining.

You start by selecting Control Panel's **Desktop** icon. When the Desktop dialog box appears, look for the Wallpaper area, and browse through the selection of wallpapers in the File drop-down list box. When you see one that sounds cool, select **OK**. You get dropped back into the Control Panel, and Windows displays the new wallpaper.

By the Way . . .

Some of this wallpaper stuff is great. I really like ARCHES.BMP, MARBLE.BMP, and, my personal favorite, CHESS.BMP. (You may not have CHESS.BMP if you have a laptop, and Windows was installed at the factory. I'm not sure why we get ripped off, but it's a big file so they may be just trying to save us some space. Thanks a lot.)

Customizing Your Mouse

For many new Windows users, the biggest obstacle to overcome when learning Windows is learning how to use a mouse for the first time. The problems range from controlling the thing, to getting double-clicks to work properly, to just finding the darn pointer! For the most part, these problems often resolve themselves as people get used to the little rodent. However, the Windows programmers were thoughtful enough to include some customization options so people could set up the mouse just the way they like.

To see these options, select the **Mouse** icon in the Control Panel. You'll see the Mouse dialog box shown here.

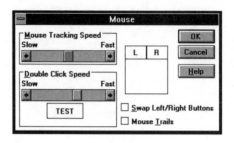

Use the options in the Mouse dialog box to customize your mouse.

Controlling the Tracking Speed

When you move the mouse on its pad, Windows translates this movement and tracks the mouse pointer on your screen accordingly. How quickly the mouse moves across the screen is called the *tracking speed*. If this speed is out of whack (for example, if you move the mouse furiously but the pointer just creeps along, or on the other extreme, if the slightest hand tremor causes the pointer to go racing across the screen), then your mouse is likely to end up in the nearest garbage can.

The good news is that adjusting the tracking speed is a snap. In the Mouse dialog box, take a look at the Mouse Tracking Speed control (it's called a *slider bar*). You can do two things with this option:

☞ If your mouse pointer is wailing around the screen, slow it down by dragging the slider bar box to the left or by clicking on the left-pointing arrow.

☞ If the pointer is too slow, slide the box to the right.

By the Way . . .

You can test the new setting at any time by simply moving the mouse around.

Controlling the Double-Click Speed

One of the things that a mouse-aware program must do is distinguish between two consecutive single-clicks and a double-click. For example, if you click once, wait five seconds, and then click again, then that would qualify as two single-clicks in most people's books. But what if there is only a second between clicks? Or half a second? This threshold is called the *double-click speed*: anything faster is handled as a double-click.

You can adjust this threshold using the Double Click Speed slider bar. You have two options:

☞ If you find that Windows doesn't always recognize your double-clicks, set up a slower double-click speed by moving the Double-Click Speed slider to the left.

☞ If you find that Windows is interpreting some of your single-clicks as double-clicks, set up a faster double-click speed by moving the slider to the right.

By the Way . . .

To test the new speed, double-click on the TEST area. It reverses colors if Windows recognizes your double-click.

Happy Mouse Trails to You

Many people with laptop computers or failing eyesight complained that they had trouble finding the little mouse pointer on their screen. So Microsoft, ever sensitive, added a Mouse Trails check box to the Mouse dialog box in Windows 3.1 (not available in 3.0). When you activate this option and move your mouse, you'll see a trail of pointers. I suppose this does make it easier to see, but I use it all the time just because it's such a cool, psychedelic effect.

> ## By the Way . . .
>
> Not all mice support this feature, I'm sorry to say. If you don't see a Mouse Trails option in your Mouse dialog box, then your mouse can't display trails.

Setting Up the Mouse for Left-Handers

Most mice and the applications that use them are "handists." That is, they assume that the user is right-handed. Southpaws, if you're tired of this discrimination, you can get a small measure of revenge by swapping the left and right buttons on your mouse. All you have to do is activate the Swap Left/Right Buttons check box in the Mouse dialog box.

Customizing the Keyboard

When you press and hold a letter on your keyboard, you notice two things: first, once you press the key, there is a slight *delay* before the second letter appears; second, the subsequent letters appear at a constant rate (called the *repeat rate*). Beginning keyboardists are usually better off with a longer delay and a slower repeat rate. More experienced types, on the other hand, would probably prefer a short delay combined with a fast repeat rate.

The good news is that Control Panel allows you to change both of these values. Select the Keyboard icon to display the Keyboard dialog box.

Use the Keyboard dialog box to adjust the delay and repeat rate.

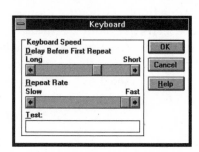

You control the delay by using the Delay Before First Repeat slider bar. Move the slider bar's box (by dragging it with your mouse or by using the left and right arrow keys) to the left for a longer delay or to the right for a shorter delay.

As you've no doubt guessed by now, the Repeat Rate slider bar controls the repeat rate. Move the slider bar's box to the left for a slower rate or to the right for a faster one.

Use the Test text box to try out your new settings. When you're done, select OK to return to the Control Panel.

The Least You Need to Know

This chapter showed you how to customize Windows to suit your own tastes. Here's a quick recap of what you need to know:

- ☞ Select Control Panel's **Color** icon to change the colors of the Windows screen. Use the Color Schemes drop-down list box to select a predefined color scheme, or make up your own by selecting the Color Palette button.

- ☞ Select the **Desktop** icon to customize the look of the desktop—the background on which Windows displays its dialog boxes and windows. In the Pattern area, select a predefined pattern from the Name list, or use the Edit Pattern button to make up your own.

- ☞ For a fancier desktop, use the Desktop dialog box' Wallpaper area to select a wallpaper file from the File list.

- ☞ Select Control Panel's **Mouse** icon to adjust four mouse options: the tracking speed, the double-click speed, mouse trails, and to switch the left and right mouse buttons.

- ☞ Control Panel's Keyboard icon allows you to control two basic keyboard characteristics: the delay and the repeat rate.

This page unintentionally left blank.

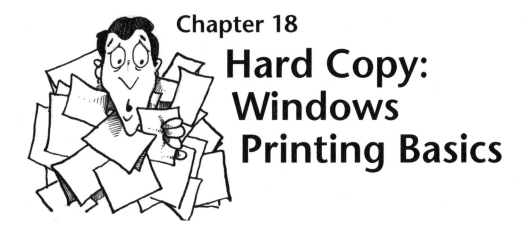

Chapter 18

Hard Copy: Windows Printing Basics

In This Chapter

- ☛ Basic printing steps
- ☛ Installing a printer in Windows
- ☛ Working with Print Manager
- ☛ A bad joke about the Show Me state and drag-and-drop revisited

I've suffered with various computers over the years, but one thing has remained constant: when I'm finished working, I need some physical, tangible proof that I really did *do* something and that this stuff isn't just all smoke and mirrors; I've gotta see some hard copy. (I figure I must have lived in Missouri, the Show Me state, in a former life.)

Happily, Windows makes printing relatively painless. You just set up your printer once, and all your Windows applications have no choice but to use that setup. This chapter shows you the basic printing procedure, and I'll also talk about how to install other printers and how to use Windows Print Manager.

Basic Printing Steps

Printing is a good example of Windows' consistent interface. Although there are some small differences between applications, the basic steps are the same.

Before printing, make sure your printer is powered up and on-line. (*On-line* means that your printer is ready, willing, and able to handle the blizzard of characters your application will be throwing at it. Most printers have some kind of On-line button that you can press, just to make sure.) In your application, pull down the File menu, and select the Print command. You'll see a Print dialog box similar the one shown here for the Write word-processor.

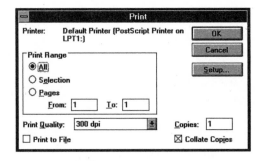

Write's Print dialog box.

The options in this dialog box will vary slightly from application to application. However, you'll almost always see two things:

☛ A text box to enter the number of copies you want. In the Write dialog box, for example, you'd fill in the Copies text box.

☛ Some controls for selecting how much of the file to print. You'll normally have the option of printing the entire file or a specific range of pages. (Write also includes a Selection option button that lets you print only the text you've highlighted.)

When you've chosen your options, select the **OK** button to start printing (some Print dialog boxes have a **Print** button, instead). If your application isn't covering the bottom of the screen, you'll see the Print Manager icon appear while your file is printing. I'll tell you more about Print Manager later in this chapter.

Installing a Printer

In the bad, old DOS world, every program deals with the printer in its own way. This means that you have to perform some kind of printer setup for every application you use. Windows changes all that because Windows itself handles all the printing chores. When you print from a Windows application, all the application does is pass everything over to Windows and say, "Here, *you* do it." This has two major advantages. First, it means that, as you saw earlier, the steps required to print something in Windows are more or less the same for all applications. Second, it means that the only program that needs to know about your printer is Windows itself. Your Windows applications couldn't care less; they're just along for the ride.

If your printer *isn't* in the list, then you have three choices:

☞ Check your printer manual to see if the printer works like (or *emulates*) another printer. If it does, see if you can find the emulated printer in the list.

☞ Select one of the list's catch-all printers. For example, select **Generic/Text Only** for a dot-matrix printer or PostScript Printer for, of course, a PostScript printer.

☞ If your printer comes with a disk, select **Install Unlisted or Updated Printer**.

Printer installation is normally handled during the Windows setup program. If you skipped that step, or if you have a new printer, then you need to follow these steps to install your printer:

1. From Program Manager, start **Control Panel** from the Main group, and then select the **Printers** icon to display the Printers dialog box.

2. If you already have some printers installed, select the Add button to expand the dialog box to the one shown here (if you have no printers installed, you can skip this step).

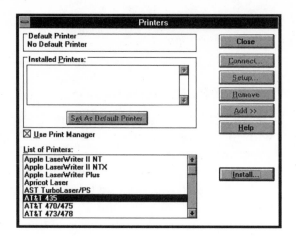

*The expanded
version of the
Printers dialog box.*

You can navigate the List of Printers quickly by pressing the first letter of the printer name you're looking for. For example, pressing **T** takes you to the Tandy LP-1000 printer.

A *port* is the name of the connection where you plug in the cable for a device, such as a mouse or printer.

3. The List of Printers lists dozens of printers that Windows recognizes. Find the name of your printer, and then select Install. One of two things will happen:

    ☞ If the file containing the printer information that Windows needs is already on your hard disk, then the printer name will appear in the Installed Printers list. In this case, you can skip ahead to step 5.

    ☞ If the printer information *isn't* on your hard disk, Control Panel will prompt you to insert one of your Windows installation disks.

4. If necessary, place the disk in the appropriate drive (change the displayed drive letter, if it's wrong), and then select **OK**. Control Panel copies the printer file to your hard disk.

5. Select the Connect button. The Connect dialog box appears.

6. Select your printer port from the Ports list, and then select **OK**. Your printer is now installed.

> ## By the Way . . .
> If you're not sure which port is the correct one, check the printer cable connection at the back of your computer. Some thoughtful computer companies actually label their ports, so look for something like LPT1 or COM2. If there are no labels, your computer manual should tell you. If you're still not sure, just choose LPT1, and cross your fingers.

7. Select **Close** to return to Control Panel.

What's Wrong with This Picture?

Suppose you want to print something, but when you pull down the File menu, the Print command is *dimmed*. You highlight it, but try as you may, you can't get it to do anything. What's wrong?

Answer: You need to install a printer in Windows. This happened to me once, and I spent hours fiddling with my printer cables and cursing Windows' ancestry. The problem, I found out later, is that I'd neglected to tell Windows about my printer. This is a no-no. Fortunately, installing printers in Windows isn't too bad, as the preceding section demonstrated.

Setting Up a Default Printer

If you install more than one printer (you can install as many as you like; it doesn't matter to Windows), then you need to designate one of them as the *default* printer. The default printer is the one all your Windows applications will assume you're printing to. You can do this from the Printers dialog box (select the **Printers** icon if you're back in Control Panel). In the Installed Printers list, just highlight the printer you want as the default, and then select the Set As Default Printer button. The name of the printer appears in the Default printer box.

Selecting a Different Printer in an Application

Whenever you print in a Windows application, the program always assumes you want to use the default printer, as described in the previous section. If you want to use a different printer, select the Print Setup command from the application's File menu. In the Print Setup dialog box that appears, you'll see a list of the installed printers. Select the one you want to use, and then select **OK**.

Working with the Print Manager

When you print from a Windows application, the application notifies a program called Print Manager that a print job is pending. To get you back to your application faster, Print Manager performs a nifty bit of trickery. It borrows the file, makes a copy of it, then hands control back to the application. While you continue working, Print Manager prints the copy of the file in the background (that's why you see the Print Manager icon at the bottom of the screen whenever you print).

You normally don't ever have to bother with Print Manager. It goes about its business behind the scenes, and it's usually best to leave it that way. However, there are times when you might want to cancel a print job or change the order in which the files will print, and you need to access Print Manager for that.

Starting Print Manager

If a print job is in progress, switch to Print Manager from your application (either double-click on the **Print Manager** icon, or hold down **Alt**, and press **Tab** until you see the Print Manager box). Otherwise, select the **Print Manager** icon from Program Manager's Main group. As you can see, Print Manager lists each of your installed printers and any print jobs in progress or pending.

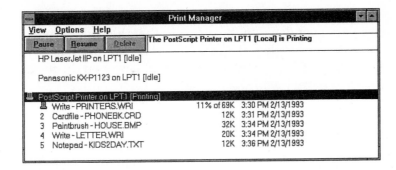

Print Manager lists your printers and any outstanding print jobs.

Pausing Printing

If you need to add paper to your printer or change the ribbon, you can tell Print Manager to hold its horses. Just highlight the name of the printer that's printing (you can click on it with your mouse or use the up and down arrow keys), and then select the **Pause** button. When you're ready to go again, select the **Resume** button.

Deleting Print Jobs

One of the nice things about Print Manager is that you don't have to wait until one print job is finished before sending another one. If the printer is busy, Print Manager just puts the new job in a queue to print it out later. If you accidentally print the wrong file, or if you simply change your mind, you can delete a file from the queue. Just highlight the appropriate file in Print manager, and then select the **Delete** button. Print Manager plays it safe and displays a dialog box asking if you're sure you want to stop printing the file. Select **OK** to remove the file from the queue.

Changing the Print Order

In Print Manager, you'll notice that, with the exception of the file currently printing, each file has a number beside it. This number tells you the print order for the jobs. This order is not set in stone, however. If you need to, you can move files up or down in the queue so that they print sooner or later. With a mouse, all you do is drag the file to the new position. With your keyboard, highlight the file, hold down the **Ctrl** key, then use the up or down arrow keys to move the file.

Changing the Print Priority

Printing files in the background is a good example of Windows' multi-tasking capabilities. Once Print Manager has a copy of the file, you're free to get back to work. However, this luxury does come with a price. To process the print job, Windows has to divide its attention between the Print Manager and your application. This tends to make both the printing *and* your application a little slower than they would be on their own.

Fortunately, you have some control over this. You can use Print Manager to tell Windows how much priority to give to your print jobs. Higher priority means that your printing will be faster, but your application will be slower. Lower priority speeds up your application, but slows down the printing.

To set the priority, pull down Print Manager's Options menu, and select either Low Priority, Medium Priority, or High Priority.

Using Drag-and-Drop to Print Files

In Part IV, "Using File Manager," I told you about some of the new "drag-and-drop" features that you get with Windows 3.1. One of the coolest uses for drag-and-drop is to print a file without even opening the appropriate application! Sound like voodoo? Well, I suppose it is, but it's darn good voodoo. All you need to do is make sure Print Manager is running, and then, in File Manager, find the file you want to print. (Refer back to Chapter 12, "File Manager Basics," to learn how to find files.) Now just drag the file over to the Print Manager and drop it (that is, let go of the mouse button). Windows opens the appropriate application, invokes the print command, and then closes the application. All you do is sit back and wait for your file to print. Neat, huh?

The Least You Need to Know

This chapter gave you the lowdown on printing in Windows. Here are a few points to memorize for tomorrow's pop quiz:

☞ Printing is basically the same in most Windows applications. Just pull down the **F**ile menu, and select the **P**rint command. Fill in the Print dialog box options, and select **OK**.

☞ Use the Control Panel's Printers setting to install printers in Windows.

☞ The Print Manager prints your files in the background. You can use Print Manager to pause your printer, delete print jobs, or change the queue order.

☞ If you have Windows 3.1, you can print a file from File Manager by dragging the file and dropping it on Print Manager.

This page unintentionally left blank.

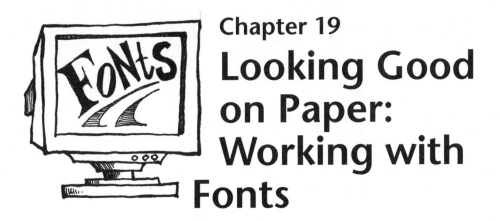

Chapter 19

Looking Good on Paper: Working with Fonts

In This Chapter

- ☞ Font basics, including the lowdown on those new-fangled TrueType fonts
- ☞ Selecting different fonts
- ☞ Tips for using fonts like a pro
- ☞ Using the cool Character Map program to add silly symbols to your documents
- ☞ Adding new fonts to your system
- ☞ Some good maternal advice and fascinating tales of flying buttresses and cars as clothes

"The least you can do is *look* respectable." That's what my mother always used to tell me when I was a kid. This advice holds up especially well in these image-conscious times. If you don't look good up front (or if your work doesn't look good), then you'll often be written off without a second thought.

When it comes to looking good—whether you're writing up a memo, slicking up a spreadsheet, or polishing up your resume—fonts are a great place to start. This chapter gives you the skinny on what fonts are, how to use them, and how to add new ones to your system.

Just What the Heck Is a Font, Anyway?

Before I started using Windows, I didn't think too much about the individual characters that made up my writings. To me, an *a* was an *a*. End of story. Windows changed all that. Suddenly, it was easy to produce an *a* that looked, well, different. Suddenly, it was easy to make a really BIG *a*, if that was what I wanted, or an italic *a*, or a bold **a**. In other words, I had discovered *fonts*.

Fonts are to characters what architecture is to buildings. In architecture, you look at certain features and patterns, and if you can tell a geodesic dome from a flying buttress, you can tell whether the building is Gothic or Art Deco or whatever. Fonts, too, are distinguished by a unique set of features. Specifically, there are four things to look for: the typeface, the type size, the type style, and the character spacing.

The Typeface

Any related set of letters, numbers, and other symbols has its own distinctive design called the *typeface*. Typefaces, as you can see here, can be wildly different depending on the shape and thickness of characters, the spacing, and the mood of the designer at the time.

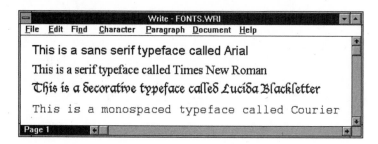

Some example typefaces.

Typefaces come in three flavors: *serif, sans serif,* or *decorative.* A serif typeface contains fine cross strokes (typographic technoids call them *feet)* at the extremities of each character. These subtle appendages give the typeface a traditional, classy look. Times New Roman is a common example of a serif typeface.

A sans serif typeface doesn't contain these cross strokes. As a result, sans serif typefaces usually have a cleaner, more modern look (check out Arial in the picture on the preceding page).

Decorative typefaces are usually special designs used to convey a particular effect. So, for example, if your document really needs a Gothic atmosphere, Lucida Blackletter would be perfect.

The Type Size

The *type size* just measures how tall a font is. (The standard unit of measurement is the *point,* where there are 72 points in an inch.) So, for example, the individual letters in a 24-point font would be twice as tall as those in a 12-point font. (In case you're wondering, this book is written in a 10-point font.)

Technically, type size is measured from the highest point of a tall letter, such as "f" to the lowest point of an underhanging letter, such as "g."

The Type Style

The *type style* of a font refers to attributes, such as **bold** and *italic.* Other type styles, (often called type *effects*) are <u>underlining</u> and ~~strikeout~~ (sometimes called "strikethru") characters. These styles are normally used to highlight or add emphasis to sections of your documents.

The Character Spacing

The *character spacing* of a font can take two forms: *monospaced* or *proportional.* Monospaced fonts reserve the same amount of space for each character. For example, take a look at the Courier font shown earlier. Notice how skinny letters such as "i" and "l" take up as much space as wider letters, such as "y" and "w." While this is admirably egalitarian, these fonts tend to look like they were produced with a typewriter (in other words, they're *ugly*). By contrast, in a proportional font, such as Arial or Times New Roman, the space allotted to each letter varies according to the width of the letter.

Okay, So How Does TrueType Fit In?

Imagine a world where individual cars, like clothes, could only fit people of a certain size. If you were 5'10", you'd be too big to fit into a car designed for a person who was 5'6", and too small for a car designed with someone 6'2" in mind. Dealers would need huge tracts of land to park all the models they'd need to keep in stock. If the land wasn't available, you'd only see a minimal selection to cover the normal size ranges of society.

This bizarre scenario is actually a good description of font technology before the advent of TrueType and other font management programs. For any combination of typeface and type style, you had to have a separate file on your system for each type size. If you wanted to use say, 8-point Courier italic, you'd have to have the appropriate file. Changing to 12-point Courier italic would require that your application load another file. Switching to Courier bold meant a whole new set of files. And these were just the fonts that you displayed on your screen. If you wanted to print anything, you had to have completely separate collection of files. Ay carumba!

All these files, of course, took up acres of precious hard disk real estate. If you didn't have the room, you had to go without some fonts.

Scalable Fonts to the Rescue

But just as some genius came up with the idea of adjustable car seats, so, too, do we now have *scalable* fonts. Put simply, a scalable font is one that contains only one representation of each character. If you want a different size, a font management program kicks in and automatically *scales* the characters to the new size. It does this for both screen and printer fonts, too, so when the dust clears, you need only one file for each font. Whew!

TrueType is Scalable

TrueType, to get to the point, is a scalable font technology that you get with Windows 3.1. You get both a font manager program and a collection of TrueType fonts for it to work with (TrueType has no effect on non-TrueType fonts). Here are a few other benefits of TrueType:

☞ It doesn't cost anything. Instead of spending your hard-earned money on a third-party type manager (such as Adobe Type Manager), you get TrueType free with Windows.

☞ Because they're scalable, TrueType fonts look good at large type sizes. Other fonts, while they may print okay, display ugly, jagged lines on your screen.

☞ You can exchange files with other users of Windows 3.1 without hassle. With other types of fonts, you never know if someone else will be able to view or print your documents properly.

☞ TrueType fonts will print on any printer that Windows supports. Other fonts are often printer specific, so if you switch printers you have to switch fonts.

Selecting Different Fonts in Applications

Okay, enough theory. Let's get down to business and see how you go about selecting different fonts in your programs. The hardest part is finding where your application hides its fonts. In Paintbrush, for example, you pull down the Text menu and select the Fonts command, but in Write, you'll find Fonts in the Character menu. Other applications don't even have a Fonts command. In Word for Windows, for example, you select the Character command from the Format menu. (So much for Windows' consistent interface!)

In any case, once you've found the appropriate command, you'll see a dialog box that looks something like the Font dialog box.

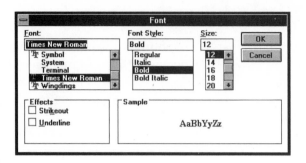

*The Font dialog box
from Paintbrush.*

From here, selecting the font you want is easy. First, use the Font list box to select the typeface. (Yeah, I know, it should be called the "Typeface" list. Ah, well.) Just so you know, the ones with the "double-T" symbol beside them are the TrueType fonts.

> ## By the Way . . .
> As you're selecting your font options, keep your eyes on the Sample box. It'll give you an idea of what your font will look like.

Once you've settled on a typeface, you need to select a type style (in Paintbrush, you'd use the Font Style list), the type size (the Size list), and any extra effects (Paintbrush has two: Strikeout and Underline). Once you're done, select **OK** to return to the application. If you highlighted some text before starting, the application will convert the text to the new font. Otherwise, the application will display your typing in the font.

> ## Put It to Work
> Using different font sizes and styles is an easy way to fool people into thinking you're a competent professional. For example, you can make your titles and section headings stand out by using a bold font that's larger than your regular text. Italic is good for things like company names and book titles, and you can also use it for emphasizing important material.

Getting Silly with the Character Map

A given typeface covers not only the letters, numbers, and symbols you can eyeball on your keyboard, but dozens of others, besides. For example, were you stumped the last time you wanted to write "Dag Hammarskjöld" because you didn't know how to get one of those ö thingamajigs? I thought so. Well, hang on to your hats because I'm going to show you an easy way to get not only an ö, but a whole universe of weirdo symbols.

It all begins with one of the new accessories that comes with Windows 3.1: the Character Map. Go ahead and start it from Program Manager's Accessories group, and you'll see a window like the one shown here.

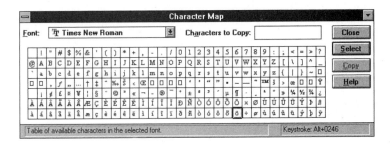

The Character Map window.

The layout is pretty simple: the squares show you all the symbols available for whatever typeface is displayed in the Font box. If you select a different typeface, a whole new set of symbols is displayed.

To use a symbol from Character Map in an application, you first select the symbol you want by double-clicking on it with your mouse or by using your keyboard's arrow keys to highlight it and then pressing Enter. The symbol will appear in the Characters to Copy box. When you're ready, select the Copy button to copy the character to the Clipboard (Windows' temporary storage area for copied things). Finally, return to your application, position the cursor where you want the character to appear, and then select Paste from the Edit menu.

By the Way . . .

Foreign characters are only the beginning of what you can get from Character Map. You should also check out typefaces, such as Wingdings or Symbol for such exotica as astrological signs, currency symbols, and clock faces.

Avoiding the "Ransom Note" Look

The downside to Windows' easy-to-use fonts is that they can sometimes be *too* easy to use. Flushed with your new-found knowledge, you start throwing every font in sight at your documents. The result, as you can see, is usually a mess.

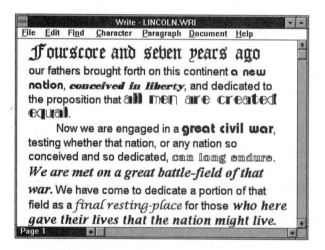

Overdone fonts can give even the most solemn text the dreaded "ransom note" look.

The problem, of course, is that there are just too many different fonts in one document. It turns even the most profound and well-written documents into a real dog's breakfast. (It's known in the trade as the "ransom note" look.) Here are some tips to avoid overdoing your fonts:

☞ Never use more than a couple of typefaces in a single document. Anything more looks amateurish and will only confuse the reader.

☞ If you need to emphasize something, bold or italicize it in the *same* typeface as the surrounding text. Avoid using underlining for emphasis.

☞ Only use larger sizes for titles and headings.

☞ Avoid bizarre decorative fonts for large sections of text. Most of those suckers are hard on the eyes after a half dozen words or so. Serif fonts are usually very readable, so they're a good choice for long passages. The clean look of sans serif fonts makes them a good choice for headlines and titles.

Adding New Fonts

Windows 3.1 comes with various fonts including five TrueType font collections (Arial, Courier New, Symbol, Times New Roman, and Wingdings). This is usually fine for most people, but there are lots of inexpensive font collections on the market these days. If you buy one of these collections, here's how to add the fonts to your system:

1. Select the **Control Panel** icon from Program Manager's Main group, and then select the **Fonts** icon. Control Panel displays the Fonts dialog box, as shown below.

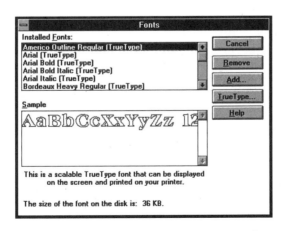

Use Control Panel's Fonts dialog box to add new fonts to your system.

2. Select the Add button. The Add Fonts dialog box appears.

3. Insert the disk containing the font files, and then select the appropriate disk drive from the Drives list. Windows reads the font names from the disk and displays them in the List of Fonts list box.

4. To install all the fonts on the disk, choose the Select All button. Otherwise, in the List of Fonts box, use either of these techniques to highlight the fonts you want to install:

   With your mouse, hold down the **Ctrl** key and click on the fonts.

   OR

   With your keyboard, press **Shift+F8** and then, for each font, move to it using the up and down arrow keys, and then press the **Spacebar**. When you're done, press **Shift+F8** again.

5. When you're ready, select **OK** to return to the Fonts dialog box.

6. Select **OK** to return to Control Panel.

The Least You Need to Know

This chapter introduced you to fonts in Windows. Here's a replay of some of the highlights:

- ☞ A font is a unique set of characters with a specific typeface, type style, type size, and character spacing.

- ☞ TrueType fonts are scalable so you only need one file per font.

- ☞ Most applications that work with text give you some way of selecting different fonts.

- ☞ You can use the Character Map to paste unusual symbols into your documents.

- ☞ Use the Control Panel's Fonts icon to add new fonts to your system.

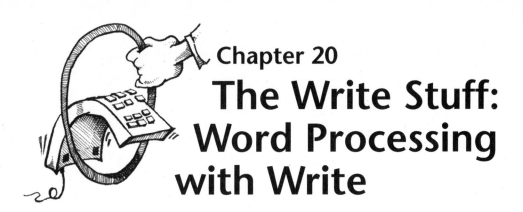

Chapter 20
The Write Stuff: Word Processing with Write

In This Chapter

☛ Getting around in Write

☛ Editing text

☛ Formatting text

☛ Formatting paragraphs

☛ Opening, saving, and printing Write documents

☛ A vast number of tips and tricks for getting the most out of Write

Write is the word processor that comes free with Windows. Such a deal! Granted, Write may not have all the fancy-schmancy features you get in the more glamorous word processors, but it'll handle simple day-to-day stuff like memos, letters, and even resumes without a complaint. So, unless you're a professional word jockey, Write will get the job done. This chapter gets you up to speed with this useful little program.

Getting Started

To start Write, select the **Write** icon from Program Manager's Accessories group. Here's a view of the Write window with a file already loaded.

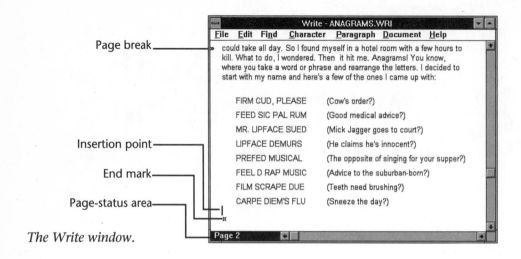

Page break

Insertion point

End mark

Page-status area

The Write window.

The Write window is a pretty simple affair with only the following unique features:

Insertion point This blinking vertical bar indicates the spot where your typing will appear.

Page break This mark indicates the point where one page ends and another begins.

End mark This mark indicates the end of the document. You can't move the insertion point past this mark.

Page-status line Once you break your document into pages (I'll tell you how to do it later on), this area tells you which page you're on. (Technically—and somewhat bizarrely—it tells you which page the *top line of the window* is on.)

Opening a Document

When you first start Write, you get a new, blank document to work with. If you prefer to work with an existing document, you need to open it. Begin by selecting the Open command from Write's File menu to display the Open dialog box. Pick out the file you want and then select **OK** to open it. (Take a look back at Chapter 7, "Day-to-Day File Drudgery," if you need more details on using the Open dialog box.)

Opening Non-Write Files

To make our lives more complicated, every word processor has its own format for the documents you create. Write is no exception, and it distinguishes its own files by adding the extension WRI to their file names. This explains why, when you display the Open dialog box in Write, these are the only files you see in the File Name list.

The different word processing formats are, of course, incompatible with each other. Fortunately, most word processors are smart enough to be able to read at least some documents in other formats. With Write, you have two ways to open files that don't end in WRI:

☛ Select a different format from the List Files of **Type** drop-down list box.

☛ Enter an appropriate description in the File Name box. For example, to list only files that end in BAT, you'd type ***.bat**, and press **Enter**.

To Convert or Not to Convert?

When you open a non-Write file, Write displays this dialog box to ask if you want to convert the file to the Write format.

When you try to open a non-Write file, Write asks if you want to convert it to the Write format.

If you're just examining the file, don't convert it (that is, select the No Conversion button). You may end up with some weird characters on the screen, but converting it to Write's format will make the file unreadable to anything but Write. This holds true even for simple text files, especially text files that end with the letters BAT, SYS, or INI. These are important configuration files for your system and converting them to Write format could cause all kinds of unpleasant results.

Entering Text

Unlike some of today's big bucks word processors, Write doesn't require a degree in rocket science to get up and running. Once you've loaded the program (and, if necessary, opened a file), you can simply go ahead and start typing. The characters you enter appear at the insertion point.

If you're used to typing with a typewriter, you may be tempted to press the Enter key when you approach the end of a line. Fortunately, you don't have to bother because Write handles that chore for you. When you hit the end of a line, Write automatically *wraps* the text onto the next line. Even if you're smack in the middle of a word, Write will automatically move the entire word onto the next line. The only time you need to press **Enter** is when you want to start a new paragraph.

> ### By the Way . . .
> If your document is wider than the Write window, the entire document will scroll to the right as you reach the edge of the window. If you find this annoying (as I do), increase the size of the window or, better yet, just maximize the whole thing. (See Chapter 8, "Why They Call It 'Windows,'" for more info on sizing and maximizing windows.)

Navigating a Document

For the terminally verbose, Write can handle documents as large as your computer's memory will allow. When your documents become several pages or more in length, however, you'll need some way to navigate them quickly. If you use a mouse, you can move the insertion point by clicking on the appropriate spot inside the window. To move to other parts of the document, use the scroll bars. (Need a scroll bar refresher course? Head back to Chapter 7, "Day-to-Day File Drudgery," to get all the facts.)

From the keyboard, you can use the techniques outlined in the following table to navigate a document.

To move . . .	Press . . .
Left or right one character	Left arrow or right arrow
Left or right one word	Ctrl+left arrow or Ctrl+right arrow
To the beginning or end of a line	Home or End
Up or down one line	Up arrow or down arrow
Top or bottom of the window	Ctrl+Page Up or Ctrl+Page Down
Up or down one screen	Page Up or Page Down
To the beginning or end of the document	Ctrl+Home or Ctrl+End

Selecting Text

When editing and formatting a Write document, you'll often need to select a group of characters or lines to work with. (Selected text appears as white letters on a dark background.)

To select text with a mouse, use any of these techniques (take a deep breath):

- ☛ To select any group of characters, position the pointer to the left of the first character, hold down the left mouse button, then drag the mouse over the text.

- ☛ To select a word, double-click on it.

- ☛ To select a line, click beside the line in the left margin.

- ☛ To select a sentence, hold down the **Ctrl** key and click anywhere in the sentence.

- ☛ To select a paragraph, double-click beside the paragraph in the left margin.

- ☛ To select the entire document, hold down Ctrl and click anywhere in the left margin.

Keyboard lovers can get in on this action as well by using the following techniques:

- ☛ To select any group of characters, place the insertion point to the left of the first character, hold down the **Shift** key, then use the arrow keys to grab what you need. (You can also use **Page Up** and **Page Down** if you have a lot of ground to cover.)

- ☛ To select a word, place the insertion point at the beginning of the word, hold down **Shift** and **Ctrl**, then press the right arrow key.

- ☛ To select a line, position the insertion point at the beginning of the line, hold down **Shift**, and press **End**.

- ☛ To select the entire document, place the insertion point at the beginning of the document, hold down **Shift** and **Ctrl**, and then press **End**.

Editing Text

Your Write documents will require some basic maintenance. This normally involves selecting a section of text and then deleting, cutting, copying, or pasting it.

> ## By the Way . . .
> If you make a mistake editing text, *immediately* select the **Undo** command from Write's **Edit** menu.

Press **Ctrl+X** to cut highlighted text quickly.

Deleting Stuff

The most basic document editing involves deleting single characters. This is a breeze: to delete the character to the left of the insertion point, press the **Backspace** key (if you don't see any key with the word "Backspace" on it, look for a left-pointing arrow (◄), instead); to delete the character to the right of the insertion point, press the **Delete** key.

If you need to get rid of larger chunks of text, highlight the offending material, and then press the **Delete** key.

Copying Stuff

If you need to make a copy of a section of text, highlight it, select the Copy command from the Edit menu, position the insertion point where you want the copy to appear, and then select the Edit menu's Paste command.

To copy highlighted text quickly, press **Ctrl+C**. To paste it quickly, press **Ctrl+V**.

By the Way . . .

For (slightly) greater detail about cutting, copying, and pasting text, see Chapter 7, "Day-to-Day File Drudgery."

Moving Stuff

If you want to move some text from one part of the document to another, highlight it, select the Edit menu's **Cut** command, position the insertion point where you want the text to appear, and then select **P**aste from the Edit menu.

By the Way . . .

If you need to copy or move a lot of text between two Write documents, just start up a second copy of Write and use it to open the other file. Then all you do is cut or copy the text from the original Write window, switch to the second window, and then paste it. See Chapter 10, "The Real Fun Begins: Starting Applications," for instructions on switching between applications.

Formatting Text

Write's Character menu gives you an impressive array of text formatting commands. Here's a table that summarizes most of them.

Format	Character menu command
Regular text	Regular (or press F5)
Boldface text	Bold (or press Ctrl+B)
Italic text	Italic (or press Ctrl+I)
<u>Underlined text</u>	Underline (or press Ctrl+U)
Smaller text	Reduce Font
Larger text	Enlarge Font
Different fonts	See the section titled "Using Different Fonts," later in this chapter

To format existing text, highlight it and then select the appropriate command from the Character menu.

Formatting Paragraphs

Although the content of your documents is important, how the documents look on the page is equally (if not more) important. Why? Because in these busy times, people will simply ignore a document if it looks cramped and uninviting.

To avoid this fate, use Write's various paragraph formatting options to make yourself look good on paper.

Setting Paragraph Alignment

Write's Paragraph menu offers four different paragraph alignment options:

Left	All lines in the paragraph are aligned with the left margin.
Centered	All lines in the paragraph are centered between the margins.

Right   All lines in the paragraph are aligned with the right
                   margin.

Justified   All lines in the paragraph are aligned with both the
                   left and right margins.

To use these commands, simply position the insertion point anywhere inside the paragraph, and then select the command.

Setting Paragraph Spacing

The **Paragraph** menu also lets you set up the spacing for your paragraphs. There are three choices:

Single Spacing   There is no space between the lines in the para-
                        graph.

1 1/2 Lines Spacing   There is half a line of space between each line in
                        the paragraph.

Double Spacing   There is an extra line of space between each line
                        in the paragraph.

Setting Tab Stops

Documents look much better if they're properly indented and if their various parts line up nicely. One easy way to do this is to use Tabs instead of spaces whenever you need to create some room in a line. Why? Well, a single space can take up a different amount of room depending on the font, the type size, and so on. So your document can end up looking pretty ragged if you try to use spaces to indent your text. Tabs, on the other hand, are fastidiously precise. When you press the Tab key, the insertion point moves ahead either exactly half an inch or to the next Tab stop.

Here are the steps you need to follow to set your own Tab stops:

1. Select the Document menu's Tabs command. The Tabs dialog box appears, as shown here.

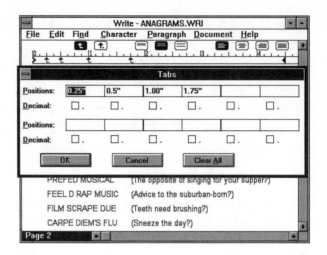

The Tabs dialog box.

2. Use the **Positions** boxes to enter your Tab stops (in inches). If you want to use a Tab to line up numbers with decimal points, be sure to activate the appropriate **Decimal** check box.

3. Select **OK**. Write adds the stops to the document. The Tab stops appear in the Ruler, if it's displayed.

Formatting Paragraphs from the Ruler

If you have a mouse, you can use Write's ruler to format your paragraphs easily. To display the ruler, pull down the Document menu and select the **Ruler On** command. As you can see, the ruler displays a number of buttons that represent the various paragraph formatting options.

Mouse users can take advantage of the ruler to format their paragraphs easily.

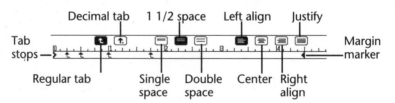

To set the alignment or spacing of a paragraph, click anywhere inside the paragraph and then click on the appropriate button in the ruler. To set tab stops, select the appropriate tab style (normal or decimal), and then click the ruler where you want to set the tab.

By the Way . . .

To hide the ruler, select the **Ruler Off** command from the **Document** menu.

Using Different Fonts

As you saw in Chapter 19, "Looking Good on Paper: Working with Fonts," fonts are an easy way to improve the look of your documents. Here are the steps to change a font in a Write document:

1. Highlight the text you want to work with.

2. Select the Fonts command from the Character menu. Write displays the Fonts dialog box.

3. Use the Font list box to select another font. As you move through the fonts, watch the Sample box to see what each font looks like.

4. If you also want to set the bold and italic attributes, select the appropriate option from the Font Style list.

5. If you'd like larger type, select a size from the Size list.

6. Select **OK**. Write reformats the selection.

Saving Your Work

Saving your work is easy, so there's no excuse for not doing it as often as you can. All you do is pull down Write's File menu, and select the Save command. If you're saving a new document, the Save As dialog box will appear. Use the File Name text box to enter the name you want for the file. The name must be no longer than eight characters, and you have to follow the DOS naming rules that I outlined in Chapter 7. (You don't have to bother adding an extension. Write will append the "WRI" automatically.)

Put It to Work

If you're ever asked to save a document as pure text (or ASCII text), select Save As from the File menu, and in the Save As dialog box, select the **Text Files** option from the Save File as Type list.

Printing Your Work

Once you've finished with a document, you'll want a hard copy to show off to your friends and colleagues. Make sure your printer is turned on and on-line, and then follow these steps:

1. Select the Print command from the File menu. The Print dialog box appears.

2. Use the Print Range area to select how much of the document you want to print. If you want the whole shebang printed, make sure the All option is activated. If you've highlighted a section of text to print, activate the Selection option. If you only want to print certain pages, activate the Pages option, and then enter the appropriate page numbers in the From and To boxes.

3. Use the Copies text box to enter the number of copies you want to print.

4. Select **OK**. Write prints the document.

By the Way . . .

If you plan to print only certain pages, you should first make sure Write's page markers—they're the double arrows (»)—are accurate. You do this by selecting the Repaginate command from the File menu.

The Least You Need to Know

This chapter gave you a basic introduction to Write, Windows' powerful, little word processor. Here's a summary of the fun stuff:

- ☞ You start Write by selecting the **Write** icon from Program Manager's **Accessories** group.

- ☞ Use the **File** menu's **O**pen command to open an existing Write document.

- ☞ When editing text in Write, first highlight the text, and then select the appropriate command from the **Edit** menu.

- ☞ Write's **Character** menu contains a whole mess of commands you can use to add formatting to your text.

- ☞ Use the commands in the **Paragraph** menu to format your paragraphs.

This page unintentionally left blank.

Chapter 21

Nurturing Your Inner Child with Paintbrush

In This Chapter

- ☞ Navigating the Paintbrush window
- ☞ Drawing lines, boxes, circles, and other shapes
- ☞ Drawing freehand lines
- ☞ Editing your drawings
- ☞ More ways than you can shake a stick at for reliving your youth

If you enjoyed finger painting when you were a kid, you'll get a kick out of Paintbrush, Windows' drawing program. Oh sure, you can use it for practical stuff like logos, charts, and whatnot, but to my mind, Paintbrush's real reason for being is sheer fun. Think about it: all you do is select a "tool" to work with and then just wiggle your mouse around the screen. Magically, you get all kinds of cool shapes and patterns. Throw in a few colors and you have a recipe for hours of entertainment.

Starting Paintbrush

To start Paintbrush, select the **Paintbrush** icon in Program Manager's **Accessories** group. You'll see the Paintbrush window shown here.

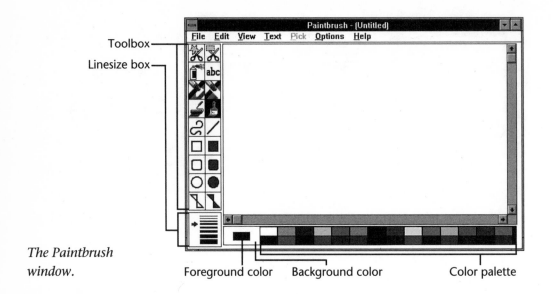

The Paintbrush window.

Foreground color   Background color   Color palette

The Paintbrush Window

There is a lot of stuff in the Paintbrush window, so let's take a close look at its various features.

The Toolbox This section contains the various "tools" that you use to create or edit your drawings. Here's a picture of the Toolbox that tells you the names of each tool (I'll show you how to use each one as we go along).

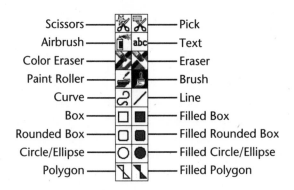

The Paintbrush Toolbox.

The Linesize Box The lines in this box represent the available thicknesses for some of the tools, including the Brush, the erasers, the Airbrush spray, and the borders of the various objects. To select a different line size, click on the appropriate line.

The Color Palette The Color Palette shows the available colors and patterns you can use for drawing or filling shapes. Paintbrush displays the currently selected foreground and background colors to the left of the palette. To select a new foreground color, click on one of the color rectangles in the palette. To select a new background color, right-click on a color.

The Drawing Area This is the large, blank area that takes up most of the Paintbrush window. This is where all the fun happens; that is, it's where you draw and paint your objects.

Navigating the Screen

Navigating the Paintbrush screen with a mouse is easy: you just click on the tool, line size, and colors you want (remember to right-click to get a new background color). If you don't have a mouse, you can navigate Paintbrush by pressing **Tab** or **Shift+Tab** to move between the screen areas. When you're in the area you want, use the arrow keys to move the pointer among the selections, and then press the **Ins** key to select the tool, line size, or color. In the Color Palette, press **Delete** to select a new background color.

> ### By the Way . . .
> If you select a new background color, it doesn't go into effect until you start a new drawing by selecting **New** from the **File** menu (you can also double-click on the **Eraser** tool).

Most of the tools require you to hold down the left mouse button while drawing. If you make a mess during the drawing, you can start again by simply clicking the right mouse button *before* you release the left mouse button. (This doesn't work with the Brush and Airbrush tools.) To get rid of everything you've drawn with the current tool, select **Undo** from the **Edit** menu.

Drawing with Paintbrush

The best way to approach Paintbrush is simply to have fun fooling around with the various tools and colors. However, there *is* a basic method you can use for each tool. You begin by selecting the tool from the Toolbox. Then, if applicable, you select a line width from the Linesize box and a color from the Color Palette. Now just move the pointer into the drawing area and draw the shape you want.

The next few sections show you how to use several of the Paintbrush tools. You'll find Paintbrush way more fun with a mouse, but if you *have* to use your keyboard, you can simulate a mouse by using the substitutions outlined in the following table.

To simulate . . .	Press . . .
Clicking the left button	Insert
Double-clicking the left button	F9+Insert
Clicking the right button	Delete
Dragging the mouse	Insert+arrow keys

Drawing Lines, Boxes, and Circles

You can use the Line, Box, Rounded Box, and Circle/Ellipse tools to create most of the basic building blocks for your drawing. (If you want your objects filled in with the current foreground color, use the Filled Box, Filled Rounded Box, and Filled Circle/Ellipse tools, instead.) To use them, first select the tool, the line width, and the color you want to work with. Then move the pointer into the drawing area and position it where you want the shape to start. (The pointer changes to a cross.) Now press and hold down the left mouse button, and then drag the pointer until the object is the size and shape you want. Finish by releasing the mouse button.

By the Way . . .

To draw a perfect square or circle, or to draw a line that is horizontal, vertical or on a 45-degree angle, hold down the **Shift** key while drawing.

Put It to Work

Paintbrush's boxes and lines are perfect for drawing company organization charts. Use the Text tool (described later on) to add people's names and job titles.

Drawing Curves

For your nonlinear moods, Paintbrush has a Curve tool for drawing wavy lines. It's actually a bit tricky to use, so you may need to play around with it a bit. Here are the steps to follow:

1. Select the **Curve** tool, the line size, and the color you want to use.

2. Position the pointer where you want the curve to start, then press and hold down the left mouse button.

3. Drag the mouse until the line is the length you want it and then release the button.

4. Drag the mouse again to curve the line. When you've got the curve you want, release the button.

5. If you want to add a second curve to the line, drag the mouse again and release the button when you're done.

Drawing Polygons

Polygon is just a fancy mathematical term for a collection of straight lines that forms a closed object. (A triangle is a common example of a polygon.) Follow these steps to create a polygon:

1. Select the **Polygon** tool (or if you want your shape filled with the current foreground color, select the Filled Polygon tool) as well as the line width and color you want to work with.

2. Move the pointer into the drawing area, and position it where you want the polygon to start. The pointer changes to a cross.

3. Press and hold down the left mouse button, and then drag the pointer until the first side is the length and angle you want.

4. Release the mouse button.

5. Position the pointer where you want the next side to end.

6. Click the left mouse button. Paintbrush draws a line from the end of the last line to the pointer.

7. Repeat steps 5 and 6 to define the other sides of the polygon. To finish the shape, connect the last side with the beginning of the first side.

Drawing Freehand Lines

As you've seen, Paintbrush makes it easy to draw lines, circles, and polygons. Too easy. For some real fun, try using the Brush tool to draw freehand lines. Begin by selecting the **Brush** tool along with the line width and color you want to use. Move the pointer into the drawing area and position it where you want to start drawing. (The pointer changes to a dot that's the same size as the line width.) Now press and hold down the left mouse button, and then drag the pointer to start drawing. When you're done, release the mouse button.

> ## By the Way . . .
> You can get some interesting effects if you use a different brush shape. Just double-click on the **Brush** tool to display the Brush Shapes dialog box. Select one of the six shapes, and then select **OK**.

Put It to Work

You can use Paintbrush to create new wallpapers for your Windows desktop. (To get the lowdown on wallpaper, refer back to Chapter 17, "Have It Your Way: Customizing Windows.") After creating a drawing, make sure you save it in your WINDOWS directory. Then, when you load Control Panel, the drawing will appear in the list with the other wallpaper files.

Filling Shapes with Color

The Paint Roller tool will fill in any closed shape with the current foreground color. The name of this tool is a bit misleading because it doesn't work like a paint roller at all. Instead, it's more like a paint *can* where you pour the color into the area.

In any case, it's pretty easy to use. Just pick out a color, select the **Paint Roller** tool, and then click anywhere inside the shape.

Using the Airbrush Tool

The Airbrush tool (as its icon shows) is actually more like a can of spray paint. As shown, this is useful for satisfying those graffiti urges without breaking the law.

If the shape has even the tiniest gap, the paint will leak out and fill in any closed area that surrounds the original shape (this usually means the entire drawing area). This will happen more times than you think, so it's important to know what to do. First, don't panic. Next, after counting to ten or chanting your mantra or whatever it is you do to calm yourself, immediately select the Undo command from the Edit menu. Finally, return to the object, and close the gap that caused the leak.

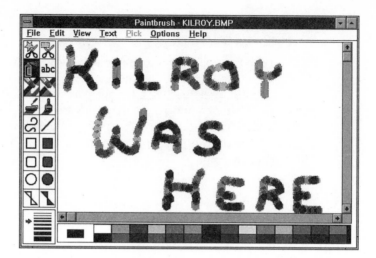

The Airbrush tool works like a can of spray paint.

After selecting the Airbrush tool, select a color and a line size (this will be the size of the "spray"). Move the mouse pointer into the drawing area, and then hold down the left mouse button to start spraying.

Adding Text to a Drawing

Paintbrush is mostly for your right brain, but if your left brain wants to get in on the act, you can use the Text tool to add text to a drawing. Here's what you do:

1. Select the **Text** tool from the Toolbox and a color from the Color Palette.

2. Pull down the Text menu, and select one or more text styles. You have five choices: **B**old, *Italic*, Underline, Outline, and Shadow. If you select the Shadow command, you also need to select a different background color to see the shadow.

3. Select the Fonts command from the Text menu to choose a font. (If you're not sure what fonts are all about, head back to Chapter 19, "Looking Good on Paper: Working with Fonts," for the nitty-gritty.)

4. Position the pointer at the spot where you want the text to begin, and then click. You'll see a blinking vertical bar.

5. Start typing. If you make a mistake, just press the **Backspace** key to delete it.

Cutting, Copying, and Pasting Drawings

You can apply the cut-and-paste techniques that I described in Chapter 7, "Day-to-Day File Drudgery," to Paintbrush drawings, although there are some extra steps involved in selecting stuff and pasting it.

Selecting Parts of a Drawing

If you need to cut or copy a piece of a drawing (to paste either elsewhere in the drawing or perhaps in a different application altogether), you first need to select the image you want. Paintbrush gives you two tools to do the job: the Scissors tool and the Pick tool.

You use the Scissors tool to select a randomly shaped area. After selecting the tool, move the pointer into the drawing area. Hold down the left mouse button and drag the mouse around the area you want to select. Release the button when you've completely outlined the area.

You use the Pick tool to select a rectangular area of the drawing. Select the tool and move the pointer to the upper left corner of the area you want to select. Hold down the left mouse button and drag the mouse until the lines enclose the area. Release the button when you're done.

Pasting Cut or Copied Images

Once you've cut or copied your selected image (by using the Edit menu's Cut or Copy commands), you need to paste the image from the Clipboard.

With text, you'll recall, you first position the cursor where you want the new text to appear. Paintbrush, though, doesn't have a cursor, so when you select **Paste** from the Edit menu, the image appears in the upper left corner of the drawing. To position it, move the mouse pointer inside the image, hold down the left mouse button, and then drag the image to the location you want.

> ### By the Way . . .
>
> Paintbrush, like Write, doesn't let you work with more than one drawing at a time. So, if you need to paste some or all of one drawing into another, just start up a second copy of Paintbrush, and use it to open the other drawing. You then cut or copy the image from the original Paintbrush window, switch to the second window, and then paste it. See Chapter 10, "The Real Fun Begins: Starting Applications," for instructions on switching between applications.

Erasing Parts of a Drawing

The Paintbrush tools take a little getting used to, so you'll have plenty of stray lines and shapes that you don't want in the finished drawing. Fortunately, Paintbrush has a couple of tools—the Eraser and the Color Eraser—that will remove any rogue elements.

Using the Eraser Tool

The Eraser tool does pretty much what you'd expect: it wipes out everything in its path. (This is not a tool to be wielded lightly!) To use it, select the **Eraser** tool and then select a line width. If you have a lot to erase, pick a wider line. If you want fine control, pick a thinner line. Move the pointer into the drawing area and position it near where you want to start erasing. (The pointer will change into a box.) Now press and hold down the left mouse button, and then drag the pointer to start erasing. Everything in the path of the box gets erased. When you're done, release the mouse button.

To replace the foreground color with the background color in the *entire* drawing, just double-click on the **Color Eraser** tool.

Using the Color Eraser

If you want to preserve the outlines of a drawing, or if you want to replace one color with another, the Color eraser will do the job. You use it just like the

Eraser, except that you also pick a foreground and background color. Then, when you run the tool over your drawing, it replaces anything it finds in the foreground color with the background color.

Saving a Drawing

To save your drawings, just pull down the File menu, and select the Save command. If you're saving a new drawing, the Save As dialog box will appear. Use the File Name text box to enter the name you want for the file. The name must be no longer than eight characters, and you have to follow the DOS naming rules that I outlined in Chapter 7. (You don't have to bother adding an extension. Paintbrush will add its default BMP extension automatically.)

The Least You Need to Know

This chapter showed you how to have all sorts of fun with Paintbrush, Windows' cool drawing program. Here's a summary of the important stuff:

- ☞ To start drawing with Paintbrush, select a tool from the Toolbox, select a line size and a color, if necessary, then move the pointer into the drawing area and off you go.

- ☞ With the exception of the Brush and Airbrush tools, you can start over with any tool by clicking the right mouse button before you've finished.

- ☞ Use the Pick or Scissors tools to select pieces of your drawing for cutting or copying. When you paste a selection into a drawing, you need to drag the image to its proper location.

- ☞ To erase stuff from a drawing, use the Eraser tool to erase everything and the Color Eraser to replace the foreground color with the background color.

This page unintentionally left blank.

Chapter 22
Windows' Free Lunch: The Accessories

In This Chapter

- Introducing four more accessories: Calculator, Calendar, Cardfile, and Clock

- How to use them

- Tips and shortcuts for each program

- Practical advice for everyday use

- A basic economics lesson and a foolproof method for balancing your checkbook

One of the first things I learned in my freshman Economics class was that "there is no such thing as a free lunch." This chapter will prove that the economists are wrong. In fact, Windows users get a free lunch that's a multi-course meal. We've already looked at Write (in Chapter 20) and Paintbrush (in Chapter 21), so now we'll look at the four other major accessories: Calculator, Calendar, Cardfile, and Clock.

Figuring Out Calculator

Forget your fingers! Windows gives you an easier way to add things up: the Calculator. Select the **Calculator** icon from Program Manager's Accessories group, and you'll see the window shown here.

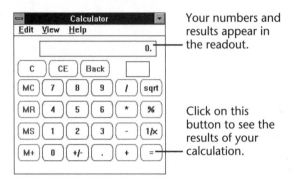

Your numbers and results appear in the readout.

Click on this button to see the results of your calculation.

The Calculator window.

As you can see, Calculator looks just like your basic calculator. It won't do rocket science, but it's good for simple operations, such as addition, subtraction, multiplication, and division.

Working with Calculator

Using Calculator is a no-brainer. You just click on the appropriate numbers and operators, and then click on the equal sign (=) to see the answer in the readout below the menu bar. For example, to add 2 and 3, you'd do the following:

1. Click on the **2** button. A "2" appears in the readout.

2. Click on the + button.

3. Click on the **3** button. A "3" appears in the readout.

4. Click on the = button. A "5" appears in the readout.

There's no problem if you prefer to use your keyboard. Simply use the numbers and operators from the numeric keypad (make sure you have Num Lock on, though). To see the results of a calculation, you can either press the equal sign (=) or the **Enter** key.

> **By the Way . . .**
> Once Calculator displays the result of a calculation in the readout, you can use it in another application by selecting the **C**opy command from the **E**dit menu (or just press **Ctrl+C**), switching to the other application, and then selecting **P**aste in the application's **E**dit menu.

The following table explains the other Calculator buttons.

Button	Description and keyboard equivalent
sqrt	Calculates the square root of the value that appears in the readout (press @ on your keyboard).
%	Calculates percentages (press %).
1/x	Calculates the reciprocal of the value that appears in the readout (press **r**).
+/-	Switches the sign of the value that appears in the readout (press **F9**).
C	Clears the current calculation (press **Esc**).
CE	Clears the value that appears in the readout (press **Delete**).
Back	Deletes the last digit entered (press **Backspace**).
MC	Clears the memory (press **Ctrl+L**).
MR	Recalls the current memory value and displays it in the readout (press **Ctrl+R**).
MS	Stores the value that appears in the readout to memory (press **Ctrl+M**).
M+	Adds the value that appears in the readout to the value stored in memory (press **Ctrl+P**).

Put It to Work

Balancing your checkbook is a mundane evil that makes root canal seem like an inviting alternative. The next time the dreaded bank statement arrives in the mail, try using Calculator to handle the math. It won't make balancing your checkbook fun (a tall order under any circumstances), but it will make the whole process a little less painful. Here's one way to reconcile your checkbook with Calculator:

1. Enter the ending balance shown on your bank statement.

2. Add any service charges and subtract any interest payments shown on the bank statement.

3. Subtract the balance showing in your checkbook register.

4. Add any deposits and subtract any checks that happened after the bank statement ending date.

5. Display the result. If it's zero, then congratulations are in order because your checkbook balances. If it's not zero, then you'll have to check everything to find the discrepancy. Good luck!

The Frightening Scientific Calculator

Calculator also includes a Scientific calculator that you can display by selecting Scientific from the View menu. This scary-looking thing is sure to warm the hearts of the tall forehead types who actually *enjoy* using things like hexadecimal numbers. The rest of us can simply shudder once or twice and then scurry back to the safety of the Standard calculator (select Standard from the View menu).

Making a Date with Calendar

Got a date and you can't be late? Got a rendezvous that you need to remember? Well, Windows' Calendar accessory can help. Select the **Calendar** icon from Program Manager's **Accessories** group to display the window shown here.

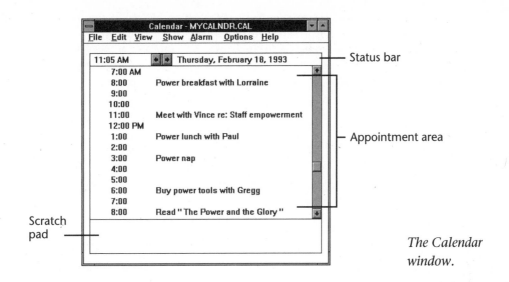

The Calendar window.

The Calendar Window

The Calendar window contains the following unique features:

Status bar	This line shows the current time and the date you're working with.
Appointment area	This area is where you enter your appointments.
Scratch pad	You can use this area to enter up to three lines of notes for each day.

Calendar is set up to look like a typical appointment book. When you first start Calendar, you see the "Day view" that displays a daily schedule at hourly intervals. If you prefer the big picture, Calendar also has a "Month view" that shows the entire month.

Press **F9** to switch to the Month view and press **F8** to return to the Day view.

Navigating the Day View

By default, Calendar opens with today's date and it shows times from 7:00 AM to 8:00 PM. You can navigate the times shown, other times, or even other days using the techniques outlined in the following table.

To move to . . .	Do this:
A later time	Click on the time.
	Press the down arrow key.
An earlier time	Click on the time.
	Press the up arrow key.
The next day	Select Next from the Show menu.
	Click on the right arrow in the Status bar.
	Press **Ctrl+Page Down**.
The previous day	Select Previous from the Show menu.
	Click on the left arrow in the Status bar.
	Press **Ctrl+Page Up**.
Today's date	Select Today from the Show menu.
Any date	Select Date from the Show menu or press **F4**, enter the date in MM/DD/YY format, and then select **OK**.
Scratch pad	Click inside the scratch pad.
	Press **Tab**.

Navigating the Month View

Select the Month command from the View menu to switch to Calendar's Month view. The following table summarizes the techniques you can use when working in Month view.

To move to . . .	Do this:
Another date	Click on the date.
	Use the arrow keys.
The next month	Select Next from the Show menu.
	Click on the right arrow in the Status bar.
	Press **Ctrl+Page Down**.

To move to . . .	Do this:
The previous month	Select Previous from the Show menu.
	Click on the left arrow in the Status bar.
	Press **Ctrl+Page Up**.
Today's date	Select Today from the Show menu.
Any date	Select Date from the Show menu or press **F4**, enter the date in MM/DD/YY format, and then select **OK**.
Scratch pad	Click inside the scratch pad.
	Press **Tab**.

Entering Appointments

Entering appointments in Calendar is easy. All you do is select the day and time of the appointment and then enter a description (you can use up to 80 characters).

Setting an Alarm

For the truly busy (or, for some of us, the absent-minded), you can set Calendar up to display a reminder and sound an alarm at a specific time. This adds an extra level of protection for those "can't miss" appointments. Simply select the time when you want to be reminded, and then select the Alarm menu's Set command. A bell icon appears next

To set an alarm quickly, select the time, and press **F5**.

to the time. When the time for the reminder arrives, Calendar sounds your computer's bell and displays a dialog box. Simply select **OK** to remove the dialog box.

Saving a Calendar

Calendar allows you to create as many different calendar files as you need. This is handy, for example, if other people use your computer because you can simply set up a Calendar file for each person. To save a file, select **Save** from the File menu. If you're saving a new file, the Save As dialog box will appear. Use the File **Name** text box to enter the name you want for the file. As usual, you can't use any more than eight characters, and you have to follow the weirdo naming rules from Chapter 7. (Don't worry about an extension. Calendar adds its "CAL" extension automatically.)

To open a saved file, select the File menu's **Open** command, and select the file you want from the Open dialog box. (For more information on opening a file, refer back to Chapter 7, "Day-To-Day File Drudgery.")

Keeping Track of Cardfile

Organized people do things like keeping their recipes in a recipe box on those 3x5 cards and their business cards in alphabetical order in a business card file. If you'd like to be more organized but you don't know if you've got it in you, don't worry; you can get Windows Cardfile accessory to do it for you.

To start Cardfile, select the **Cardfile** icon from the **Accessories** group in Program Manager. As you can see here, the Cardfile window is really just a collection of cards (they look just like those darn 3x5 index cards!).

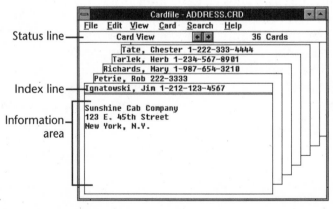

The Cardfile window.

The *Status line* below the menu bar tells you how many cards are in the file and which view is active (there are two views: the card view and the list view; I'll explain the difference later on). The cards themselves are divided into two areas: the *Index line* and the *Information area*.

The Index Line

The *Index line* is the bar along the top of each card. You can use the information in this line to sort your cards. So, for example, if you were entering addresses, you'd likely use this line for the person's name and, for quick reference, their phone number. For, say, recipes, you'd enter the name of the recipe.

The Information Area

The *Information area* holds the card information, such as addresses and recipe instructions. You generally just type in the information, but you can also paste in stuff that you've cut or copied from another application. See Chapter 7, "Day-To-Day File Drudgery," for the lowdown on cut-and-paste techniques.

Filling Out the First Card

When you first start the program, Cardfile displays a blank card ready to receive your information. To fill out this card, first select the Index command from the Edit menu to display the Index dialog box. Use the Index Line text box to enter a name or title for the card (you can enter up to 39 characters). When you're done, select **OK** to return to Cardfile. Now just enter the rest of the data in the Information area.

> **E·Z**
>
> To display the Index dialog box quickly, press **F6**.

> ## By the Way . . .
>
> When entering the Index line, keep in mind that Cardfile uses this information to sort your cards. So, for example, if you're entering names in the Index line, it's probably best to put the last name first.

Adding New Cards

Once you've completed your first card, you can add more cards by selecting the Card menu's Add command. In the Add dialog box that appears, enter the index line information in the Add text box, and then select **OK**. As before, enter the rest of the data in the Information area.

To display the Add dialog box quickly, press **F7**.

Put It to Work

Cardfile provides a handy way to create an inventory of your possessions. (Useful for insurance purposes in case of fire or theft, or if you just get a kick out of making lists.) Use the Index line for the name of the object and the Information area for any other stuff that seems appropriate (the date purchased, the value—that kind of thing). You can make one big list or break everything up into separate files (books, CDs, cubic zirconia jewelry, and so on).

Navigating Cardfile

Cardfile always keeps your cards in alphabetical order according to the information on each card's Index line. You can either scroll through your cards or display specific ones. If you have a mouse, you can use either of the following techniques to navigate your cards:

Click on a visible card to bring it to the front of the pile.

OR

Click on the arrows in the status line to scroll through the cards one at a time.

If you prefer the keyboard, use the keys outlined in the following table.

To display . . .	Press:
The next card	Page Down
The previous card	Page Up
The first card	Ctrl+Home
The last card	Ctrl+End
The first card that begins with a specific letter	Ctrl+Shift+letter

Searching for Names

If you have a lot of cards, you'll probably find the one you want faster by using Cardfile's Search feature. Just select the Goto command from the Search menu. In the Go To dialog box, use the Go To text box to enter some or all of the index line of the card you want to find and then select **OK**.

To display the Go To dialog box quickly, press **F4**.

Switching to the List View

A quick way to navigate Cardfile is to use the List view that displays only the individual index lines. To switch to List view, simply select the View menu's **List** command.

Deleting Addresses

Your files will be easier to manage if you delete any unwanted cards (such as anyone who forgets to send you a birthday card). All you do is display the appropriate card and then select the Delete command from the Card menu. When Cardfile asks if you're sure you want to delete the card, select **OK**.

Saving a File

Once you've completed a few cards, you should save your work. To save a file, select Save from the File menu. If you're saving a new file, the Save As dialog box will appear. Use the File Name text box to enter the name you want for the file. (You know the drill by now: no more than eight characters; follow the DOS naming rules from Chapter 7.) Again, don't bother adding an extension. Cardfile will add its default "CRD" extension automatically.

To open a saved file, select Open from the File menu, and then select the file you want from the Open dialog box. (Chapter 7, "Day-To-Day File Drudgery," tells you everything you need to know about opening files.)

Doing Time with Clock

Windows is so much fun that you may lose track of time (stop laughing!). To help out, you can use Windows' little Clock accessory to display the time on your screen. Just select the **Clock** icon from Program Manager's Accessories group to see the window shown here.

The Clock accessory.

Clock doesn't do you much good in the middle of the screen if you're using other applications, so most people minimize it (it still shows the date and time when minimized). You do this by clicking on the Clock window's **Minimize** button or by pulling down Clock's **Control** menu (by pressing **Alt+Spacebar**) and then selecting the Minimize command.

If you still can't see it (that is, if you're working with an application full-screen), select Always on Top from the Control menu. This keeps Clock visible at all times.

If you prefer your clocks to have hands, select the Analog command from Clock's **Settings** menu. Clock is only useful, of course, if the date and time are accurate. If you need to set your computer's date and time, select the **Control Panel** icon from Program Manager's **Main** group, and then select the **Date/Time** icon. Use the **Date** and **Time** fields to make your changes, and then select **OK**.

A Recorder Recording Session

You've probably seen articles or reports on what's being termed the "plague of the '90s": repetitive-stress injuries (such as Carpal Tunnel Syndrome) caused by excessive thumping on computer keyboards. (Computers, it seems, aren't satisfied with just messing up our heads; they've now targeted other body parts, as well.)

While there's no shortage of preventive measures being proffered (including the use of wrist rests, maintaining correct posture, and—my personal favorite—taking frequent breaks), you can save all kinds of anatomical wear-and-tear simply by eliminating unnecessary typing and mousing. One of the best ways to do this is to get to know a Windows tool that can reduce tasks that normally require dozens of keystrokes or mouse clicks into a simple key combination. Really. This tool is called Recorder, and it's the subject of this section.

How does Recorder work? It's quite simple, really. Recorder can "memorize" any sequence of keystrokes and mouse movements, and then play them back at will. By assigning a shortcut key combination to the "recording," you can replay the whole shebang just by pressing a couple of keys. Ah, my wrists feel better already.

SPEAK LIKE A GEEK

Any recorded sequence of mouse clicks or keystrokes is called a **macro**.

The biggest problem you'll face with Recorder is that if you botch the recording, you have to start the whole thing from scratch. (Sadly, Recorder doesn't let you edit an existing macro.) For complex recordings, you might consider a practice run or two to make sure you're comfortable with the keystrokes you need to perform.

Brass Tacks Time: Recording a Macro

Without further ado, let's get right down to business and see just how you go about recording a macro. To give you something concrete to get your hands on, we'll go through an example: recording a long section of text that you use regularly. This could be your company name, a report title, a bit of boilerplate text, or a good joke you use a lot. For starters, open your word processor and position the cursor where you want to type your text. Now crank up Recorder by selecting the **Recorder** icon in Program Manager's **Accessories** group, and then follow these steps:

1. Pull down Recorder's Macro menu, and select the Record command. The Record Macro dialog box appears, as shown below.

You use the Record Macro dialog box to enter the particulars for your macro.

2. In the Record Macro **Name** text box, enter a name for the macro. (The name can be as long as 40 characters.)

3. Use the controls in the Shortcut Key group to assign a shortcut key for the macro. You build the key combination by selecting one or more of the **Ctrl**, **Shift**, and **Alt** check boxes, and then either entering a letter or number in the text box, or selecting a key from the drop-down list. For example, if you activate **Ctrl** and **Shift**, and enter **T** in the text box, your shortcut key will be **Ctrl+Shift+T**.

4. Use the **Playback** group to determine how Recorder should play the macro. You have the following options:

To The options in this drop-down list determine where Recorder plays back the macro. If you select **Same Application**, the macro only runs in the application you used for the original recording. **Any Application** tells Recorder to play back the macro in any application. For our example, select **Same Application**.

Speed This drop-down list's options determine how fast Recorder plays back the macro. **Fast** plays the macro at top speed, while **Recorded Speed** runs the macro at the same tempo you used during the recording. Only choose **Recorded Speed** when your macro has to wait for an operation (such as a file search in File Manager) to finish before moving on. For the example, select **Fast**.

Continuous Loop You only activate this check box when you want Recorder to play back the macro continuously. Leave this option unchecked for the example.

Enable Shortcut Keys When this check box is activated, Recorder allows you to run other macros you've recorded by pressing their shortcut keys. Although we don't need this feature for the example, it doesn't hurt to leave this option turned on.

5. Use the Record Mouse drop-down list to tell Recorder whether you want to record just keystrokes (**Ignore Mouse**), just mouse actions—including mouse actions performed while holding down a key—(**Clicks + Drags**), or both (**Everything**). Recorder is at its most reliable when you use only keystrokes for your macros, so you'll usually select **Ignore Mouse** for this option.

TECHNO NERD TEACHES

Why is Recorder unreliable when you use mouse clicks? The problem is that when you click, Recorder memorizes the position of the mouse relative to either the screen or the active window (as given by the setting in the **Relative to** drop-down list). But this position may be way off if, when you run the macro, the window has changed size or position, or you're using a different screen resolution.

6. If you like, you can also use the Description box to enter a detailed explanation of what the macro does. In our example, for instance, you might want to mention that you need to have your word processor up and running before playing this macro.

7. Select the Start button. Recorder minimizes itself to an icon. The icon flashes on and off to let you know that a recording is in progress.

8. Enter the keystrokes necessary to perform the operation you want to automate. In our example, you'd first switch to your word processor (using **Alt+Tab**), and then type in the text.

9. When you're done, pause Recorder either by pressing **Ctrl+Break**, or by clicking on the flashing Recorder icon. The Recorder dialog box appears, as shown in the following figure.

This dialog box appears when you press Ctrl+Break or click on the Recorder icon.

10. Activate the Save Macro option, and then select **OK**. If you prefer to continue the recording (say, after making some adjustments), activate **Resume Recording**, instead. If the recording is a total fiasco, choose Cancel Recording to forget the whole thing.

When you've finished a recording, you're returned to the Recorder window, and your macro's name and shortcut key are displayed. You're free to add as many macros as you like to a Recorder file. However, you should save your macros for posterity after each recording. To do this, select the File menu's Save command, enter a name for the file (don't bother with an extension; Recorder adds its .REC extension automatically), and then select **OK**.

How to Run a Macro

The whole purpose of Recorder macros, of course, is to play back their contents at will. To do this, first start Recorder and open the Recorder file that contains the macro you want to run (by using the File menu's Open command). You can now run the macro using either of the following techniques:

☞ If the macro has a shortcut key, switch to the application you want to play the macro back in, position the cursor (if necessary), and then press the shortcut key combination.

☞ In the Recorder window, highlight the macro you want to run, and select the **Macro** menu's **Run** command. You can also simply double-click on the macro.

If you need to stop a macro in progress, press **Ctrl+Break**, and then select **OK** in the dialog box that appears.

The Least You Need to Know

This chapter gave you the goods on five of Windows' free accessories: Calculator, Calendar, Cardfile, Clock, and Recorder. Here's a quick review of the important stuff:

☞ Use Calculator for simple math calculations. Select the **Calculator** icon from Program Manager's **Accessories** group.

☞ Calendar is useful for keeping track of daily appointments. Select the **Calendar** icon in the **Accessories** group.

☞ Use Cardfile to keep lists of addresses, recipes, and anything else that comes to mind. Double-click on the **Cardfile** icon in the **Accessories** group.

☞ Clock is a simple, little program that just shows you the current date and time. You fire it up by selecting the **Clock** icon in the **Accessories** group.

☞ Recorder can save you hours of drudgery by automating mundane tasks. To start Recorder, select the **Recorder** icon in the **Accessories** group.

This page unintentionally left blank.

Chapter 23
Getting Wired with Terminal

In This Chapter

- ☛ Setting up your modem
- ☛ Dialing online services
- ☛ Transferring files to and from online services
- ☛ An example session with a real bulletin board
- ☛ Your personal on-ramp to the information superhighway

As you've no doubt figured out by now, computer nerds thrive on jargon and buzzwords. These terms range from the useful (such as *multimedia* and *drag-and-drop*) to the downright silly (*GUI* and *boot* come to mind). Fortunately, most jargon never makes it past the narrow confines of each nerd's subspecialty (which means the rest of us don't have to know about scary-sounding things like *TCP/IP* and *client-server*).

Occasionally, however, the odd buzzword makes it into the mainstream—where, tragically, it's quickly trampled to death from media overkill. (I call it the "cachet-to-cliché" syndrome.) The most spectacular example of this was the phrase "user-friendly" that appeared *ad nauseam* a few years back. The current champ in the overused-phrase category is "information superhighway." Heck, the thing doesn't even exist yet, and we're already sick of hearing about it!

TECHNO NERD TEACHES

To use Terminal, you need to have a modem attached to one of your computer's serial ports, and you need a phone line attached to the modem. Confused already? Hey, it can happen. For fast relief, I'd suggest you pick up a copy of *The Complete Idiot's Guide to Modems and Online Services* by Sherry Kinkoph. It's coming soon to your local bookstore.

But just as "user-friendly" was a good idea before it was knocked silly (after all, who'd want to use something that was "user-hostile?"), so too is the information superhighway a good idea obscured by hype. In this chapter, we'll ignore the hype, and I'll show you how to use Windows' Terminal accessory to tap into the existing services (such as bulletin board systems and large-scale data marketplaces such as CompuServe) that are the precursors of the info autobahn.

Starting Terminal

Starting Terminal is as easy as starting any other accessory: in Program Manager, open the **Accessories** group and double-click on the **Terminal** icon. If Terminal asks you to select a default serial port, select the port your modem is attached to and then select **OK**. When Terminal loads, you'll see the window shown in the figure. Not much to look at, is it? Well, that's in keeping with Terminal's Spartan nature. This is a real bare-bones communications program that lacks most of the nice features you get in commercial applications (but hey, whaddaya want for nothing?).

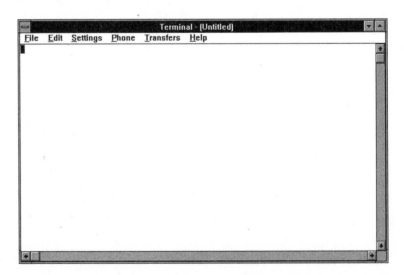

The Terminal window.

Entering a Phone Number

The first thing to do is tell Terminal which phone number you want to dial. You do this by pulling down the **Settings** menu and selecting the Phone Number command. You'll see the Phone Number dialog box, shown in the next figure. In the **Dial** text box, type the phone number, and then press **Enter** (you can ignore the other controls in this dialog box). Here are a few points to keep in mind when entering a phone number:

☞ If the number is long distance, be sure to enter both the country code and the area code.

☞ You can enter dashes and parentheses to make the number more readable, but Terminal ignores them.

☞ If you need to dial 9 to get an outside line, enter a **9** and a comma (,) before the phone number. The comma tells the modem to pause for two seconds before dialing the number, which should be enough time to get the outside line; if not, enter a second comma to pause for four seconds. For example, the following entry dials 9, pauses for two seconds, and then dials a long distance number: 9,1-123-555-1234

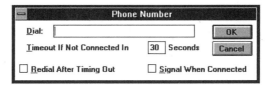

Use the Phone Number dialog box to enter the phone number you want Terminal to dial.

Getting Terminal Ready for Action

We now turn to the "Tower of Babel" problem in modem communications. Modems, you see, have the darnedest time talking to each other. Even the simplest exchange requires jumping through a few bizarre and hopelessly technical hoops. The problem isn't that each modem speaks a different "language," but that all modems can speak many different dialects of the same language. These dialects are called *communications settings*, and they're critical if you hope to get anywhere with this stuff.

The basic idea is that the settings your modem uses must be identical to those used by the remote modem. If they're different, chaos reigns, and communication is usually impossible. How do you know which settings the other modem uses? That's a good question! Many BBS operators and information services have a voice line you can call to ask about the proper settings. Failing that, there are a couple of common settings you can try.

TECHNO NERD TEACHES

Whenever you dial in Terminal, you'll see some incomprehensible letters and numbers appear inside the Terminal window. These hieroglyphics are commands that Terminal sends to your modem. For example, when you dial, you usually see a command that begins with ATDT and ends with the phone number. The AT part is short for ATtention; it acts as a sort of "Ahem!" command. The DT stands for Dial Tone, and it tells the modem to get a dial tone before dialing the number. The line after each of these "AT" commands is the modem's response (such as "OK"). Happily, you can ignore all this stuff.

To set the communications settings, pull down the Settings menu and select the Communications command. You'll see the Communications dialog box, shown in the following figure. My, doesn't that look like fun! Here's the bare minimum you need to know about this gobbledygook:

Baud Rate: This is the rate at which data will be transferred between the two modems (the higher the better). Most modems today operate at 2400 baud, but 9600-baud modems are becoming the standard.

Data Bits: In the vast majority of cases, you'll choose either 7 or 8 in this section.

Parity: Here, the usual settings are either **None** or **Even**. If you select 8 data bits, you must select **None** (Terminal does this for you automatically).

Stop Bits: This is almost always set to 1.

Connector: This is the serial port your modem is connected to.

Here are the two setups that will work 99% of the time:

☞ 2400 baud, 8 data bits, no parity, 1 stop bit (this is usually abbreviated as 2400,8,N,1). We'll be using this setup to dial in to the Microsoft Download Service.

☞ 2400 baud, 7 data bits, even parity, 1 stop bit (this is usually abbreviated as 2400,7,E,1).

Once you've entered your settings, select **OK** to return to the Terminal window.

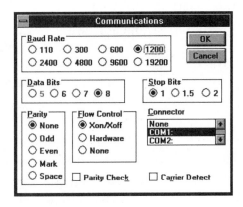

The Communications dialog box: a finalist for the Scariest-Looking Dialog Box award.

The File Transfer Thing

Depending on which service you call, you can do all kinds of fun things online. For example, you can have "chats" with other people who have dialed in to the same service, send electronic mail, or look up information in one or more of the service's databases. Or you can send a file to the service, or receive a file from the service, just to name a few.

The steps you use to perform the first three example actions will vary from service to service. Most BBSs have an online help system you can use to find out what the heck you're supposed to do next. If you need to receive a file from the service (or, more rarely, send one of your own files to the service), you'll generally need to slog through the following steps:

1. Move to the appropriate file transfer area. All BBSs have different sections you can move in and out of. For example, there might be sections for browsing information, getting help, leaving messages, and so on. You'll usually get a menu of choices; look for a menu item such as Download (if you're receiving), Upload (if you're sending), or Files.

2. Tell the service you want to receive or send a file (how you do this will depend on the service). You'll be asked to enter the name of the file. If you're receiving a file and you're not sure of the name, most services allow you to browse through their files to find the one you want.

3. You'll also be asked which *transfer protocol* you want to use. This isn't as scary as it sounds; Terminal can only use two of these protocol things, and there's one you'll use almost all the time (I'll explain everything you need to know a little later).

4. Tell Terminal you want to perform a file transfer (I'll discuss this in detail in a sec).

5. When the transfer is complete, you'll usually have to press **Enter** or some other key to let the service know you're back.

The next couple of sections take a closer look at steps 2 through 4.

Following Protocol

In diplomacy, *protocol* defines the rules and formalities that smooth communications between nations. As we've seen, just to get two modems talking to each other requires perfect synchronization of communications settings. If we now want to actually exchange data—well, that just adds a whole new level of complexity.

The good news is that this complexity is something you and I can safely ignore, because the world's modem nerds have worked out various solutions. These solutions are called *protocols*; in the same way that diplomatic protocols make cultural exchanges easy, communications protocols are designed to make it easy for two modems to exchange data. The only thing we have to do is make sure both modems are using the same protocol. Otherwise, we'd end up like two diplomats trying to perform different ceremonies at the same time: things just won't mesh properly.

Here's the way it works. When you let the online service know you want to receive or send a file, it will eventually display a list of the protocols it can use, and ask you to select the one you want to use during the transfer. Which one should you choose? Well, Terminal only supports two protocols: XModem/CRC and Kermit, so your choices are limited. However, I've yet to encounter a BBS that doesn't support at least XModem/CRC, so that's the one you'll use most of the time.

To tell Terminal which protocol to use, pull down the **Settings** menu and select the **Binary Transfers** command. You'll see the Binary Transfers dialog box, shown below. Select the protocol you want, and then select **OK** or press **Enter**. You choose the protocol either before you dial up (if you know which one you'll need in advance) or while you're online. If I'm not sure which one I need, I usually wait until the service displays its list of available protocols.

Terminal gives you a choice of two protocols to use in your online diplomatic missions.

Receiving and Sending Files

Once you've told the online service the name of the file you want to receive or send, and you've selected the protocol to use, the service will say something like **Ready to send/receive file. Please initiate file transfer.** At this point, pull down the Transfers menu and select one of the following commands:

Receive Binary File   Select this command when you want to receive a file from the service. The dialog box that appears is called Receive Binary File, and it lets you enter a name for the file and a location.

Send Binary File   Select this command when you want to send a file to the service. Terminal displays a dialog box named Send Binary File that lets you choose the file to send.

Both of these dialog boxes use the same layout as the Open dialog box you've probably seen *ad nauseam* by now. Once you've specified a file, select **OK** or press **Enter** to begin the file transfer. Terminal displays the progress of the transfer at the bottom of the window (see below). If for any reason you need to abort the transfer before it's complete, you can either select the Stop command from the Transfers menu or click on the **Stop** button at the bottom of the progress bar.

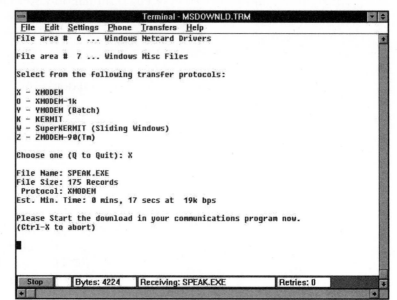

```
┌─────────────────────────────────────────────────────────────────┐
│ ─                   Terminal - MSDOWNLD.TRM                   ▼ ▲ │
├─────────────────────────────────────────────────────────────────┤
│ File  Edit  Settings  Phone  Transfers  Help                     │
│ File area #  6 ... Windows Netcard Drivers                     ▲ │
│                                                                   │
│ File area #  7 ... Windows Misc Files                             │
│                                                                   │
│ Select from the following transfer protocols:                    │
│                                                                   │
│ X - XMODEM                                                        │
│ O - XMODEM-1k                                                     │
│ Y - YMODEM (Batch)                                                │
│ K - KERMIT                                                        │
│ W - SuperKERMIT (Sliding Windows)                                 │
│ Z - ZMODEM-90(Tm)                                                 │
│                                                                   │
│ Choose one (Q to Quit): X                                         │
│                                                                   │
│ File Name: SPEAK.EXE                                              │
│ File Size: 175 Records                                            │
│  Protocol: XMODEM                                                 │
│ Est. Min. Time: 0 mins, 17 secs at  19k bps                       │
│                                                                   │
│ Please Start the download in your communications program now.     │
│ (Ctrl-X to abort)                                                 │
│                                                                   │
│ ▊                                                                 │
│                                                                 ▼ │
├──────┬───────────────┬─────────────────────┬──────────────┬──────┤
│ Stop │ Bytes: 4224   │ Receiving: SPEAK.EXE │ Retries: 0   │    ▲ │
├──────┴───────────────┴─────────────────────┴──────────────┴──────┤
│ ◄                                                               ► │
└─────────────────────────────────────────────────────────────────┘
```

Once you start a file transfer, Terminal displays this progress bar at the bottom of the window.

When the transfer is complete, Terminal returns control to the service, and you can continue with other service options or log off.

Saving Your Settings

Terminal lets you save your settings (including the phone number and protocol) in a special file you can open at any time. This allows you to create a separate file for each online service you'll be using. Once you've entered the data for a particular service, select the **Save** command from the File menu. In the Save dialog box that appears, enter a name for the file that's eight characters long or less (Terminal will add its TRM extension automatically). Select **OK** or press **Enter** to save the file.

When you need to use one of the settings files, select the File menu's Open command, select the file you want to use from the Open dialog box, and then select **OK** or press **Enter**.

An Example Online Session

To get a feel for life online, let's go through an example session using the Microsoft Product Support Download Service bulletin board. This BBS contains mostly updated files that work with Microsoft products, and best of all, it's free (except for the long distance charges, of course; note, however, that many BBSs also charge an access fee). We'll be downloading (receiving) a file named SPEAK.EXE. This file contains a device driver that lets your system play fancy-shmancy sounds even if you don't have a sound board.

Here are the settings we'll need for this session:

Phone Number	1-206-936-6735
Baud Rate	1200, 2400, or 9600 (depending on the maximum baud rate of your modem)
Data Bits	8
Parity	None
Stop Bits	1
Connector	Select the appropriate serial port for your computer
Protocol	XModem/CRC

Be sure to save these settings before you continue (I named my settings file MSDOWNLD.TRM).

Practicing Safe Downloading

Although many bulletin boards test their software for viruses, you shouldn't take this for granted. Always download files into an empty directory (or even onto an empty floppy disk) where you can easily run a virus program to check for diseased files. (The Anti-Virus program you get with DOS 6 will do the job nicely. See Chapter 24, "Wielding the DOS Tools," to find out more.)

Even if you don't have any anti-virus software, you should still place your downloads in an empty directory so you can check out all the files you end up with. This is, in fact, a must for downloading the PC Speaker driver file. If you don't have an empty directory, use File Manager to create a new directory called DOWNLOAD.

Logging On

With your settings entered and saved, you're ready to go. First, make sure your modem is turned on and the cables are attached properly. Now just select the Phone menu's Dial command to get the ball rolling. Note that you don't pick up the receiver in this case. In modem-to-modem communications, the two modems will do most of the talking; if your input is needed (say, to enter a password), you'll use your computer's keyboard to send messages to the other modem.

When the other modem answers the call, you'll probably hear a cacophony of strange (and annoying) sounds. This is normal behavior as the two modems exchange pleasantries. If all goes well, the sounds will cease and the modems will continue their conversation in blissful silence. Terminal will also display a **CONNECT** message (such as CONNECT 9600) to let you know the modems are connected.

If you have call waiting on the phone line you'll be using, you should turn it off before starting an online session. Why? Well, because the call waiting beep can throw your modem for a loop and possibly disrupt communications. In most phone systems, you disable call waiting by pressing ***70** (if you're not sure, check with your phone company). Call waiting resumes normal operation when you complete your online call.

The Microsoft BBS (like most services) then asks you to enter your name. Just type in your full name and press **Enter**. You may also be asked other questions (such as where you're calling from). Enter the pertinent data and press **Enter** each time. If you're asked a yes-or-no question, press **Y** or **N** (as appropriate) without pressing **Enter**.

You'll then get several screenfuls of what's known as *read me* information. These notes give you updates about the service and other tidbits the operators think you may be interested in. Press **Enter** after each screen to move on. Eventually, you'll see the Microsoft Download Service Main Menu.

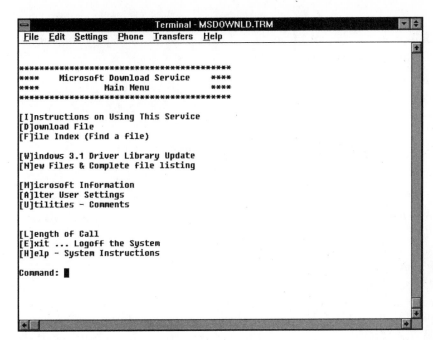

```
Terminal - MSDOWNLD.TRM
File  Edit  Settings  Phone  Transfers  Help

*******************************************
****    Microsoft Download Service    ****
****              Main Menu            ****
*******************************************

[I]nstructions on Using This Service
[D]ownload File
[F]ile Index (Find a file)

[W]indows 3.1 Driver Library Update
[N]ew Files & Complete file listing

[M]icrosoft Information
[A]lter User Settings
[U]tilities - Comments


[L]ength of Call
[E]xit ... Logoff the System
[H]elp - System Instructions

Command: █
```

The Main Menu of the Microsoft BBS.

Notice that each menu item has one letter surrounded by square brackets ([]). These letters act just like the underlined letters in Windows' pull-down menus: you press the letter to select the menu option. For example, to enter the service's Help system, you'd press **H**.

In our case, we want to download a file, so press **D**. The service then displays a list of options related to downloading. We want to get right to the file transfer, so press **D** again, and press **Enter**. (Yes, it *is* a little confusing that sometimes you have to press **Enter** and sometimes you don't. Ah, well, that's life in the fast lane of the information superhighway!)

The Microsoft BBS now asks you to enter the name of the file you want to receive. Type **SPEAK.EXE** and press **Enter**. The service takes a few seconds to search its file areas for the appropriate file, and then displays a list of the protocols you can use. Hmmm, there's no option for XModem/CRC. That's no problem because you're allowed to use plain XModem instead (*don't* use XModem-1K). To select this protocol, press **X**. The service displays the following message:

Please start the download in your communications program now.

That's our cue to tell Terminal to start the transfer. Select the Receive Binary File command from the Transfers menu to display the Receive Binary File dialog box. You need to do two things:

☞ Change the directory to **C:\DOWNLOAD** (or whatever you named the empty directory you'll be using for downloads).

☞ In the File Name text box, type **SPEAK.EXE**.

Always make sure you hang up when you've finished an online session. This will help you avoid running up a large tab in either long distance charges or online fees for services, such as CompuServe, where you pay by the minute.

When you're done, take a deep breath, and select **OK** or press **Enter**. Terminal displays the progress bar at the bottom of the window, and starts receiving the file.

The transfer will take a minute or two, depending on the speed of your modem. When it's done, you'll be returned to the Microsoft BBS screen. Press **Enter** to return to the Main menu. To exit the service, press **E**. Your last task is to hang up the phone. You do this by selecting the **Hangup** command from the **Phone** menu.

Extracting the Speaker Driver

To make file transfers quicker, most BBSs store files in a compressed format. SPEAK.EXE is the compressed form of the device driver we need. To use this driver, you need to *decompress* the file. This is, fortunately, very easy in this case, as the following steps show.

1. Start File Manager.

2. Select the directory where you received SPEAK.EXE (your download directory).

3. In the file list, double-click on **SPEAK.EXE**, or highlight it and press **Enter**. A message appears on your screen warning you to use an empty directory (you're okay on this), and you're asked if you want to extract (decompress) the files.

4. Press **Y**. The files are decompressed, and you're returned to File Manager.

5. Press **F5** to refresh the screen and see all the files that were hiding in SPEAK.EXE (you'll probably now have six files in the directory).

6. Select all the files and move them to the C:\WINDOWS\SYSTEM directory.

7. Exit File Manager and follow the instructions for installing the PC Speaker driver, as outlined in the next section.

Installing the Speaker Driver

Merely extracting the PC Speaker driver isn't enough to get good sound from your computer. No, you need to stick Windows' nose in it, so to speak, by following these steps:

1. Start Control Panel (by selecting the **Control Panel** icon from the **Main** program group) and then select the **Drivers** icon. Control Panel displays the Drivers dialog box.

2. Select the Add button. Control Panel displays the Add dialog box.

3. In the List of Drivers, highlight the **Unlisted or Updated Driver** option and then select **OK**. Windows will ask you to insert the disk containing the driver. For the PC Speaker driver, type **c:\windows\system** and then select **OK**.

TECHNO NERD TEACHES

If your I-Way travels take you to CompuServe, why not pay a visit to the Macmillan Computer Publishing Forum to say hello (type **GO PHCP** at any CompuServe **!** prompt). Better yet, why not drop me a line. My e-mail address is 70033,541. (If you're on some part of the Internet other than CompuServe, send your e-mail to 70033.541@compuserve.com or to paulmcf@hookup.net.)

4. Windows then displays a list of the drivers it found. Highlight the PC speaker driver and then select **OK**. The PC Speaker Driver Setup dialog box appears.

5. Enter the settings you want (the defaults are usually fine), and then select **OK**.

A Note About ZIP Files and Other Online Oddities

Many BBS files are compressed in what's called a *ZIP format*. These files are compressed using a program called PKZIP, and you can recognize them by looking for a .ZIP extension (such as SOMEFILE.ZIP). To decompress (or unzip, as the cognoscenti say) these files, you need another program called PKUNZIP. Most bulletin boards carry both programs. They're *shareware*, so if you use them regularly, you should send the small registration fee to the program's authors (the program provides all the details).

In some cases, though, you'll find that BBS files have an EXE extension (like SPEAK.EXE). These are also compressed files, but you don't need an extra program to decompress them. As you did with SPEAK.EXE, you decompress these files just by selecting them in File Manager.

The Least You Need to Know

This chapter showed you how to get online with Windows' Terminal accessory. Here's a look back at some of the stuff you downloaded into your brain in this chapter:

- ☞ To start Terminal, select the **Terminal** icon in Program Manager's **Accessories** group.

- ☞ To enter a phone number, select the **Settings** menu's **Phone Number** command and enter the number in the dialog box that appears.

- ☞ To enter the communications settings for the service you'll be dialing, select the **Communications** command from the **Settings** menu and enter the appropriate settings in the dialog box.

- ☞ If you need to select a file transfer protocol, select the **Settings** menu's **Binary Transfers** command. In the dialog box, select either **X**Modem/CRC or **K**ermit.

- ☞ To dial the modem, pull down the **Phone** menu and select the **Dial** command.

- ☞ If you want to receive a file, wait until the BBS tells you to start the transfer and then select Receive Binary **File** from the **Transfers** menu. To send a file, select the Send **Binary** File command from the **Transfers** menu.

Chapter 24
Wielding the DOS 6 Tools

In This Chapter

- ☛ Preserving precious data with Backup
- ☛ Eradicating nasty viruses with Anti-Virus
- ☛ Recovering trashed files with Undelete
- ☛ A brief history of a war you probably missed

When Windows was released in the mid-eighties, the computer world immediately divided into two opposing camps: DOS diehards and Windows wonks. There were regular skirmishes in the letters sections of computer magazines and on computer bulletin boards with both sides extolling the virtues of their way of doing things. The war of words raged on until, finally, the marketplace crowned a victor: Windows applications now substantially outsell their DOS counterparts.

DOS certainly isn't dead yet, but it appears to be on its last legs. History, I think, will record that the fatal blow came with the release of DOS 6 which included—heresy of heresies for DOS mavens—three *Windows* utilities. This was, if nothing else, a tacit acknowledgment that Windows is the superior approach.

In preparation for a rousing chorus of "Ding Dong, DOS is Dead," this chapter looks at the three Windows programs you get with DOS 6: Backup (which makes backup copies of the data on your hard disk), Anti-Virus (which can check for and fumigate viruses on your system), and Undelete (which can recover a file that was accidentally deleted). You should find all of these programs in Program Manager's **Microsoft Tools** group.

Microsoft Backup: A Seat Belt for Your Data

A couple of years ago I switched on my computer anticipating a normal day's writing. Instead, I heard some strange, unnatural clunking noises emanating from my machine, and then saw the following ominous message:

Hard disk failure

My reaction to this stark reality is unprintable, but let's just say I was more than a little upset. Why? Not because it was going to cost me big bucks to repair my hard drive or get a new one, but because I had months of work on the disk that I hadn't backed up. Oh sure, I'd planned to get around to it some day, but my procrastination always won out in the end. (Even to this day, my motto—for everything *except* backing up my data—remains "Never put off until tomorrow what you can put off until the day after tomorrow.")

The lesson here, of course, is that hard disk crashes are a fact of computing life, so you need to protect your precious data at all costs. What's that? Backing up is a pain in the you-know-what? Well, the good news is that the Microsoft Backup utility that comes with DOS 6 removes much of the drudgery normally associated with backups. You just select the files you want to archive and the program will copy them to floppy disks. Then, if your hard disk should burst into flames, you can use Backup to restore your data from the disks. The next few sections tell you everything you need to know.

Getting Backup Up to Speed

To start Backup, select the **Backup** icon from Program Manager's **Microsoft Tools** program group. Alternatively, you can start Backup by pulling down File Manager's Tools menu and selecting the **Backup** command. If you're starting Backup for the first time, you're asked if you want to "automatically configure" the program. Select Yes to perform the configuration (see the next section).

Doing the Configuration Thing

To make sure your backups are reliable, Backup will configure itself to your system. This process is a bit of a pain, but it's worth the extra peace of mind. (If you selected No when you were asked about performing the configuration, you can still change your mind. In the Backup window, select the Configure button and then select the Auto Floppy Configure button.)

Backup first asks you to remove any disks you may have in your computer's disk drives. When you're ready, select **OK**. The program then displays the Compatibility Test dialog box. (If you don't see this dialog, select the Compatibility Test button in the Configure screen.)

This test is just a practice backup that will be used to make sure your data can be backed up and restored without mishap. Use the Drive To Test drop-down list to select the disk drive you'll be using for your backups. Then select the **Start** button to perform the test.

TECHNO NERD TEACHES

Which drive should you use for backups? Well, the best choice is the one that has the higher capacity (see Chapter 15, "Disk Driving," to learn about disk capacity). You can fit more data on these disks so your backups will use fewer disks and the whole ordeal will be over faster.

Backup then displays a long-winded message telling you not to use the disk drive while the backup and restore operations are in progress. Duh.

Grab a couple of floppy disks that contain no useful data (Backup will overwrite any existing files, so be sure the disks contain only expendable data) and insert one of them into the disk drive you selected earlier. When you're ready to go, select **OK**.

If the disk contains data, Backup displays a partial list of the files. If you want to overwrite the files, select the Overwrite button. If you don't want to use this disk after all, slip another disk in the drive and then select the Retry button.

Backup then displays the Backup Progress dialog box, and starts copying files to the floppy disk. When the disk is full, you'll hear a beep, and you'll see the message **Insert diskette #2** in the Drive A: or Drive B: box (depending on which drive you're using). Remove the first disk, and place the second disk in the drive. (If you wait too long before inserting the second disk, or if Backup can't automatically detect the second disk in the drive, you'll see a dialog box telling you to insert the disk. In this case, you need to select **OK** to proceed.) If Backup detects files on the new disk, you'll have to go through the same overwrite/retry rigmarole.

When the second disk is done, Backup lets you know, and asks you to reinsert the first disk. The program will now attempt to restore the files it backed up. Insert the first disk, and then select **OK**. As you've probably guessed, when the first disk is done, you'll be asked to reinsert the second disk. (Don't worry, you're almost done.) Just fire the disk into the drive to continue (again, if you wait too long, a dialog box will appear and you'll need to select **OK**).

After a few seconds, Backup reports that the "Compare phase" of the compatibility test is done. Select **OK**. Yet another dialog box appears (yes, this *is* getting ridiculous!) to tell you that you can now safely perform your backups. Hallelujah! (Didn't someone say this was supposed to be an "automatic" configuration? Sheesh!) For the last time, select **OK** to return to the Backup window. Select the Backup button to display the Backup screen (see below).

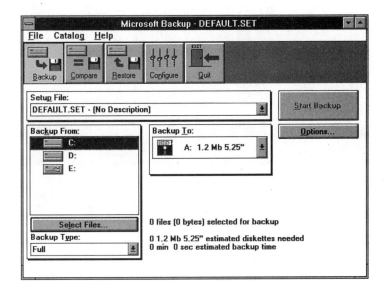

You'll be using the Backup screen to select the files to back up and the floppy disk to use for the backup.

Selecting the Files to Back Up

The next step in your backup chore is to select the files you want to include in the backup. The first thing to do is make sure your hard disk is highlighted in the Backup From list (you don't have to do anything if the list only displays one drive).

To select the specific files, click on the Select Files button. After a few seconds, Backup displays the Select Backup Files window, as shown in the following figure.

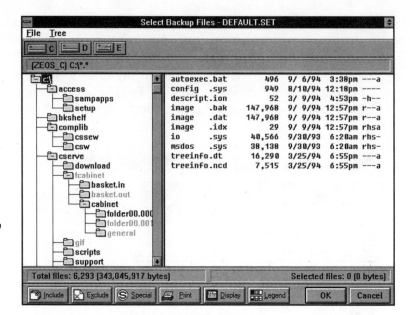

*Use the Select Backup
Files screen to select
the files you want to
include in your
backup.*

Before proceeding, you need to ask yourself which files you want to include in the backup. Your first inclination might be to include every file, just to be safe. The problem with this approach is that even a small hard disk contains enough data to fill a couple of dozen floppies. Believe me, shuffling that many disks in and out of your machine every time you do a backup will get old *real* fast. "Sorry, I'd like to do a backup but I have to de-louse my Rottweiler."

No, what we need is a different approach, one that will encourage you to back up your hard disk regularly. You'll recall that back in Chapter 12, "File Manager Basics," I told you the files in your computer can be divided into two categories: program files (the ones that run your applications) and data files (the ones you create when you use those applications). Of the two, only your data files are irreplaceable; after all, you can always reinstall the applications if your hard disk goes kaput. So a more realistic backup strategy is one where you back up *only* your data. The good news is that it's the program files that take up most of your hard disk real estate. So backing up only data will drastically reduce the number of floppy disks you need (as well as the time it takes to perform the backup).

Okay, now that we have all that straightened out, let's see how we implement such a strategy. You use the **Select Backup Files** window to include and exclude files from the selection. So the first thing you need to do is include all your data files in the selection. There are two ways to do this:

☞ To include an individual file, first use the left side of the window to select a directory. (You can either click on the directory or use the up and down arrow keys.) Then, on the right side of the window, double-click on the file you want to include. (From the keyboard, press **Tab** to move to the right side, use the up and down arrows to highlight the file, and then press the **Spacebar**.)

☞ To select a group of files, highlight the directory containing the files and then select the Include button. This displays the Include/Exclude Files dialog box. If you want to include every file in the directory, select the Add button and then select **OK**. More likely, you'll only want to include files with certain extensions (such as your data files). For example, if you're in your word processor directory and all your documents use the DOC extension, then you'd enter ***.doc** in the File text box. Similarly, you might use ***.xls** or ***.wks** for your spreadsheet files, ***.wri** for your Write files, ***.bmp** for your Paintbrush files, and so on. Select Add and then select **OK** to return to the Select Backup Files window.

Once you've selected all your data files, select **OK** to return to the Backup window.

Starting the Backup

Well, we're just about ready to roll. The only other task that remains is to make sure you select the appropriate floppy drive in the Backup To list (you should select the same drive you used earlier in the configuration). When you're ready, follow these steps to back up your data:

1. Gather the appropriate number of floppy disks for the backup (the Backup screen tells you approximately how many you'll need), and then place one of the disks in the drive. Again, Backup will overwrite any files on the disk, so make sure it contains no valuable info.

TECHNO NERD TEACHES

You can also make backups easier by taking advantage of the different backup types (found in the Backup Type drop-down list). The **Full** option backs up all the selected files. The **Incremental** option backs up only those files that have changed since the last full or incremental backup. Choose **Differential** to back up only files that have changed since the last full backup.

2. Select the Start Backup button. Backup displays the message about not accessing the drive during the backup. I'd recommend activating the Disable this message check box so you won't have to read this silliness again. Select **OK** to continue.

3. If the disk contains data, Backup will display a warning. Select **Overwrite** or **Retry**, as appropriate. The Backup Progress window that appears lets you keep track of the backup.

4. Depending on the number and size of the files you selected, Backup will occasionally prompt you to enter more disks. When you're done with a disk, you should label it for future reference (e.g., **Backup Disk #1**).

Restoring Your Data

If some unforeseen disaster should occur, you'll need to restore your data from the backups. Here are the steps to follow:

1. Use the Backup Set Catalog drop-down list to select the appropriate backup catalog. A *catalog* is just a list of the files you included in your backup. How do you know which catalog to select? Well, you need to look at two things: first, check out the extension of the catalog's filename. **FUL** denotes a Full backup; **INC** denotes an incremental backup; and **DIF** denotes a Differential backup. Second, look at the date and time provided for each catalog.

2. In the Restore From list, make sure the drive you normally use for your backups is selected.

3. In the Restore To list, select where you want the files restored. (You'll normally select Original Locations, but you can also select Alternate Drives or Alternate Directories. For the latter, Backup prompts you for the new locations during the restore.)

4. Choose the Select Files button and select the files you want to restore (this is similar to selecting files for a backup).

5. Select the **Start Restore** button. If a message appears warning you about accessing the floppy drive during the restore, select **OK** to continue. After a few seconds, Backup will prompt you to enter one of the disks from your backup (this is why you need to label your disks).

6. Insert the disk and then select **OK**. Backup starts the restoration. You may be prompted to insert one or more other disks from the backup set.

Exiting Backup

When you're done with Backup, you can use either of the following methods to exit the program and return to Program Manager:

- ☛ Pull down the File menu and select the Exit command.
- ☛ Select the **Quit** button.

In the Exit Backup dialog box that appears, select **OK.**

Guarding Against Viruses

Viruses are tiny little software programs that—like their biological namesakes—exist only to invade hosts and reproduce themselves (where, for a digital virus, a "host" is any hard disk or floppy disk). In fact, virus hackers prefer to call the products of their black art "self-propagating, autonomous computer programs."

Once they've invaded a system, viruses exhibit a remarkable range of behavior. Many are relatively benign: the Joshi virus locks up your computer once a year (on January 5th), and won't let you do anything until you type the phrase "Happy Birthday Joshi"; the Sunday virus freezes your machine on Sundays and orders you to go out and have some fun.

Most viruses, though, are downright nasty. They get their jollies by altering existing data, or by trashing it altogether. Although some of these malevolent creations have innocent-sounding names such as Michelangelo and Christmas, most sport monikers that more directly reflect their wicked intentions: Armageddon, Beast, Black Monday, Dark Avenger, and Darth Vader are good (or should I say evil) examples.

Although virus infections are, fortunately, still relatively rare, they *do* happen. That Microsoft decided to bundle an anti-virus program with its operating system is an indication that the problem is a real one and should be taken seriously.

Starting Anti-Virus

Okay, now that I've scared the living daylights out of everyone, it's time to get down to business. To start DOS 6's Anti-Virus program, open the **Microsoft Tools** group in Program Manager and then select the **Anti-Virus** icon. You'll see the Microsoft Anti-Virus window, as shown below. (You can also start Anti-Virus from File Manager by pulling down the Tools menu and selecting the Anti-Virus command.)

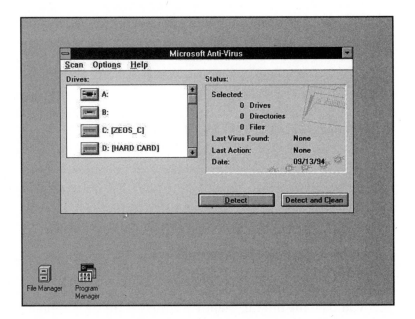

The Microsoft Anti-Virus window.

Detecting and Cleaning Viruses

To be safe, you should use Anti-Virus to perform a checkup on your system regularly. I'd recommend running the program at least once a month or anytime your computer seems to behave strangely (I know, I know: computers *always* behave strangely).

To get started, you first need to use the **Drives** box to select the drive (or drives) you want to scan. Use either of the following methods to select a drive:

☞ With your mouse, click on the drive.

☞ With your keyboard, press **Tab** until one of the drives is highlighted, use the up and down arrow keys to highlight the drive you want to scan, and then press the **Spacebar**.

Anti-Virus will take a few seconds to read the disk's information. When it's done, select the Detect and Clean button. Anti-Virus first scans your system's memory (to check for viruses that may be skulking in the shadows) and then proceeds to check every file on the drive you selected. The scan takes a few minutes, so this would be a good time to go grab a cup of coffee or something. When its chores are complete, Anti-Virus displays a Statistics dialog box that tells you the number of files that were infected and cleaned.

TECHNO NERD TEACHES

If you think there are only a few viruses out there, think again. There are, in fact, *hundreds*. To see for yourself, pull down the **S**can menu and select the **Virus List** command. This displays the Virus List dialog box that gives you information on all the known viruses. At the very bottom of the list you'll see the total number of viruses. In my case, the number is—brace yourself—1,234! (There are more viruses discovered every day, so your number may be different.)

Some Anti-Virus Tips

Besides using Anti-Virus regularly, here are a few other tips to help keep your system disease-free:

☞ Most viruses are transmitted from machine to machine via floppy disks, so you should always be careful about which used disks you trust in your computer. If you've inherited some old disks, you can make sure there are no viruses lurking in the weeds by formatting each one before you use them (see Chapter 15, "Disk Driving," to learn how to format a floppy disk).

☞ Trust no one when it comes to loading programs on your machine. Whether they come from family, friends, or a BBS, use Anti-Virus to scan the files *before* using them on your hard disk.

☞ Keep your virus list up to date. The DOS 6 manual has a coupon in the back that you can use to send away for virus updates. As you read this, there are probably dozens, maybe even hundreds, of amoral scum-nerds designing even nastier viruses. Regular updates will help you keep up.

Exiting Anti-Virus

With your hard disk checked out and your peace of mind restored, you can exit Anti-Virus by selecting the Exit Anti-Virus command from the Scan menu.

Undeleting Accidentally Erased Files

It's an old saw that there are two types of computer users: those who have accidentally deleted files and those who will. If it has happened to you, you know only too well that sinking feeling you get in the pit of your stomach when you realize you've just consigned your life's work to nothingness.

When this happened to the world's programmers once too often, they decided to do something about it. The result was software that could actually undelete a trashed file. Now, with DOS 6, the capability is available to us Windows users in the form of the Undelete application.

If you have a file you need to undelete, head *immediately* to the "Undeleting a File" section of this chapter. The sooner you attempt to undelete the file, the better your chances of success.

Starting Undelete

Windows gives you two ways to crank up the Undelete program: In Program Manager, open the **Microsoft Tools** group and select the **Undelete** icon; In File Manager, pull down the File menu and select the Undelete command. In either case, you'll see the Undelete window shown in the figure.

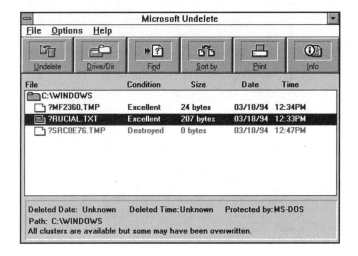

The Undelete window.

Protecting Your Files

Undelete can do a better job of recovering your files if you tell it you want them protected. In this case, "protection" just means that Undelete keeps track of certain types of information for every file you delete. When you need to recover a file you blew away by accident, Undelete uses this information to bring the file back from the dead. Follow these steps to set up deletion protection:

1. Pull down the Options menu and select the Configure Delete Protection command. Undelete displays the Configure Delete Protection dialog box.

2. Undelete gives you three protection options. Select the Delete Sentry option (this is, by far, the safest and most reliable scheme), and then select **OK**. Undelete displays the Configure Delete Sentry dialog box, as shown in the figure.

Undelete gives you all kinds of ways to configure the Delete Sentry.

3. You can ignore most of this stuff, but you'll probably want to change the value in the text box named Limit disk space for deleted files to. The suggested value is 20%, which is absurdly high. I'd suggest changing this to a more reasonable 5%. If you're running out of room on your hard drive, you might want to go as low as 2% or 3%. (Keep in mind, though, that the lower the number, the fewer files Delete Sentry can protect.)

TECHNO NERD TEACHES

Delete Sentry works by creating a new directory on your hard drive (called SENTRY). When you delete a file, Delete Sentry actually moves it to the SENTRY directory. Undeleting (as you'll see later in this chapter) is then a simple matter of restoring the file to its original directory.

4. Select the Drives button, select the drive you want to protect (usually this will be your hard drive), and then select **OK** to return to the Configure Delete Sentry dialog box.

5. Select **OK**. Undelete lets you know it needs to update something called an "autoexec.bat" file. Be thankful you don't have to worry about such things, and just go ahead and select **OK** to let Undelete handle this chore for you.

6. Undelete next tells you to reboot your computer. Select **OK**, exit Undelete (see "Exiting Undelete," coming right up), exit Windows, and then reboot (the easiest way to reboot is to press **Ctrl+Alt+Delete**).

Undeleting a File

The Undelete window shows a list of the recently deleted files for the selected directory. If you deleted the file from a directory other than the one shown (which is usually either WINDOWS or DOS), your first order of business is to display the proper directory. Begin by selecting Undelete's **Drive/Dir** button. In the Change Drive and Directory dialog box that appears, select the directory you want and then select **OK**.

In the list of deleted files, highlight the file you want to recover. If the file was deleted before you set up the Delete Sentry protection, you'll need to take into account the fact that the first letter of the file name has been changed to a question mark. For example, if you deleted a file named CRUCIAL.TXT, it will appear as ?RUCIAL.TXT.

Now take a look at the file's condition (the second column of the file list). If it says **Perfect** or **Excellent**, you'll be able to recover the entire file; if it says **Good**, you can probably recover the file, but you may lose some data; if it says **Poor** or **Destroyed**, you're out of luck.

If the file is in Perfect, Excellent or Good condition, select the Undelete button. One of two things will happen:

Why is there a question mark in front of files deleted without Delete Sentry? Well, when DOS deletes a file, it saves time by simply changing the file's first letter to a special character. This character signifies that the disk area used by the file is now available to other data. (This is why, if you're not using Delete Sentry, you should waste no time before trying to undelete the file: another file may overwrite your data and it will then be lost for good.) Recovering the file is a simple matter of restoring the original first letter.

- ☞ If the file was deleted after you set up Delete Sentry, Undelete recovers the file immediately.

- ☞ If the file name is missing its first letter, Undelete asks you to enter the original letter. Type the letter and then select **OK**.

Exiting Undelete

To exit Undelete, pull down the File menu and select the Exit command.

The Least You Need to Know

This chapter showed you how to use the Windows tools that come with DOS 6: Backup, Anti-Virus, and Undelete. Here's a summary:

- ☞ To start Backup, either select the **Backup** icon from the **Microsoft Tools** group, or pull down File Manager's Tools menu and select the **Backup** command.

- ☞ To make your backup chores easier and faster, back up only the data files you create with your applications.

- ☞ To start Anti-Virus, select the **Anti-Virus** icon from the **Microsoft Tools** group, or select Anti-Virus from File Manager's Tools menu.

- ☞ Start Undelete by selecting the **Undelete** icon from the **Microsoft Tools** group, or by selecting the **U**ndelete command from File Manager's **F**ile menu.

- ☞ For the highest level of deletion protection, configure Undelete to use the Delete Sentry method.

Chapter 25

An Introduction to Windows for Workgroups

In This Chapter

☛ Checking out Windows for Workgroups' new File Manager and Print Manager

☛ Logging on to a workgroup

☛ Sharing directories and printers

☛ Monkeying around with network settings

☛ A brief workgroup primer that'll have you surfing your "net" in no time

If your computer came with a copy of Windows for Workgroups instead of regular Windows, you're probably asking yourself, "What the heck is a workgroup, and how does it affect me?" Well, the good news is that you can run Windows for Workgroups without having to bother with any of this workgroup networking nonsense. It's actually a bit faster than plain-vanilla Windows, and it adds a few bells and whistles to File Manager and Print Manager. This chapter will take you through all these improvements.

And hey, if you're a budding network administrator and you've hooked up a couple of machines at home or at the office, we'll also look at some simple network stuff: sharing files, sharing printers, and more.

TECHNO NERD TEACHES

When you start Windows for Workgroups, you may see a dialog box complaining about not having any network hardware installed. If you have no intention of doing any full-blown networking, you can avoid this missive by starting Windows for Workgroups with the command **WIN /N**.

The New, Improved File Manager

The first thing you'll notice when you start Windows for Workgroups is, well, nothing. Program Manager looks and works as it always has; the accessories (Write, Paintbrush, etc.) are no different; and your applications operate in the normal fashion (albeit, as I've said, a little faster). No, you won't see much of a difference between regular Windows and Windows for Workgroups until you crank up File Manager. When you do, you'll see the window shown in the following figure.

Toolbar —

The spiffy new version of File Manager you get in Windows for Workgroups.

A Review of the New Stuff

The most obvious of File Manager's new features is the *Toolbar* that appears below the menu bar. (Your Toolbar may appear different, depending on which Windows for Workgroups features you have loaded.) You may have come across a Toolbar or two in your other Windows applications. If so, this one works the same way; if not, the idea is simple: each "button" represents a specific File Manager task, and you select one of these tasks simply by clicking on the button with your mouse. For example, the drop-down list on the left contains a list of each drive on your computer. You can display a drive just by selecting it from this list. (I know, I know: it's a lot easier just to click on one of the drive icons. As you'll see below, however, the new File Manager lets you hide the drive icons to give you more room to display files and directories.) Here's a summary of what some of the other Toolbar buttons represent (I'll talk about the rest of the buttons later in this chapter):

Displays filenames only.

Displays all the details for each file.

Sorts files alphabetically by filename.

Sorts file alphabetically by extension.

Sorts files by size (from largest to smallest).

Sorts files by date (from latest to earliest).

The Toolbar makes things so easy that it's worth the price of admission alone. However, the new version of File Manager has a few other tricks up its digital sleeve:

☞ The Options menu has three new commands that let you control what you see in the File Manager window. The Toolbar command toggles the Toolbar on and off; the Drivebar command toggles the drive icons on and off; and the Status Bar command toggles the status bar on and off.

☞ Speaking of the status bar, one nice little touch is that it displays large file and disk sizes in megabytes (MB) instead of the hard-to-read kilobytes (KB) of the regular File Manager.

Can't remember what a Toolbar button does? Instead of guessing, just move the mouse pointer over the button and then press and hold down the left mouse button. The status bar at the bottom of the window displays a brief description of what the button will do.

☞ There's a new **Mail** menu for sending electronic mail.

☞ The **Window** menu has a new Tile Horizontally command that tiles directory windows one on top of the other.

☞ The **Options** menu has a new Customize Toolbar command. I'll show you how to customize the Toolbar in the next section.

Customizing File Manager's Toolbar

One of the many things that's always bugged me about computers is that they always force you to work *their* way. We're the ones who have to change to accommodate whatever bizarre hoops our software wants us to jump through. So it's always a welcome relief to find a program that can actually be changed to suit the way *we* work. The Windows for Workgroups File Manager falls into this category, because you can customize the Toolbar to exclude features you don't use, and include features you use most often.

You can also display the Customize Toolbar dialog box by double-clicking on the Toolbar background.

For example, if you don't use Windows for Workgroups' networking features, you can easily remove the four network-related buttons and replace them with buttons that crank up tasks you use regularly, such as copying or searching.

To see how this customization stuff works, pull down the Options menu and select the Customize Toolbar command. You'll see the Customize Toolbar dialog box, as shown below.

These are the buttons you can add to the Toolbar.

These are the buttons already on the Toolbar.

Use the Customize Toolbar dialog box to remake File Manager's Toolbar in your own image.

Customize Toolbar

Available Buttons:		Toolbar Buttons:			
Separator		Separator			Close
📁 File - Move...		View - Sort by Name			Reset
📋 File - Copy...		View - Sort by Type		Add ->	Help
✕ File - Delete...		View - Sort by Size		<- Remove	
File - Rename...		EZ View - Sort by Date			Move Up
File - Properties...		Separator			Move Down

The Customize Toolbar dialog box has two lists. The Available Buttons list shows the buttons you can add to the Toolbar. (A *separator*, by the way, is just a small space between buttons.) The Toolbar Buttons list shows you the buttons that are already on the Toolbar. Here's a rundown of the techniques you can use to create your own, personalized Toolbar:

☞ To get rid of an existing Toolbar button, highlight it in the Toolbar Buttons list, and then select <-**R**emove.

☞ To add a new button to the Toolbar, highlight the one you want in the Available Buttons list, and then select **A**dd->.

☞ To change the order the buttons appear on the Toolbar, highlight a button in the Toolbar Buttons list, and then select either Move **U**p (to move the button up in the list and to the left on the Toolbar) or Move **D**own (to move the button down in the list and to the right on the Toolbar).

☞ If you make a mess of things and you want to start over, select **R**eset to restore the default Toolbar.

When you're done, select Close to return to File Manager.

The New, Improved Print Manager

Windows for Workgroups has also applied a serious makeover to Print Manager. The most obvious alterations include a revamped Toolbar (similar to the one in File Manager), a beefed up menu bar, and a new status bar (see the figure below).

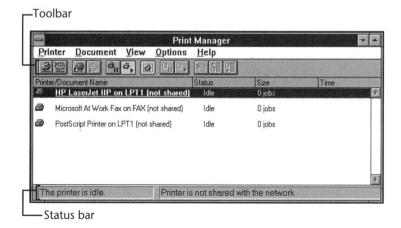

The Windows for Workgroups Print Manager.

The new Toolbar is a big improvement over the dinky three-button job you get in the regular Windows Print Manager. Here's a rundown of some of the shiny new buttons (I'll talk about the rest of the buttons later in this chapter):

Pauses printing for the highlighted printer.

Resumes printing for the highlighted printer.

Specifies the default printer.

Pauses printing for the highlighted document.

Resumes printing for the highlighted document.

Deletes the highlighted document from the print queue.

Moves the highlighted document to the top of the print queue.

Moves the highlighted document to the bottom of the print queue.

Besides the Toolbar, the new Print Manager has a fistful of other improvements:

☞ The new status bar at the bottom of the window tells you what's happening with the highlighted printer (whether or not it's printing, and whether or not it's shared with the network). It will also display a description of a Toolbar button if you place the mouse pointer over the button, and then press and hold down the left mouse button. When you're done, move the mouse pointer off the Toolbar and then release the left mouse button.

☞ In the **Printer** menu, use the **Pause Printer** and **Resume Printer** commands to stop and restart the highlighted printer (to add more paper, for example). You can also use the **Set Default Printer** command to make the currently highlighted printer the default printer used by all your Windows applications. (Recall from Chapter 18, "Hard Copy: Windows Printing Basics," that you have to do this from the Control Panel in regular Windows).

- ☞ The commands in the new Document menu let you pause and resume individual documents, delete a document from the queue, and move documents up or down in the queue.

- ☞ In the Options menu, use the Toolbar and Status Bar commands to toggle the Toolbar and status bar, respectively, on and off. You can also use the Font command to change the font used in the Print Manager window.

- ☞ If you want to change the priority Windows for Workgroups assigns to Print Manager, select the Options menu's Background Printing command. In the Background Printing dialog box, select either Low, Normal, or High, and then select OK.

Networking for Novices

If you'd like to take the networking plunge to hook up a couple of computers for sharing files and printers, Windows for Workgroups is probably your best way to go. Why? Well, it takes most of the pain out of connecting computers together, and you can share stuff with others in your network using the familiar File Manager and Print Manager tools we've just looked at. The rest of this chapter looks at this workgroup-related stuff, and takes you through the basics of setting up your network as well as sharing files and printers with other computers.

Half a chapter is, of course, a pitifully small amount to devote to a large topic like networking. Since I can't cover everything, I'm going to assume that you (or some nearby networking guru) has installed the necessary network hardware on your computers, and has set up Windows for Workgroups appropriately.

What's a Workgroup?

When most people think of networks (if, in fact, they ever think of them at all), the image that springs to mind is one of a central, monolithic computer that contains all the data and applications, with dozens or even hundreds of "terminals" attached to it. *Workgroups*, however, are different. A workgroup is a small group of computers connected by some kind of network cable. Each computer has its own applications and data, and the other computers in the workgroup can share these resources. In this egalitarian setup, all the computers in the workgroup are treated equally;

no one machine is "better" or more important than any other. In most workgroups, the computers are related to each other somehow. For example, all the computers in a company's accounting department could form one workgroup, while the marketing department might have their own workgroup.

Networks where all the machines have their own programs and data, and can share these with the other computers, are called **peer-to-peer** networks.

Each workgroup has a name (ACCOUNTING, for example), and each computer in the workgroup has its own name (this is usually the name of the person using the computer, but it can be just about anything you like). The workgroup name and computer name are specified when you set up Windows for Workgroups. In my case, I have two computers set up as a workgroup. My group name is LONEWOLF (the name of my company), and the two computer names are TWEEDLEDUM and TWEEDLEDUMBER.

The whole point of setting up a workgroup is so the members of the group can share their resources. For example, if you have three computers in the group, but only one printer, you can set things up so that each machine can print out stuff on the printer. Similarly, you can share files, applications, and even CD-ROM drives. Does this mean that other people in the group can just play with your machine willy-nilly? No, not if you don't want them to. *You* decide what stuff on your computer gets shared, and, for extra safety, you can set up passwords to prevent undesirables from accessing sensitive areas.

Logging On

If Windows for Workgroups is set up for networking, you can either be "on" the network or "off" it. If you're on the network, it means you can access the shared resources from the other computers in the group (and they can access yours). If you're off the network, your machine acts just like any other stand-alone computer.

When you start Windows for Workgroups for the first time, you'll eventually be pestered to enter a *logon name* and a password. Here are the steps to follow to get through this:

1. The default name shown in the Logon Name text box will be the computer name you entered during setup. If you like, you can change the logon name to something different.

2. Use the **P**assword text box to enter a password if you want to prevent others from getting into your copy of Windows for Workgroups. Passwords can be up to 14 characters long, and they should be something you can easily remember. When you enter the password, the letters are displayed as asterisks (*) for security reasons (you never know who might be peeking over your shoulder!).

If you're not concerned about security (if you've set up a workgroup at home, for example), you can avoid being hassled to enter a logon password simply by leaving the password fields blank. If you've already set up a password, see "Changing the Network Settings," later in this chapter, to learn how to remove it.

3. Select **OK**. Windows for Workgroups asks if you want to create a "password-list file." This file keeps track of all the passwords you have to enter to get to the shared resources on other computers in your workgroup.

4. Select **Y**es. The Confirm Logon Password dialog box appears.

5. Re-enter your password in the **C**onfirm New Password text box, and then select **OK**. Windows for Workgroups finishes loading.

When you start Windows for Workgroups in the future, all you'll have to do is enter your password. If, however, you change your logon name (as I'll show how to do a little later), you'll have to repeat the whole process.

Sharing Stuff Part I: Directories

Okay, now that you've logged on to the network, what happens next? Well, you need to do two things: set up the resources on your computer so other people in the group can share them, and connect your computer to those resources that other people are sharing.

We'll begin by looking at sharing files and directories through File Manager. Here are the steps you need to follow:

1. With File Manager loaded, highlight a directory you want to share.

2. Pull down the **Disk** menu and select the Share As command. File Manager displays the Share Directory dialog box (as shown in the following figure).

    You can also display the Share Directory dialog box by clicking on this button in File Manager's Toolbar.

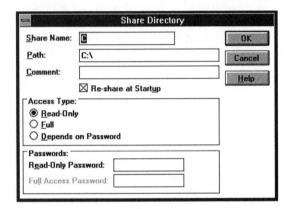

Use the Share Directory dialog box to share a directory with your workgroup pals.

3. You can leave most of the options in this dialog box as is, but the controls in the Access Type group are particularly important because they specify what the others in your workgroup can do with the shared directory:

   Read-Only   Others can only view the files and run the programs that are in the directory. They can't change files, add new files, or delete files.

   Full   Anything goes: others can run programs, view files, make changes, add new files, and delete files.

   Depends on Password   This option gives the others either read-only or full access, depending on which password they enter (see step 4).

4. If you want others to enter a password before they can access the shared directory, enter the appropriate password in either the Read-Only Password or Full-Access Password text box. (If you enter a password, don't forget to let the other people in your group know what it is.)

5. Select **OK**. If you entered a password, you'll be asked to confirm it. In this case, re-enter the password and then select **OK**. When you return to File Manager, you'll see a little hand under the directory's folder icon. This reminds you that you've shared the directory.

So the other members of your group can access one or more of your directories; now how do you get at theirs? Easy: just pull down the **Disk** menu and select the Connect Network Drive command. The Connect Network Drive dialog box appears, as shown in the following figure.

 Clicking on this button in the Toolbar will also display the Connect Network Drive dialog box.

The Connect Network Drive dialog box lets you select a shared directory from another computer in the workgroup.

The **S**how Shared Directories on list displays the name of the workgroup at the top, and the names of the computers in the group below it. (You may need to double-click on the workgroup name to display the computer names.) When you highlight the name of the computer you want to work with, its shared directories appear in the Shared Directories on list. Now just highlight the directory you want to use, and then select **OK**. If the directory is protected with a password, the Enter Network Password dialog box will appear. Enter the password and then select **OK**. (Make sure you activate the **S**ave this Password in Your Password List check box. This will prevent Windows for Workgroups from prompting you for a password each time you connect to this drive.)

File Manager adds the directory as a new drive. For example, if your system currently has drives A, B, and C, the new directory will appear as drive D. Just click on the new drive, and its files will appear like magic.

Sharing Stuff Part II: Printing

Sharing a printer among several computers in a workgroup isn't all that different from sharing directories. First off, you'll need to start Print Manager. How you proceed depends on whether you're sharing your printer with others in the group, or if you want to connect with a shared printer from another computer.

To share your printer, highlight the printer name in Print Manager, and then select the **P**rinter menu's **S**hare Printer As command. The Share Printer dialog box appears.

 You can also display the Share Printer dialog box by clicking on this button in Print Manager's Toolbar.

If you want to restrict printer access to a chosen few, enter a password in the Password text box, and then select **OK**.

If you want to be able to print to some other printer on the network, you'll need to set up a connection to it. Just pull down the **P**rinter menu and select the Connect Network Printer command. The Connect Network Printer dialog box that appears is almost identical to the Connect Network Drive dialog box you saw earlier. Use the **S**how Shared Printers on list to highlight the computer name that has the shared printer you want to use. You then highlight the printer in the Shared Printers list, select **OK**, and you're laughing (with incredulity, triumph, or encroaching insanity). You may need to enter a password to connect the printer. The shared printer will appear on your printer lists, so it's easy enough just to select it, and then print to it.

For some unfathomable reason, Print Manager doesn't ask you to confirm the password you enter in the Share Printer dialog box. So, to avoid any unpleasantness when others try to use your printer, you'll need to be extra careful when entering the password.

Mouse users can also display the Connect Network Printer dialog box by clicking on this Toolbar button.

Changing the Network Settings

Want to change your computer's workgroup name? Need to redo your logon password because your kids have hacked their way onto your system? For these and many other kinds of network alterations, follow these steps:

1. Start Control Panel by double-clicking on the **Control Panel** icon in Program Manager's **Main** group.

2. Double-click on the **Networks** icon. Control Panel displays the Microsoft Windows Network dialog box.

3. Make your adjustments to the following settings, as necessary:

   Computer Name   Your computer's workgroup name.

   Workgroup   The name of the workgroup your computer is part of.

   Comment   This text appears beside the computer name in the Connect Network Drive and Connect Network Printer dialog boxes.

   Default Logon Name   The logon name that appears when you log on to the network.

   Log Off   Select this button to log off the network. If, as described below, you elect not to log on automatically when you start Windows for Workgroups, this button will say Log On, and you can use it to log on to the network.

   Startup   This button displays the Startup Settings dialog box. You can ignore most of this stuff, but you might want to deactivate the Log On at Startup check box. This prevents Windows for Workgroups from prompting you to log on to the network.

   Password   Select this button to change your logon password. In the Change Logon Password dialog box, enter your old password in the **Old Password** text box, enter your new password in the New Password text box, and then re-enter it in the Confirm New Password text box. Select **OK** when you're done.

4. Select **OK**. Depending on the changes you've made, Windows for Workgroups might tell you to restart your computer to put them into effect. If so, select the **Restart Computer** button.

The Least You Need to Know

This chapter gave you.a very brief introduction to Windows for Workgroups. Here's a review:

- ☞ Windows for Workgroups has a revamped File Manager that includes a customizable Toolbar, and several new menu commands.

- ☞ There's also a much-improved version of Print Manager that has a Toolbar, a status bar, and a number of new menus and commands that make it easier to work with your printers and print jobs.

- ☞ A workgroup is a small group of connected computers that can share resources such as applications, files, and printers.

- ☞ To share a directory with your fellow workgroupies, select the Share **As** command from File Manager's **D**isk menu.

- ☞ To connect to a shared directory on another computer, select the **D**isk menu's **C**onnect **N**etwork Drive command.

- ☞ For printers, select the **S**hare Printer command in Print Manager's **P**rinter menu to share your printer. To use a shared printer on another machine, select the **P**rinter menu's **C**onnect Network Printer command.

- ☞ To change network settings such as your computer's workgroup name, select the **Network** icon in Control Panel.

Chapter 26
@#$*%! Troubleshooting Common Application Problems

In This Chapter

- ☛ Handling Program Manager woes
- ☛ Common File Manager complaints
- ☛ Tackling low-memory mishaps
- ☛ Avoiding General Protection Fault errors
- ☛ Dealing with various application aberrations

One of the biggest problems with computers is that it's so easy to grow dependent on the things. Most people, after they've used one for a little while, wonder how they ever did without it (I know this may seem hard to believe for some of you, but it really does happen). So it's all the more traumatic when our once-trusty software sidekicks start doing strange and unpredictable things. Suddenly, in true codependent fashion, we find we can no longer function without our programs at our side. Write a letter by hand? How primitive!

So, in an effort to minimize the trauma associated with software problems, this chapter looks at a few of the ways your programs can go bad, and offers nontechnical, relatively pain-free solutions.

Disclaimer Dept.

It just isn't possible in one or two chapters to come up with a list of Windows problems that's even remotely comprehensive. If you're having trouble and you don't see a solution here, you still have a couple of options:

☞ Pick up a book dedicated to Windows troubleshooting. Can I recommend one? As a matter of fact, I can. Alpha Books also publishes a book called *Windows Woes* (written by some geek named Paul McFedries).

☞ Call Microsoft Technical Support at (206) 637-7098.

Program Manager Problems

Back in Chapter 9, I called Program Manager "your faithful Windows servant." Faithful's a good word because Program Manager—unlike a lot of other Windows applications—rarely causes a fuss. But when it *does* act weird, it's usually a big problem—because it means you can't do anything else. This section takes a look at the few things that can go wrong with Program Manager.

You've lost all your Program Manager groups. Through some disaster (such as powering down your computer before exiting Windows, or maybe even a virus) you may wake up one day and find that you've lost all your Program Manager groups. Instead of recreating the groups yourself, you can get Windows to reconstruct the original program groups (Main, Accessories, Games, and so on) for you. All you do is select the **Run** command from Program Manager's File menu, type **SETUP /P** in the Run dialog box's Command Line text box, and then select **OK**. Windows will go ahead and restore the original groups.

Your groups and icons aren't the same as when you last exited Windows. When you exit most Windows applications, they're smart enough to ask you whether or not you want to save your changes. Program Manager doesn't give you a choice; it's all or nothing. Your changes are either saved *every* time you exit, or they never are. If you want your changes saved, pull down the Options menu, and take a look at the Save Settings on Exit command. If there's no check mark beside it (to indicate that it's active), go ahead and select it.

A more common scenario is when you want a default group arrangement to appear every time you start Windows. Here's how you set this up:

1. Arrange your groups the way you'll want them to appear whenever you start Windows.

2. Hold down the **Shift** key, pull down the File menu, and select the Exit Windows command. This is just a shortcut method for saving your Program Manager settings; it doesn't actually exit Windows.

3. Pull down the **Options** menu and deactivate the **Save Settings on** Exit command. (The command should now have no check mark beside it.)

That's all there is to it. By deactivating the **Save Settings on Exit** command, Program Manager will always load the default settings you saved earlier.

When you try to load an application, Windows reports that it "Cannot find file *x* **or one of its components."** Back in Chapter 11, "Program Manager: Creating New Groups and Items," I showed you how to add new icons to Program Manager's groups. You'll recall that Windows uses the text in the Command Line box (in the Program Item Properties dialog box) to find the file that starts the application. The *x* in the error message just cited is the Command Line text, and the error means that Windows can't locate the file you specified. To solve the problem, open the icon's Program Item Properties dialog box (by highlighting the icon and pressing **Alt+Enter**), and then edit the Command Line text as follows:

☞ Make sure the filename is spelled correctly.

☞ Add the appropriate extension to the filename (usually .EXE), if it doesn't have one.

☞ Add the drive and directory where the file resides (e.g., **C:\WP\WP51.EXE**).

☞ If you're not sure about all this, select the **Browse** button and choose the file from the Browse dialog box that appears.

File Manager Foul-ups

Once you get the hang of File Manager, you'll probably find it's one of the Windows applications you use the most. But of course, the more you use it, the better chance there is of some operation going up in flames. The next few sections take you through some common File Manager complaints.

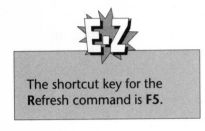

The shortcut key for the Refresh command is **F5**.

File Manager Isn't Showing You the Correct Information

Sometimes what File Manager *thinks* is in a directory or on a disk is not what is actually there. (Short attention span, I guess.) You can give File Manager a poke in the ribs by selecting the **Win**dow menu's **R**efresh command.

You Have Problems Trying to Copy, Move, Delete, or Rename a File on a Floppy Disk

As explained in Chapter 13, "File Finagling," File Manager makes it easy to copy or move files to and from a floppy disk. However, there are some situations where you might run into problems:

Is the disk full? File Manager, rightly so, won't allow you to copy or move a file to a disk unless there is sufficient space. If the disk is full, delete any unneeded files, or use another disk.

Is the disk write-protected? When a floppy disk is *write-protected*, it means you can't copy or move files to the disk or delete or rename files on the disk. Here's how to tell whether or not a disk is write-protected:

- When a 5 1/4-inch disk is not write-protected, you'll see a small notch in the side of the disk. If the notch is covered with tape, simply remove the tape to disable the write-protection.

- For a 3 1/2-inch disk, write-protection is controlled by a small, movable tab on the back of the disk. If the tab is toward the edge of the disk, then the disk is write-protected. To disable the write-protection, slide the tab away from the edge of the disk.

File Manager Won't Let You Copy a Disk

Here are a few solutions if you're having trouble copying a floppy disk:

Make sure the disk is inserted properly. If you're using 3 1/2-inch disks, make sure they're inserted all the way into the drive. If you're using 5 1/4-inch disks, make sure the drive door is closed.

Is the destination disk write-protected? File Manager won't copy files to a disk that is write-protected. Check the disk and disable the write-protection as described earlier in this chapter.

Are the two disks the same type? File Manager's Disk Copy feature is designed to work only with two disks that have the same capacity and are of the same type. (I explained disk capacity and disk types back in Chapter 15, "Disk Driving.") If you have two different types of disk drives, then you can still copy a disk. Simply use the same drive as both the source and destination.

Windows Tells You There Is "Insufficient Memory" to Run an Application

Memory is to Windows what money is to an investor. The more you have, the more things you can do, but if you run out, well, you're out of luck. This section presents a few solutions for those times when memory is scarce.

Close down what you don't need. The most obvious (but the least convenient) solution is to close any running applications that you really don't need. The bigger the application, the more memory you'll save.

Delete the contents of the Clipboard. When you cut or copy a selection in a Windows application, the program stores the data in an area called the Clipboard. If you're working with only a few lines of text, this area remains fairly small. Cutting or copying a graphic image, however, can increase the size of the Clipboard to several hundred kilobytes or more. If you've run out of memory, a large Clipboard may be the problem. To release this memory, try one of the following methods:

☛ If you have an application running, highlight a small section of text (a single character or word will do) and select Copy from the Edit menu. This replaces the current Clipboard with a much smaller one.

☛ In Program Manager, select the Clipboard Viewer icon from the Main group. When the Clipboard Viewer window appears, select the Edit menu's Delete command.

Release some "system resources." *System resources* are two small (64K) memory areas that Windows uses to keep track of things like the position and size of open windows, dialog boxes, and your desktop configuration (wallpaper, etc.). You can have megabytes of free memory but you'll still get "Insufficient Memory" errors if you run out of system resources! How can you tell if your system resources are getting low? In Program Manager, pull down the **Help** menu and select the About Program Manager command. As you can see below, the About Program Manager dialog box tells you what percentage of the system resource areas is still available. Problems develop when this number drops below 20%.

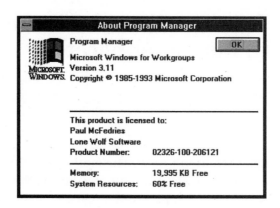

The About Program Manager dialog box tells you what percentage of system resources is still available.

Here are a few tips for preserving your system resources:

☛ In Program Manager, don't open any program groups you don't need. In fact, many people reduce their total number of program groups to one or two. See Chapter 11, "Playing with Program Manager," to learn how to delete program groups.

☛ When working with Windows applications, don't leave open any unnecessary document windows. Also, turn off features such as status bars, rulers, and icon bars if you don't use them.

☛ When working with DOS applications, run them full-screen instead of in a window.

☛ Turn off the wallpaper on your desktop. Chapter 17, "Have It Your Way: Customizing Windows," tells you all about Windows wallpaper.

☛ Upgrade to Windows 3.1 if you haven't done so already. The new version uses system resources more intelligently than previous versions.

Load larger applications first. Because of the way Windows uses memory, you can often start more programs if you load your larger Windows applications before your smaller ones.

Upgrade to at least DOS 5. DOS versions 5 and later include two important new features that enable you to reclaim large chunks of conventional memory. These features are:

☛ The ability to load most of DOS itself into an area of memory called the *High Memory Area*.

☛ The ability to load memory-resident programs and device drivers into an area called the *Upper Memory Area*.

Depending on the setup of your system, these features can give you back dozens of kilobytes of conventional memory. (Another shameless plug: see my book *At Home with MS-DOS* to learn how to use these DOS features.) By the way, DOS 6 includes a program called MemMaker that makes all this memory mumbo-jumbo a breeze. To use it, exit Windows, type **MEMMAKER** and press **Enter**, and then follow the instructions on the screen.

Shell out the bucks to buy more memory. The ultimate way to beat memory problems, of course, is simply to add more memory to your system. (Although, as you've seen, you still need to watch that your system resources don't get too low.) Unfortunately, memory prices have risen over the past couple of years, so adding any more than a megabyte or two may break your budget. If you do decide to take the plunge, though, contact your computer manufacturer to find out the best kind of memory to add to your system.

Dealing with the Dastardly General Protection Fault

If you use Windows regularly, you're bound to come across the occasional General Protection Fault (GPF) or its cousin from Windows 3.0, the Unrecoverable Application Error (UAE). These GPFs are particularly nasty errors in that they can trash data and hang your machine. Why do they occur? Well, applications, like people, have their own "personal space" in your computer's memory. GPFs occur, basically, when one application invades the personal space of another.

What to Do When a GPF Rears Its Ugly Head

When Windows detects a General Protection Fault, all sorts of internal bells and alarms go off, and depending on how badly things are messed up, one of three things will happen:

☛ You'll see a dialog box telling you that a GPF has occurred. In some cases, this dialog box only has a **Close** button. When you select this button, Windows nixes the clumsy oaf of an application that caused the problem. If you're lucky, the dialog box will have both a **Close** and an **Ignore** button. In this case, try selecting **Ignore** a few times to get back into the application. If you're successful, immediately save your work and get the heck out of there.

☛ If your system locks up, press **Ctrl+Alt+Delete** and wait a few seconds. If the problem isn't too severe, you'll see the following message:

> **System has either become busy or has become unstable**
> **- Press any key to return to Windows and wait**
> **- Press CTRL+ALT+DEL again to restart your computer**
> **(all unsaved information will be lost)**

You can sometimes press any key and wait things out, but more often than not you'll have to bail out altogether (by pressing **Ctrl+Alt+Delete** to display the above message, and then pressing **Ctrl+Alt+Delete** again to reboot).

☞ If your system locks up with a particularly ugly GPF, pressing **Ctrl+Alt+Delete** brings up the following message:

> **This Windows application has stopped responding to the system**
> **- Press ESC to cancel and return to Windows**
> **- Press ENTER to close this application (all unsaved information will be lost)**
> **- Press CTRL+ALT+DEL again to restart your computer (all unsaved information will be lost)**

If Windows managed to intercept the rogue program in time, you can usually press **Esc** to return to the application, save your work, and then exit. Otherwise, press **Enter** to shut down the application. As a last resort, you can press **Ctrl+Alt+Delete** to reboot and start over again.

Even if you manage to recover from a GPF, you're not out of the woods yet. Your system is probably unstable, so you should always exit Windows and reboot your machine.

How to Avoid Those Nasty GPFs

This section looks at a number of ways to prevent GPFs (or UAEs if you're still using Windows 3.0) from happening:

Upgrade your DOS version. GPFs can result from using the wrong version of DOS. You need to check two things:

☞ Are you using the version of DOS that was designed for your computer? Some companies (such as IBM and Compaq) remake DOS in their own image, so to speak, for use on their machines. If you have such a system, make sure you're using the appropriate DOS version.

☞ If your computer uses generic DOS, you need at least version 3.1 (although version 3.3 is a more realistic minimum). If you're using version 4, I'd strongly suggest moving up to a later version (preferably version 6.22).

To find out which version of DOS you're using, open a DOS window, type **VER**, and press **Enter**.

Check to see if Windows was set up for the wrong computer type. Part of the Windows setup involves specifying the computer type. (This may have been done automatically by the Setup program if you chose the Express installation.) You may need to rerun the Setup program to change this setting. Here are the steps to follow:

1. Exit Windows.

2. In the WINDOWS directory, type **SETUP** and press **Enter**.

3. Use the up arrow key to highlight the **Computer** setting, and then press **Enter**. Setup displays a list of computers (see below).

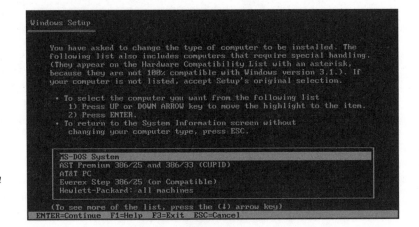

Use this Setup screen to select the type of computer you have.

4. If applicable, select your computer type from the list and then press **Enter**. Otherwise, press **F3** twice to exit Setup.

5. Press **Enter** to accept the new configuration, and then follow the prompts on the screen.

If you're running an application written for Windows version 2, upgrade to a newer version. Programs designed to run under Windows version 2 will not run properly in versions 3.0 or 3.1. Upgrade to a newer version of the program, if possible.

Use ScanDisk or Chkdsk to weed out disk errors. Corrupted or damaged files on your hard disk are another common source of GPFs. To check for (and fix) these problems, exit to DOS, type **SCANDISK /AUTOFIX / NOSAVE** (if you have DOS 6.2 or higher) or **CHKDSK /F** (if you have an earlier version of DOS), and then press **Enter**. In the latter case, if DOS asks if you want to save some files, press **N** to select No.

Keep an eye on your system resources. You can bet your bottom dollar that a GPF is just around the corner if your system resources head below the 20% mark. Keep an eye on them (as described earlier in this chapter) if you're working with large applications.

Use Dr. Watson to see if a single application is causing the problem. Many GPFs are the result of bug-ridden applications that have run amok. If you have one of these sloppily programmed rogues, complain long and loud to the developer and demand a (bug-free) upgrade.

How can you tell if a single program is causing all your GPFs? Well, if Windows always crashes while you're performing the same operation in the same application, then you can pretty well narrow down the cause. If the crashes seem to be more random, then you need to do a little more legwork. Fortunately, Microsoft has made tracking down the source of GPFs much easier by including a utility called Dr. Watson with Windows 3.1.

Dr. Watson is a memory-resident utility that only kicks into life when a GPF occurs. Dr. Watson creates a text file (it's called DRWATSON.LOG and you'll find it in your main Windows directory) that records all the technical details about Windows' state at the time of the crash. It will also ask you what you were doing when the crash occurred and add this to the log. Although the information recorded by Dr. Watson is way too technical for our purposes, the good people in your application's tech support department will know what to do with it.

TECHNO NERD TEACHES

When you create your Dr. Watson program item, you enter **DRWATSON.EXE** in the Command Line text box of the Program Item Properties dialog box.

The best way to use Dr. Watson is to have it running in memory at all times. Most people, therefore, create an icon for Dr. Watson in their Startup group.

Windows reports that an application has "violated system integrity." This error is a more serious version of the General Protection Fault. In this case, your only option is to reboot and start over. Use the solutions described earlier. In particular, make sure you check your hard disk for file errors (by running ScanDisk or Chkdsk).

The Least You Need to Know

This chapter gave you some solutions to some common Windows problems. Here are the highlights:

☞ If, by some mishap, you lose all your Program Manager groups, select **R**un from the **F**ile menu, and type **SETUP /P** in the **C**ommand Line text box. When you select **OK**, Windows reconstructs your original groups.

☞ Press **F5** in File Manager to update the contents of a window.

☞ If an application is dead in the water, press **Ctrl+Alt+Delete** to let Windows know. Press **Enter** to shut down the application and return to Windows.

☞ If you don't have enough memory to run an application, you can try things like closing other programs, reducing your use of system resources, or deleting the contents of the Clipboard.

Chapter 27

Miscellaneous Pains in the You-Know-What

In This Chapter

- ☛ Solutions for installation troubles
- ☛ Mouse and keyboard conundrums
- ☛ Patching up printing problems
- ☛ Dealing with video woes
- ☛ A veritable cornucopia of computer complaints (and their solutions)

I wish I could tell you that applications were the only thing that can go kaput in Windows. Unfortunately, there's a whole host of accidents waiting to happen, and you're bound to be tripped up by at least some of them. This chapter looks at the most common problems that fall into this miscellaneous category, including woes related to Windows installation, the mouse and keyboard, printing, and your video display.

Installation Impediments

Windows' installation program is easier than most, and it usually goes pretty smoothly. If, however, you have some unusual software running on your machine—or a hardware combination that Windows hasn't seen before—you could run into problems. Here are a few solutions to try if Windows' installation program is hanging, or it plops you back out to the DOS prompt:

A computer **hangs** when it locks up tight as a drum and no amount of keyboard banging, mouse clicking, or verbal abuse will make it do anything.

Remove all memory-resident programs. By far the most common cause of installation hangups is a clash between Setup and a *terminate-and-stay-resident* (TSR) program. Try starting the installation with the command **SETUP /T**. This tells Setup to check for conflicting TSRs. If conflicts are found, Setup will give you instructions on how to proceed.

Turn off Setup's hardware-detection scheme. If TSRs aren't the problem, then Setup may be choking during its "auto-detection" phase. During this phase, the program tries to save you some time by automatically detecting the type of hardware on your system. Unfortunately, if Setup makes a mistake your computer will hang. (This is especially true if Setup chooses the wrong option for your video display.) To turn off auto-detection, use the command **SETUP /I** to begin the installation. Setup will display a standard configuration. Select the settings appropriate for your computer, and then continue with the installation.

If Setup always hangs when it switches to Windows Mode, try a different display driver. Setup is actually two programs in one. The first program (called DOS Mode Setup) analyzes your system and installs the files needed to start Windows. The second program (Windows Mode Setup) actually runs in Windows; it installs the rest of the Windows files, and configures applications such as Program Manager. If Setup fails when switching from DOS Mode to Windows Mode, then it's likely Setup is using an incorrect display driver. Use the command **SETUP /I** to prevent Setup from automatically selecting a display driver. When Setup displays the system settings (as described earlier), select the correct display option for your system. If you're not sure about this, select a generic driver (such as VGA or EGA). If the problem persists, contact the manufacturer of the video board and ask them about it. They may need to send you a new video driver that is compatible with Windows 3.1.

If you can't find a setting appropriate for your hardware, contact either the manufacturer or Microsoft for a driver. Windows communicates with your hardware using a small chunk of software called a *device driver*. If your hardware doesn't appear in the Setup lists, then you need to get the appropriate driver. The best source to contact is the manufacturer of the device. Otherwise, Microsoft themselves maintain an extensive device-driver library. While you're waiting for the driver to arrive, you may still be able to install Windows by selecting generic devices from the hardware lists in Setup. Here are some suggestions:

For this . . .	Select this:
Computer	MS-DOS System
Display	VGA or EGA
Mouse	Microsoft
Keyboard	Enhanced 101 or 102 key US
Printer	Generic/Text

Mouse Mishaps

A mouse makes Windows so much easier to use that many people never learn how to work the program from the keyboard. This can present real problems, though, if your mouse decides to go wacko on you. (I once saw an otherwise-composed individual panic when his mouse quit on him during a Windows presentation, and he didn't have a clue about Windows keyboard techniques.) The next few sections show you how to respond to various mouse problems.

Your Mouse Pointer Is Doing Weird Things

Some people would say that the mouse pointer *always* does weird things, but some of the weirdness may not be your fault. If you find your mouse isn't responding, or if the pointer is racing all over the screen, it's usually easy to fix:

Is the mouse plugged in? Yeah, I know, this seems pretty simple-minded, but the Number One rule when troubleshooting any device is to first ask, "Is it plugged in?" You'd be surprised how often the answer is a sheepish "No."

Try a mouse pad with a firmer feel. A nice, firm mouse pad is essential for consistent mouse movements. If the pad is too soft, the roller sinks in too deep, which can cause it to stick.

Have you cleaned the little guy lately? If your mouse is behaving errati-cally, all you may need to do is clean its insides. A well-used mouse can take in quite a collection of dust, crumbs, and other alien substances which can play havoc on its delicate constitution. Your mouse documenta-tion should tell you the proper cleaning procedure. If your mouse has a roller ball, you can also follow these steps:

1. Remove the cover on the bottom of the mouse.

2. Remove the roller ball.

3. Using a cotton swab with isopropyl alcohol or water, clean the rollers and other contact areas. (I also find a pair of tweezers is handy for pulling out the mini dust bunnies that accumulate inside the rollers.)

4. Wipe off any excess liquid, and then replace the ball and cover.

If all else fails . . . You can often help your mouse regain its sanity by simply exiting and restarting Windows. If this still doesn't work, try exiting Windows and rebooting your computer.

Windows Doesn't Always Respond to Your Double-Clicks

If Windows ignores some of your double-clicks, you likely need to slow down the *double-click speed*. Refer back to Chapter 17, "Have It Your Way: Customizing Windows," to learn how to do this.

You Have Trouble Seeing the Mouse Pointer

If you use a laptop or if your eyesight isn't what it used to be, then you may be having trouble keeping track of the little mouse pointer. You may be able to make things a bit better by telling Windows to display "trails" as you move the mouse. You can find complete instructions in Chapter 17.

The Mouse Pointer Moves Too Slowly or Too Quickly

The speed at which the pointer moves across the screen is governed by the *mouse tracking speed*. If this just doesn't feel right, you can change this setting to one that's more comfortable. Once again, check out Chapter 17 to get the nitty-gritty.

Correcting Keyboard Kinks

Although Windows' interface is generally easier to use with a mouse, a keyboard is still a necessity. And while the vast majority of keyboard problems are hardware-related, there are a few problems you can take care of yourself.

Your Keyboard Is Too Slow

Back in Chapter 17, "Have It Your Way: Customizing Windows," I showed you how to use the Control Panel to set your keyboard's delay and repeat rate. If your keyboard feels too slow, use the techniques I outlined in that chapter to decrease the delay and increase the repeat rate.

Your Keyboard's F11 and F12 Keys Don't Work

If Windows is set up with a keyboard driver for an "AT-style" or "XT-style" (84- or 86-key) keyboard, then you won't be able to use the F11 and F12 keys. To fix this, follow these steps:

1. In Program Manager, open the **Main** group and select the **Windows Setup** icon. The Windows Setup window appears.

2. Pull down the Options menu and select Change System Settings. Setup displays the Change System Settings dialog box, as shown below.

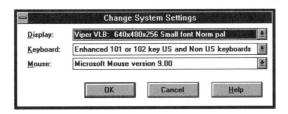

Use the Change System Settings dialog box to select a device driver.

3. In the Keyboard drop-down list, select the **Enhanced 101 or 102 key US and Non US keyboards** option.

4. Select **OK**. A dialog box appears, telling you that you need to restart Windows.

5. Select the Restart Windows button to restart Windows.

Your Numeric Keypad Numbers Don't Work

Most of the keys on a numeric keypad have two types of characters: a number and a navigation symbol (the arrow keys, Home, End, Page Up, and Page Down). The Num Lock key is used to toggle a numeric keypad between these two types of keys. If you can't get any numbers, simply press **Num Lock** to activate them. Most keyboards also have a NUM LOCK indicator that lights up when Num Lock is turned on.

Printing Perplexities

As I explained back in Chapter 18, "Hard Copy: Windows Printing Basics," Windows makes printing easy because your applications get to pass their printing bucks to Windows, which then handles all the dirty work. This, unfortunately, doesn't mean that printing is trouble-free. If you're having problems getting your printer to print, the next few sections tell you what to do.

Windows Reports That the Printer Is "Offline or Not Selected"

Windows reports this error when it can't communicate with the printer. Here are a couple of solutions.

Make sure your printer is powered up and on-line. Before starting any print jobs, check the following:

- ☞ Your printer is powered up.
- ☞ It's on-line (this means that it's ready to receive output). Most printers have an "On-line" button you can select.
- ☞ The cable connections are secure.
- ☞ There's paper in the printer.
- ☞ There's no paper jam.

Tell Windows to be more patient. Depending on the print job, some printers will take an extra long time to process the data that Windows sends it. If they take *too* long, Windows will assume that the printer is "off-line" and you'll get an error. To fix this, follow these steps:

1. Load Control Panel, and select the **Printers** icon. Control Panel displays the Printers dialog box.

2. In the Installed Printers list, highlight the printer you're using, and then select the Connect button to display the Connect dialog box.

3. Increase the number in the Transmission Retry box, as shown below (the maximum value is 999 seconds).

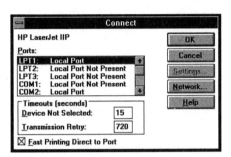

Use Control Panel's Connect dialog box to tell Windows to wait longer before giving a printer-error message.

4. Select **OK** to return to the Printers dialog box, and then select **Close** to return to Control Panel.

You Can't Select the Print Command from an Application's File Menu

Most Windows applications that can print include a Print command in their File menu. If this command is "dimmed" (that is, it appears in a light gray text, and you can't highlight it), it means you have no printer installed in Windows. Skip back to Chapter 18, "Hard Copy: Windows Printing Basics," to learn how to install a printer.

Curing Video Ills

Your video display may be the most important component of your system since you're forced to look at it for hours on end every day. This is especially true for us Windows users, since one of Windows' most appealing features is its good-looking, graphical interface. But the fanciest interface in the world isn't worth a hill of beans if your display is displaying garbage. If you're having video trouble, the following sections show you how to adjust your set.

Dealing with Distorted Displays

If your display goes snaky on you, try any of these solutions to bring things back to normal:

Reinstall the video driver. One of the most common causes of display problems is a corrupt video driver. (In this case, the "driver" is the program that translates the otherwise-incomprehensible junk inside your computer into something readable on your screen.) You can usually fix the problem by reinstalling the driver. Since your display is distorted, you can't use the Setup program within Windows itself. Instead, follow these steps:

1. Press **Alt+F4** and then **Enter** to exit Windows (you may need to do this several times if you have any applications running).

2. Change to your main Windows directory. (You do this by typing **CD\WINDOWS** and pressing **Enter**.)

3. Type **SETUP** and press **Enter**. The Windows Setup screen appears, as shown in the following figure.

```
Windows Setup

     If your computer or network appears on the Hardware Compatibility List
     with an asterisk next to it, press F1 before continuing.

     System Information
          Computer:          MS-DOS System
          Display:           VGA
          Mouse:             Microsoft Mouse version 9.00
          Keyboard:          Enhanced 101 or 102 key US and Non US keyboards
          Keyboard Layout:   US
          Language:          English (American)
          Codepage:          English (437)
          Network:           No Network Installed

          Complete Changes:  Accept the configuration shown above.

     To change a system setting, press the UP or DOWN ARROW key to
     move the highlight to the setting you want to change. Then press
     ENTER to see alternatives for that item. When you have finished
     changing your settings, select the "Complete Changes" option
     to quit Setup.

   ENTER=Continue  F1=Help  F3=Exit
```

If you can't see what's going on in Windows, use the DOS version of the Setup program to set things right.

4. Use the up arrow key to highlight the **Display** setting, and then press **Enter**. A list of display drivers appears.

5. Highlight the item you want, and then press **Enter**. (If you're not sure which one to pick, **VGA** is a safe choice.) Depending on the item you choose, Setup may ask you if you want to use the current driver, or it may ask you to insert a disk.

6. Follow the instructions on-screen until you return to the Windows Setup screen.

7. Press **Enter** to return to the DOS prompt.

8. Type **WIN** and press **Enter** to restart Windows.

Switch to a lower-resolution driver. If you're having problems with, say, a SuperVGA driver, use Setup (the DOS version) to switch to a VGA driver. If your display is okay with the lower-resolution driver, then you need to contact the manufacturer for an updated driver for the higher resolution.

Exit and restart Windows. Sometimes a display problem is nothing more than a temporary mental lapse on Windows' part. Try exiting Windows (press **Alt+F4** and **Enter**) and restarting. If this still doesn't work, exit Windows, turn off your machine, and then turn it back on again.

The Least You Need to Know

This chapter took you on a tour of some miscellaneous Windows woes. Here's a recap:

☞   If your computer hangs during installation, try running Setup with either the command **SETUP /T** (to check for memory conflicts) or the command **SETUP /I** (to turn off hardware detection).

☞   If your mouse is acting strange, it may need cleaning. Also, check that it's properly plugged in. Other mouse problems can often be resolved just by customizing the mouse settings (double-click speed, tracking speed, etc.).

☞   If your keyboard feels too slow, use Control Panel to adjust the delay and repeat rate to more comfortable levels.

☞   If Windows won't print, make sure the printer is plugged in, powered up, and on-line. You can also use Control Panel to increase the Transmission Retry setting to a more reasonable level.

☞   If your display has gone snaky on you, exit Windows, run the DOS version of Setup, and choose the VGA driver.

This page unintentionally left blank.

Speak Like a Geek: The Complete Archive

286, 386, 486   These are the aficionado's cool short forms for the *80286*, *80386*, and *80486* microprocessors. The microprocessor is the head honcho chip inside your computer that controls the whole shebang. Most people describe it as the "brain" of the computer, so you can think of these numbers as your computer's IQ. In that sense, a 386 machine is "smarter" than a 286, but a 486 is the genius of the group (at least it was until the Pentium came along). To get the most out of DOS programs in Windows, you really should have a 386 or better computer. See *386 enhanced mode*.

386 enhanced mode   Fancy-shmancy mode that lets Windows do things like DOS multitasking, running DOS programs in a window, and more. Windows runs in this mode automatically if you have a 386 or better computer.

accessory   One of the mini-applications that comes free with Windows. For information on using some of the accessories, check out Chapter 20, "The Write Stuff: Word Processing with Write," Chapter 21, "Nurturing Your Inner Child with Paintbrush," and Chapter 22, "Windows' Free Lunch: The Accessories."

active window   The window you're currently slaving away in. You can tell a window is active by looking at its title bar: if the bar shows white letters on a dark background, the window is active. (Inactive windows show dark letters on a white background, unless you changed your colors.)

application   Software that accomplishes a specific, practical task. It's the same thing as a program.

application window   A window containing a running application, such as Program Manager or Write.

ASCII text file   A file that uses only the American Standard Code for Information Interchange character set (which is just techno-lingo for the characters you see on your keyboard).

Background mode   A mode where a program continues performing a task "behind the scenes." Typical background tasks are spreadsheet recalculations, document printing, and modem file transfers.

boot   Computer geeks won't tell you to start your computer, they'll tell you to *boot* it. This doesn't mean you should punt your monitor across the room. The term *booting* comes from the phrase "pulling oneself up by one's own bootstraps," which just means that your computer can load everything it needs to operate properly without any help from the likes of you and me.

byte   Computerese for a single character of information. So, for example, the phrase *This phrase is 28 bytes long* is, yes, 28 bytes long (you count the spaces, too).

cascade   A cool way of arranging windows so that they overlap each other but you can still see each window's title bar.

cascade menu   A menu that appears when you select certain pull-down menu commands.

character spacing   The amount of space that a font reserves for each character. In a *monospaced font*, every character gets the same amount of space, regardless of its true width. In a *proportional font*, the space allotted to each letter varies according to the width of the letter.

check box   A square-shaped switch that toggles an option in a dialog box on or off. The option is toggled on when an X appears in the box.

click   To quickly press and release the left mouse button.

Clipboard   A utility that holds data temporarily during cut-and-paste operations.

command button   A rectangular doohickey (usually found in dialog boxes) that, when chosen, runs whatever command is spelled out on its label.

commands   The options you see in a pull-down menu. You use these commands to tell the application what you want it to do next.

Control menu   A menu common to every Windows window that you use to manipulate various features of the window. You activate the Control menu by clicking on the Control-menu box in the upper left corner of the window, or by pressing **Alt+Spacebar** (for an application window) or **Alt+hyphen** (for a document window).

Control-menu box   The icon for the *Control menu*. It appears as a square in the upper left corner of a window.

data files   The files used by you or your programs. See also *program files*.

delay   The amount of time it takes for a second character to appear when you press and hold down a key.

desktop   A metaphor for the Windows screen. Starting a Windows application is similar to putting a folder full of papers (the application window) on your desk. To do some work, you pull some papers out of the folder (the document windows) and place them on the desktop. The Windows desktop metaphor is so prevalent that most people (geeks and otherwise) refer to the Windows screen as simply the *desktop*.

destination disk   The disk to which you're copying another disk (which is called the *source disk*).

device driver   Small program that controls the way a device (such as a mouse) works with your system.

dialog boxes   Ubiquitous windows that pop up on the screen to ask you for information, or to seek confirmation of an action you requested (or sometimes just to say "Hi").

directory   A storage location on your hard disk for keeping related files together. If your hard disk is like a house, a directory is like a room inside the house. See also *subdirectory*.

directory window   A File Manager window.

disk   See *floppy disk*.

document window   A window opened within an application. Document windows hold whatever you're working on in the application.

double-click   To quickly press and release the left mouse button *twice* in succession.

double-click speed   The maximum amount of time between mouse clicks that Windows will allow for a double-click to be registered.

drag   To press and *hold down* the left mouse button and then move the mouse.

drag-and-drop   Technique that lets you run commands (such as Copy) or applications simply by dragging files or icons to strategic screen areas.

drop-down list box   A list box that normally shows only a single item, but when selected, displays a list of options.

extension   The three-character ending to a DOS file name. The extension is separated from the main name by a period.

file   An organized unit of information inside your computer. If you think of your hard disk as a house, then files can be either servants (your applications) or things (data used by you or by a program).

floppy disk   A portable storage medium that consists of a flexible disk protected by a plastic case. Floppy disks are available in a variety of sizes and capacities.

focus   The window that has the attention of the operating system (that is, Windows).

font   A character set of a specific typeface, type style, and type size.

font management program   A software program that scales font characters automatically to the size you select.

formatting   The process of setting up a disk so the computer can read information from it and write information to it.

fritterware   Any software that causes you to fritter away time fiddling with its various bells and whistles.

group   A window within Program Manager that contains a collection of program items.

hard disk   The main storage area inside your computer. In the computer house analogy, the hard disk is equivalent to the inside of the house.

icons   The little pictures that Windows uses to represent programs and files.

insertion point cursor   The blinking vertical bar you see inside a text box and a word processing application, such as Write. It tells you where the next character you type will appear.

kilobyte   1,024 bytes. To be cool, always abbreviate this to "K."

list box   A small window that displays a list of items such as file names or directories.

maximize   To increase the size of a window to its largest extent. A maximized application window fills the entire screen. A maximized document window fills the entire application window.

megabyte   1,024 kilobytes or 1,048,576 bytes. The cognoscenti write this as "M" or "MB" and pronounce it "meg."

memory-resident program   A program that stays in memory once it is loaded, and works "behind the scenes." The program normally responds only to a specific event (such as the deletion of a file) or a key combination. Also called *terminate-and-stay-resident* (TSR) programs.

menu bar   The horizontal bar on the second line of an application window. The menu bar contains the application's pull-down menus.

microprocessor   See *286, 386, 486*.

minimize   To reduce a window to an icon.

multitasking   The ability to run several programs at the same time. It simply means that Windows, unlike some people you may know, can walk and chew gum at the same time.

option buttons   Dialog box options that appear as small circles in groups of two or more. Only one option from a group can be chosen.

peer-to-peer   A network where all the computers have their own applications and data, and each machine can access the resources on the other machines in the network. Windows for Workgroups is a peer-to-peer networking scheme.

point   Move the mouse pointer so that it rests on a specific screen location.

port   The connection that you use to plug in the cable from a device, such as a mouse or printer.

program group   See *group*.

program item   An application icon within a program group.

program files   The files that run your programs. See also *Data files*.

pull-down menus   Hidden menus that you open from an application's menu bar to access the commands and features of the application.

RAM   Stands for random-access memory. The memory in your computer that DOS uses to run your programs.

repeat rate   After the initial delay, the rate at which characters appear when you press and hold down a key.

scalable font   A font where each character exists as an outline that is scaled to different sizes. Examples of scalable fonts that come with Windows are Arial, Courier New, and Times New Roman. Scalable fonts require a software program called a *type manager* to do the scaling. Windows 3.1 comes with its own type manager: TrueType.

scroll bar   A bar that appears at the bottom or on the right of a window whenever the window is too small to display all of its contents.

shell   Applications, such as Program Manager, that insulate you from the inner workings of your computer.

subdirectory   A directory within a directory.

system resources   Two small (64K) memory areas that Windows uses to keep track of things like the position and size of open windows, dialog boxes and your desktop configuration (wallpaper and so on).

text box   A screen area you use to type in text information, such as a description or a file name.

text editor   A program that lets you edit files that are text-only. The Windows text editor is called NotePad.

title bar   The area on the top line of a window that displays the window's title.

tracking speed   How quickly the mouse pointer moves across the screen when you move the mouse on its pad.

TrueType   A *font management program* that comes with Windows 3.1.

type size   A measure of the height of a font. Type size is measured in *points*; there are 72 points in an inch.

type style   Character attributes, such as regular, bold, and italic. Other type styles (often called type *effects*) are underlining and strikeout characters.

typeface   A distinctive graphic design of letters, numbers, and other symbols.

window   A rectangular screen area in which Windows displays applications and documents.

word wrap   A word processor feature that automatically starts a new line as your typing reaches the end of the current line.

workgroup   A small collection of computers connected by networking cable in a peer-to-peer setup. A typical workgroup consists of related computers (such as the machines from a company's accounting or marketing department).

write-protection   Floppy-disk safeguard that prevents you from changing any information on the disk. A 5 1/4-inch disk normally has a small notch in its side. If the notch is covered with tape, the disk is write-protected. Simply remove the tape to disable the write-protection. For a 3 1/2-inch disk, a small movable tab on the back of the disk controls the write-protection. If the tab is toward the edge of the disk, then the disk is write-protected. To disable the write-protection, slide the tab away from the edge of the disk.

Index

Symbols

– (minus sign) in directories, 116, 133
* (asterisk) in directories, 133
+ (plus sign) in directories, 116, 133
... (ellipsis), 41
1 1/2 Lines Spacing (Paragraph menu) command, 207
3 1/2-inch floppy disks, 142-145
5 1/4-inch floppy disks, 142-145
286 microprocessors, 160-162, 309
386 microprocessors, 158-162, 309
486 microprocessors, 309

A

About Program Manager command (Help menu), 292
About Program Manager dialog box, 292
accessories, 309
  Calculator, 226-228
  Calendar, 228-232
  Cardfile, 232-236
  Character Map, 195-196
  Clock, 236, 237
  Paintbrush, 213-223
  Write, 199-210
active option buttons, 49
active windows, 71-72, 309
Add (Card menu) command, 234
Add dialog box, 234, 255
Add Fonts dialog box, 198
adding Toolbar buttons, 277
addresses (Cardfile), deleting, 235
Airbrush tool, 219-220

Alarm (F5), 231
Alarm menu, Set command, 231
alarms, setting, 231
aligning paragraphs, 206-207
alphanumeric keypad, 29-30
Always on Top (Control menu) command, 236
Analog (Settings menu) command, 237
Anti-Virus command (Tools menu), 266-267
application windows
  arranging on-screen, 95-96
  filling with single window, 77
applications, 310
  Anti-Virus, 267
  automating file opening startup, 122-123
  closing, 291
  exiting, 97
  insufficient memory error message, 291-293
  linking, 162-165
  Print Manager, 184-186
  sharing data between, 156-162
  shells, 315
  starting, 5, 90-92
  switching between, 7-8, 92-95
  Undelete utility, 127-129
  violated system integrity error message, 298
  windows, 310
Appointment area, Calendar, 229
appointments, entering in Calendar, 231
Arrange Icons (Window menu) command, 85
arrow keys in dialog boxes, 47
arrowheads beside commands, 41
ASCII text file, 310
asterisk (*) in directories, 133
attributes (type styles), 191
Auto Arrange (Options menu) command, 85
auto-detection (Setup), 300

L–M

Mr. Biddle
and the
Squirrel's Tale

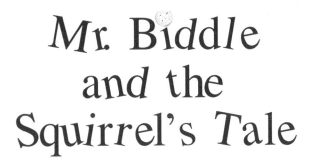

Mr. Biddle and the Squirrel's Tale

By Anne Mason

Anne Mason

Copyright © 2017 by Anne Mason

This book is a work of fiction. Names, characters, places, and incidents either are products of the author's imagination or are used fictitiously. Any resemblance to actual events or persons, living or dead, is entirely coincidental.

Photographer: Jim Zuckerman

Design: 3SIXTY Marketing Studio

Indigo River Publishing
3 West Garden Street Ste. 352
Pensacola, FL 32502
www.indigoriverpublishing.com

Ordering Information:

Quantity sales: Special discounts are available on quantity purchases by corporations, associations, and others. For details, contact the publisher at the address above.

Orders by U.S. trade bookstores and wholesalers: Please contact the publisher at the address above.

Printed in the United States of America

Library of Congress Control Number: 2017956161

ISBN: 978-0-9990210-8-8

First Edition

With Indigo River Publishing, you can always expect great books, strong voices, and meaningful messages. Most importantly, you'll always find...words worth reading.